Books by Roger Bourke White Jr.

Tales of Technofiction Series
www.technofictionland.com

The Honeycomb Comet

Rostov Rising

Tips for Tailoring Spacetime Fabric, Vol. 1

Tips for Tailoring Spacetime Fabric, Vol. 2

Science and Insight for Science Fiction Writing

Child Champs: Babymaking in the Year 2112

Visions of 2050 – Rise of the cyber muses

Business and Insight Series
www.cyreenik-says.com

Evolution and Thought: Why We Think the Way We Do

How Evolution Explains the Human Condition

Surfing the High Tech Wave: A History of Novell 1980–1990

Goat Sacrificing in the 21st Century: How to Save the Planet from its Biggest Waste: Good Intentions Gone Bad

PROFIT FROM HISTORY

See Patterns; Make Predictions; Better Your Life

ROGER BOURKE WHITE JR.

authorHOUSE®

AuthorHouse™
1663 Liberty Drive
Bloomington, IN 47403
www.authorhouse.com
Phone: 1 (800) 839-8640

Published by AuthorHouse 05/06/2016

ISBN: 978-1-5049-7517-9 (sc)
ISBN: 978-1-5049-7516-2 (e)

Print information available on the last page.

Any people depicted in stock imagery provided by Thinkstock are models, and such images are being used for illustrative purposes only. Certain stock imagery © Thinkstock.

This book is printed on acid-free paper.

Contents

Part 3c: Case Studies—Other Memorable Times

Conclusion

01

Introduction

The goal of this book is to get history working for you. I mean that in both senses of the word *work*: working as in you can understand it better, and working as in it will bring you benefits. You can exploit your understanding to take advantage of upcoming opportunities and sleep better at nights because your world will be more understandable and predictable.

Why There Are Patterns

Patterns are things that repeat. History repeats itself because there are so many unchanging givens in our world such as the laws of physics. Likewise, human thinking at the instinctive level changes little from one generation to the next. Children will always grow up, people will always fall in love, people will always trust each other, and people will always betray each other. These constants are the foundation for patterns in history.

Why There Are Surprises

There are, nonetheless, changes. Weather changes, crops flourish and fail, and plagues come and go as has always happened. These are important changes, but the fact they occur is not surprising.

The surprises have been in the technologies humans have developed that have changed lives in surprising ways. Cars have replaced horses forever. These kinds of changes are the sources for surprises in history.

How Predicting Works

Predicting is about deciding which patterns of history will repeat next. Is this next iteration going to be the same ol', same ol' as a previous pattern, or will technology make it unfold in a different way? One of the recent dramatic changes is in the way we make war. Militant Islamics wear masks in photos and other media to avoid drone strikes. Compare how they present themselves with how Hitler and Mussolini presented themselves. All these leaders are or were pushing dramatic social revolutions among their peoples and willing to use violence to do so—that pattern is repeating. But how leaders present themselves to the public has been changed by changing technology.

Conclusion

History is a mix of repeating patterns and surprises. The repeating patterns are based on unchanging parts of our universe such as physics and human instinctive thinking (emotions). The surprises are based on the changing parts, most commonly technology and those elements of life it affects.

To predict the future, we must understand how these two basic elements interact. The better we can do that, the better we can predict. "Those who cannot remember the past are condemned to repeat it" (George Santayana, 1863–1952). A wise saying to which I'll add, "Those who learn history can use it to predict the unfolding of … what's coming up shortly, as in, current events" (Roger Bourke White Jr., (1948–).

This book deals with your future and how you can favorably influence it. It's about discovering the patterns of history, the way things repeat in similar ways. If you can identify a pattern, the right one, I should add, you're taking a big step toward understanding what's coming next, how current events will unfold.

02

This Book's Structure

This book is laid out in three parts.

Part 1: The Fabric of the Patterns

Part 1 is about the fabric these patterns of history are composed of. The fabric consists of just a few elements.

- The constants: human thinking. The most important part is instinctive thinking, examples being Us vs. Them, Blame Them, the End of the World, Ambition vs. Fairness, and Chosen People thinking and history that resonates with instincts.
- The variables: technology and circumstance. These are the parts of the patterns that change: technology, circumstances, novel and scary incidents, and lessons learned. Lessons learned come from analytical thinking, the converse of instinctive thinking.

History happens because people take action based on their thinking, the fabric. In the context of this book, human thinking falls into two broad categories: analytic thinking and instinctive thinking. Analytic thinking is learned thinking. When we learn to do arithmetic or ride a bike, we're engaging in analytic thinking. Instinctive thinking is what comes into our heads without learning it; it's fast, simple, and comfortable thinking. Falling in love is the classic example of this.

Our thinking is a product of evolution just as our bodies are. Instinctive thinking allows us to deal with situations that come up repeatedly without having to think about it. Analytic thinking is the way we figure out how to deal with new or one-of-a-kind situations.

Humans engage in a mix of these ways of thinking, but as we become technologically advanced and prosperous, we must use much more analytical thinking because technology and prosperity are novel. Humans have never experienced them before, so instinctive thinking can't provide the right answers.

But this comes with an interesting twist: technology and prosperity may be novel, but instinctive thinking doesn't go way. It's still there, offering powerful suggestions as to how we should act. The hard question for people is whether these instinctive answers are the right ones to apply in any one situation.

Human instinctive thinking is a constant; the variables are those things that change with time and circumstance. The most enduring changes are those associated with the changing technologies a community deals with. Those in the Stone Age didn't experience life the same way later sedentary farmers did, and sedentary farmers didn't experience life the same way factory workers do today. A community's technology, particularly when it changes, affects how its members live and think and thereby act.

Part 2: The Patterns

Part 2 is about the patterns in history that repeat—the consistencies, the cycles, that show up time and again.

- Panic and Blunder
- Slippery Slope
- booms and busts
- frustration and Times of Nutcases
- Big Vision
- NIMBY
- acrimony
- migrations
- unions and fairness

- aspiring to entitlement
- aspiring to progress
- merchant thinking vs. fairness thinking
- monarchy

Part 3: Case Studies

Part 3 offers concrete examples, historical events viewed through the prisms of the patterns described in part 2 that explain what has happened and how they can explain where current events are likely to lead.

Definitions

This section will describe how I use these terms in this book.

Bank Panic

A bank panic is a scary financial crisis that occurs when many people get worried about their money in a bank or other financial institution and want to withdraw it. When too many people come at the same time, the bank owners have to say, "I'm sorry. There's not enough money in the vault right now. Come back later." That's scary for the customers, and their fear can spread and create a bank panic.

Sports Thinking

Sports thinking is what people do when they have to act quickly but are trained and are familiar with the situation; they automatically know what to do. The converse is panic thinking, what goes on in people's minds when they have to act quickly but aren't at all sure what they should do.

Cheap Shots

You know what this is—unscrupulous athletes who hit or slam into unsuspecting opponents in an illegal way are guilty of this. Referees sometimes miss this, and if the offended party retaliates, and the referee catches this, they are the ones who get penalized. A cheap shot has been successfully taken.

The Curse of Being Important

This happens when a project gets mucked up because too many people are too interested in the outcome. Too many cooks spoil the broth. This curse afflicts many human activities and causes progress to slow and lots of time and money to be wasted.

03

How Big-Picture History Is Presented

Seeing history's big picture allows us to predict the future based on the present. Such predictions aren't always accurate, but they're much better than random guesses or decisions based on doctrine or opinion based on propaganda or extreme religious beliefs.

What works well is being able to see patterns in current events similar to past patterns; history does repeat itself.

The following are trends that shape the patterns. As you learn history, watch for these kinds of trends in historical events and then watch for similar patterns in current events.

History in Context

It's critical to learn the context in which historical events happen because they shape the event itself. By context, I mean,

- the kinds of human thinking decision makers engaged in;
- the current events surrounding the historical event;
- the technologies available (or not available) to those involved;
- what has been happening in the economic/financial world in the years before the historic event.

Human Thinking

Humans think before making decisions whether they do so instinctively or analytically. Which thinking was involved in any one historical event is important. Too much instinctive thinking about modern-day problems can result in big mistakes; people use that type of thinking because it's fast, easy, and comfortable, but it can result in panic and blunder.

America's response to the 9/11 disaster is an example of this; it was a horrifying event that was the first of its kind for millions. Because of this, leaders and followers alike relied on their gut feelings—instinctive thinking—to craft their responses.

The converse to the gut-feeling response is the drill response: "We've experienced this or anticipated this, so we have thought about how to respond and we are prepared." Think of school fire drills.

What the people of the community feel is more important than what their leaders feel; those leaders who go off in a direction the community considers too weird are replaced. Leaders, whether tyrants or populists, lead where the important members of their communities want to go.

Which type of thinking gets used—instinctual or analytical—depends a lot on the leader and how unusual or scary an event is. The more novel and scary an event is, the more instinctive thinking will be used. This is why the leader's ability is so important—the more experience a leader and the community have, the more drill-like and cool-headed the response will be.

Other Current Events

Historic events don't happen in isolation; other things happening at the same time can affect them as can how the people involved are feeling and the capabilities of their leaders. Knowing what else is happening in addition to a historic event can add a lot to understanding the pattern. An example of this is President Carter's dealing with the unrest in Iran that led to the Iranian Revolution of 1979; he had a lot on his plate domestically dealing with post-Watergate feelings, and high inflation/low growth "stagflation" he inherited from the Johnson- and Nixon-era presidencies. He was a busy man and a deeply devoted human rights advocate. It's not surprising that America's actions relating to Iran, its monarchist shah, and the growing chaos in the country didn't seem to get a lot of his personal attention.

Technology

Technology affects what people can and can't do. Until Europeans had sailing ships that could cross the Atlantic, they had no great interest in figuring out what was on the other side. Think of the difference between Eric the Red and Christopher Columbus. With this Eric/Christopher pattern in mind, observe what is happening to Neil Armstrong and Buzz Aldrin's stature in history. Knowing what technology was or wasn't available is vital to fleshing out the pattern of a historical event.

Financial Events

What was happening in an economy prior to a historic event gets almost no mention in conventional histories, but it's important because financial issues get very personal when it comes down to it. They affect how much money people have to spend, what kinds of jobs they have or don't have, and how confident they are about their future. Most dramatic social revolutions such as the Civil War, the French Revolution, and the Arab Spring follow a bank panic (the old term) or a deep recession. The financial condition of governments and their people is very much a part of a historical event pattern. If you want to predict a dramatic social revolution, watch the economic cycle for a severe crash. The pattern is that a revolution will follow in a few years.

Current Events Are Surprising

Those who experience a truly historical event haven't experienced it before; it's not a TV rerun. No one is sure what will happen; people can only guess. I call this the "It's inconceivable!" element of a historical event, the 9/11 disaster being a textbook example. Who had experienced planes being deliberately flown into skyscrapers before?

Watch Out for Dark Side Issues

Dark side issues are those mentioned in history but aren't part of the pattern. They are in fact distractions from it, and they can conceal the true pattern. Some common ones are Monday-morning quarterbacking, urban legends, and supporting an opinion.

Monday-Morning Quarterbacking

Monday-morning quarterbacking is when people comment on the previous day's game with the benefit of hindsight. This happens in history recounting. Someone could say, "The United States should have seen the

Japanese fleet coming to attack Pearl Harbor. If they had, the war would
have ended in six months."

It didn't happen that way. It was a terrible, surprising event for the
Americans and a triumphant, surprising event for the Japanese. If you are
telling this as history, not fiction, tell it with the Japanese doing a great job
of keeping a secret and with the Americans being surprised.

Urban Legends

Urban legends are stories that sound good to people's instincts. They
aren't closely related to what really happened, but the stories are passed on
because they just sound good. An example of this is stories about the White
Star Lines, builders and owners of the *Titanic*, having advertised the ship
as unsinkable. They didn't; they advertised it as equipped with the latest
safety features, which it was.

There are stories of stockbrokers committing suicide by jumping out
of their office windows during the 1929 stock market crash. This sounds
comfortable because the market crashed and so did these people, but in
truth, no one did.

One Side Good, the Other Evil

Few people wake up in the morning, stretch, and say, "What a great
day to do evil!" But much of history is portrayed as a matter of a good
player and an evil player in a contest. The harsh reality is that players on
both sides think they're good. To get a more-accurate big picture of a
historical contest, learn what the word *good* meant to the people on both
sides. In the Korean War as an example, the United States and the United
Nations got involved to prevent those evil Communists who had just
taken over China from also taking over South Korea. When the Chinese
intervened six months after the fighting started, it was to prevent those
evil American capitalists from moving north of the Korean border into
Manchuria and reigniting the Chinese civil war. Both sides thought they
were in the right and doing good.

Supporting an Opinion

Many documentaries today are telling, actually selling, opinions. A producer has a point of view on a topic and supports it by deciding what to show or not to the audience. The result is not a balanced viewpoint. Watch these but keep the salesmanship involved in mind. Be skeptical. Research other points of view on the topic to develop a broader and more-balanced opinion.

Conclusion

Human thinking, other current events, technologies available, and financial circumstances will compose the core of the Case Studies section of this book. I want to help others learn how to integrate the concept of patterns in their views of history so they are better able to better predict what's going to happen next in our surprising world.

Part 1

The Fabric

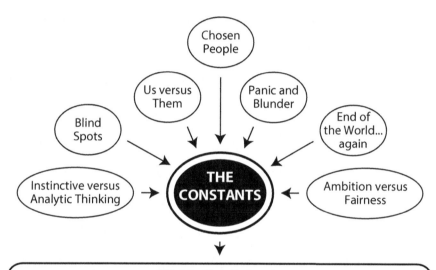

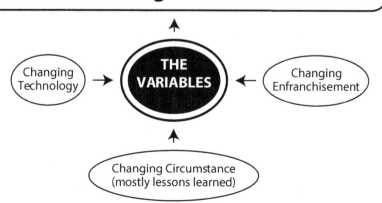

04

Human Thinking and Circumstance

The fabric in which the patterns are woven are foundational concepts that consist of two broad categories: constants in history and variables in history. The constants center on our instinctive thinking, which varies little from generation to generation; it's a powerful influence on the choices humans make when circumstances call for action. The other style of thinking in which humans engage is analytic thinking.

The variables concern changes in technology and circumstances. When these differ, the actions taken will differ. When individuals learn lessons based on this, their actions will be different—that's analytic thinking in action.

The constants include instances of instinctive human thinking such as Us vs. Them, Blame Them, End of the World, Ambition vs. Fairness, and Chosen People thinking. These are my terms for these thinking styles, and I'll define them in this part.

The variables center on changing technology and circumstance. These include changing technology, changing circumstances, the novelty and scariness of incidents, and lessons recently learned. Again, I will define these terms in following sections of this overview.

Roger Bourke White Jr.

Instinctive and Analytic Thinking

Humans engage in instinctive thinking; it's been hard-wired into us over thousands of generations. But as we have become technologically advanced and prosperous, life requires that we must use much more analytical thinking.

But we need both ways of thinking. At times, we need to think instinctively, and other times, especially when we're faced with new situations, we need to apply analytical thought.

Pattern Variables

The variables in a pattern are those elements that change with time and circumstance. The most enduring changes are those associated with the change in technology, which brings on all sorts of changes in how people think and act. If a community has just harvested a bumper crop, a harsh winter will be unpleasant but not a reason to change the rhythm of living. But if this harsh winter happens after a decade of poor harvests, it may be time for a big change in activity such as going to war or migrating elsewhere. This is the difference circumstances can make.

05

The Constants: Instinctive Thinking vs. Analytic Thinking

We are the fruits of evolution. Our bodies offer a high-performance fit for living on earth, and our thinking is just as evolved and high performance.

Thinking is a complex activity, so in these explanations, I'll simplify things dramatically. This section divides our thinking into two broad categories: instinctive thinking and analytic thinking. It will describe when and how these modes of thinking pop up in our day-to-day living and how we use them to make choices and take actions.

This will be a brief description. If you want more details, check out my *Business and Insight Series* of books.

Instinctive Thinking

Instinctive thinking is the basic kind of thinking exhibited by all animals. It is fast and simple and it covers all the basic, data-interpreting activities in which animals engage. It covers things such as reflexes, which allow us to stand, walk, and eat. It covers the basic parts of vision—converting an image that falls on the retina into a form the brain can understand. It also covers love, a thinking style which pops up without practice or training.

Instinctive thinking is hardwired. It is a product of evolution. Over thousands of generations the brain and body have become hardwired to handle routine activities and solve repeating problems. It's fast and comfortable thinking that requires little or no conscious thought.

Our instincts take thousands of generations to develop, so they don't change quickly. These days our lifestyle and circumstances are brand new so instinctive thinking has fallen behind. The instincts are still well-suited for Stone Age living, but most of us aren't living in the Stone Age anymore.

Analytic Thinking

Analytic thinking comes into play when we face new environments, events, and developments our hardwired brains haven't faced before. I'm talking about try-it-and-learn-something thinking we must engage in when we face this-hasn't-happened-before situations. We can do this because we're organisms with advanced thinking skills and can handle learning arithmetic and how to ride bicycles.

It was the growth of strong language and teaching skills that allowed our large brains to develop. If we couldn't teach, our big brains would be a waste of resources.

As a community becomes more prosperous and technologically advanced, the number of "toys" and techniques that are valuable for its people to master grows exponentially. This change puts a lot more emphasis on analytic thinking skills. This is why universal education, and lots of it, is so valuable to industrialized communities.

When Instinctive Thinking Sneaks In

Instinctive thinking will offer suggestions for action even when the situation isn't quite right for the routine solution it's suggesting. This problem gets worse the further away from a Stone Age environment we get. We have to learn to rely heavily on analytic thinking rather than acting on fast, easy answers until we're sure what the situation requires. In this way, we'll learn new and better ways to respond to such situations, and they can even become sports thinking responses.

The Instinctive Thinking Rogues' Gallery

What follows are some of the powerful versions of instinctive thinking that influence history.

Us vs. Them: whom to cooperate with and whom to betray

Back in the Stone Age, people knew who was in their community, and these were people to be cooperating with. These were Us's. Those outside the community were Them's. They could cooperate with or betray Them's. The benefits of betrayal—say, robbing a stranger—were immediate. The benefits of cooperation—say, to get a large field cleared and farmed year after year—were long term.

As a community moves from a Neolithic mind-set to an industrial mind-set, the benefits of cooperation increase, but the world of people who must be cooperated with grows larger as well. It's the difference between living off the land in a closed commune and being a road warrior in the globalized economy.

This growing size of the cooperating universe rubs the Us vs. Them instinct the wrong way. It is constantly looking for opportunities to betray.

Blame Them: dodging the problem

Closely related to Us vs. Them thinking is whom to blame when things go wrong. The fast and comfortable choice for leaders is to point to strangers; that's also a comfortable choice for followers. "It's not our problem. We don't need to figure out how fix it."

Chosen People: widening the concept of "Us"

Humans invent new thinking styles as well as new devices and techniques. One of the big challenges of moving into the Agricultural Age was getting wider cooperation. One way that has worked well is to invoke the "We are the Chosen People" concept. This is an effective way of widening the Us feeling to include more people in cooperative endeavors.

Closely related to this is Pillar of Faith thinking, a crazy belief that is useful for identifying who is part of the Chosen People and who isn't.

Panic and blunder: trying to solve novel and scary problems

When novel and scary events occur—a double whammy—people tend to panic. Panicking means they are looking for a fast solution to the scary problem. Because they are looking for a real quick answer, they focus down and consider only a handful of issues, and consider them only for a moment before deciding on a course of action. This fast decision making leads to quick solutions that are frequently terrible-looking in retrospect or to a cool-headed observer. The person blunders. But the choices were made based mostly on instinctive thinking so they feel good at the time. And this is why the blunder can still look like a good choice to the chooser even well after the crisis has passed and the huge expense of the choice is clear.

If a scary problem is not new, not novel, sports thinking can take over. As I mentioned, school fire drills are good examples of how sports thinking can be taught.

Ambition vs. Fairness

Conflicts can occur between the ambitious members of a community and those promoting fairness. The ambitious members want to work hard and get ahead, while the fairness members want to ensure the community's blessings are shared fairly. Think of those who patiently wait in line and those who try to figure out ways of avoiding the wait.

End of the World: seminomadic thinking

Periodically, someone declares the end of the world is coming, and many people mysteriously take that person seriously. This is the seminomadic instinct. Stone Age people moved when they needed something that was elsewhere, and this happened often enough that it became part of the instinctual mindset.

Food concerns: is your food safe?

Finding safe food and clean water were musts for Stone Age people. Humans became omnivores—they could eat plants and animals due to the robust digestive systems they developed. But though we have extraordinarily safe foods by Stone Age standards, we still worry a lot about food.

Protecting the children: are we doing enough?

We worry about our children's safety though they are much safer than their Stone Age counterparts.

These are examples of instinctive thinking that show up in modern day decision making. Instinctive thinking is still quite powerful.

Conclusion

These are examples of the thinking constants and variables that are part of the fabric of history. When people are determining a course of action, they will use a mix of instinctive thinking and analytic thinking.

06

Blind Spots in American Thinking

The debates on health care, the War on Drugs, climate change, and registering sex offenders are examples of blind spots in American thinking because what we've up with even after much effort isn't working. This failure is a problem because it's a huge waste of resources for little or no results and it causes members of the community to feel disenfranchised, to feel what they do is unimportant to the community and that the community isn't listening to them.

In spite of our efforts and money spent, society still faces the problems caused by criminals, corruption, and malcontents, and it's losing a sense of responsibility and importance in the debate.

Those who try to solve these problems do so for the best of reasons; they are enthusiastic and dedicated people who want the best for us all but are blind to the huge costs of the choices they promote or their bad or unintended consequences.

Root Attitudes

These blind spots are caused by root attitudes, feelings held so deeply that they are considered simply axioms—givens—by much of the community. Just imagine a man walking onto the stage wearing a black suit and a black hat and twisting a thin moustache in his fingers and smirking at a cowering young woman and waving a paper in her face.

You just *know* he's threatening her with eviction if she doesn't marry him; that's axiomatic.

Our root attitudes are based on mixing the instinctive thinking we've inherited, with the realities of our technologically advanced lifestyle. There are times when this mix produces strange and expensive results, and in spite of the ineffectiveness the results are supported for decades.

My Research

My thoughts on the foregoing are based on not science but on my life's experiences, which include anecdotes, but anecdotes can have a lot of depth. I've been around a while; I read a lot about current events, science, and history; and I've lived and worked in five countries over six decades. As I read about and experience day-to-day life in America, these are the attitudes I consider over-the-top worries that lead people to make expensive and damaging decisions in terms of not only money but also civil liberties, and they cause people to feel disenfranchised. The serious problems aren't solved; the solutions supposed to do that corrode society further.

What follows are matters Americans have been over-the-top about for one or more decades and are the result of blind spots.

Terrorism

Fear of crime and violence is ancient. Fear of terrorism is a rather new twist on this ancient worry. Modern terrorism evolved as a symbiote with modern news reporting. As TV has become more a part of our lives and as news reporters use fast and portable technology to relay their messages, there has been a revolution in what people can learn about their community, their government, and the whole world.

Much of this change has been beneficial. I attribute the relatively bloodless regime changes of the late twentieth century such as the fall of the Soviet Union to this immediacy of news reporting. It's harder for a government to hide bloody repression when most everyone has camera and even video capabilities on their cell phones. Compare easy-to-censor "News of the Week" newsreels shown at movie theaters in the 1930s and

'40s with YouTube. But the age-old news reporting instincts of "If it bleeds it leads" and "Stop the presses!" haven't died out. In fact, they've become even more vivid to audiences, and that's the root of terrorism's potency.

Terrorism is at its root violence to advertise a cause, and *advertising* is the key word. Terrorists promote causes, and they commit terrorist actions because they see it as cost-effective advertising for their causes. That terrorism is reported is of value to its perpetrators.

As an example, many Americans have a deep-rooted fear of flying, thus the media circus that surrounds every airplane crash. Americans also deeply fear suicidal people; witness the great concern caused by kamikaze pilots in World War II. Terrorists thus mix airplanes with suicide and provoke a huge media circus in response. That's a great advertising return on a tight budget.

The blind spot here is that Americans don't recognize this violence as advertising. Rather than work at reducing the advertising return of terrorism, Americans have invested heavily in developing a modern religion based on security. The most visible practitioners of this modern religion are commercial air travelers and their priesthood, the TSA.

Compare airport passenger security—something faith-based—to starting your car when you turn the key—something fact-based. If you bad-mouth airport security at the airport, you'll get a big response. But if you get in your car and bad-mouth it, it'll still start up. This is the blind spot surrounding terrorism; America doesn't recognize that it's up against advertising; instead, it's investing in a neoreligion.

Mind-Altering Experiences

Our thinking processes can be temporarily altered by drugs, drinking, falling in love, experiencing runner's high, meditating, enjoying a concert, and experiencing an adrenaline rush. Perhaps because our brains have gone through dramatic changes in recent (in an evolutionary sense) times, they easily tire of ordinary, conscious-level thinking and like to relax by doing other kinds of thinking.

Typical Americans consume alcohol or don't mind if others do, but that's not the case with fundamentalist Muslims in Saudi Arabia, for instance. A blind spot happens when those who don't like a particular mind-altering practice declare laws against it. Those who enjoy using the prohibited mind-altering technique don't see a problem and end up feeling disenfranchised, which affects the whole community. They start sneaking around to indulge. They worry about their civil liberties being curtailed by those who enforce the law and being considered criminals.

Even if an activity is harmless, if it's deemed suspicious, it must be given up; an example of this is wearing a surgical mask for health reasons and walking into a bank. "The Forfeiture Racket" by Radly Balko is an article in *Reason* magazine (February 2010) that dealt with an institutionalized craziness: the thriving practice of police seizing property that *might* be related to a crime, a $3 billion practice in 2008. Evidence can be so tenuous that charges don't even have to be filed related to the seizing. This is a gross trampling of our civil rights, but the American community doesn't see it that way.

The value of a law is diminished when smuggling grows up to support the outlawed activity; people start feeling that all people aren't being treated equally under the law, and that leads to feelings of disenfranchisement.

When police or politicians sympathize with the outlawed practice, if they think a law is crazy, that can lead to corruption that further diminishes the rule of law. And those who break the law also feel disenfranchised and become prone to justifying their lawless behavior and even violence because they don't feel a stake in the community, which suffers from the lawlessness and violence. This is vividly illustrated in the *Wall Street Journal* story "Cartel Wars Gut Juárez, a Onetime Boom Town" by Nicholas Casey (March 20, 2010) that reported on the middle-class neighborhoods of a Mexican border town being abandoned because of drug-related violence.

What I have outlined above comes at a huge cost paid for by a scared, outraged community watching others indulge in mind-altering experiences. The less-expensive choice is to recognize that mind-altering experiences come in many forms and that part of being an advanced civilization requires one side to be tolerant of such differences and the other side to be responsible about their practices.

The root of the blind spot—the deep instinct—is believing that practitioners of some kinds of mind-altering behavior can't be responsible and thus must be stopped at all costs. This is a variant of "The devil made me do it" thinking, the idea that an evil spirit of some sort can get inside people and absolve them of responsibility for their actions. In almost all cases where this defense of an action is invoked and accepted as believable by those making judgment, it's a blind spot.

The better alternative is to hold people responsible for their actions, including those done at the suggestion of any devils inside them.

Guilt

Nothing seems to turn off cost-benefit analysis thinking faster than feeling guilty. Guilt powers some of the biggest and craziest spending blind spots in American thinking.

In the 2010's, the spectacular, trillion-dollar blunder-in-the-making powered by guilt is the movement to prevent climate change, which became high profile as scientists involved declared humans had caused it. For decades before that twist was added, climate research was just another earth science; the alarmist pronouncements in the 1970s of a coming Ice Age made interesting science reading but nothing more.

Other examples of guilt-driven crazy spending include donations to charities whose spending and its results aren't monitored. At times, charities can do more to perpetuate rather than solve problems. Did America's assistance to Haiti in the decades before the earthquake of 2010 help end the poverty that made the earthquake so devastating or perpetuate it? The same questions can be asked about universal health care coverage, giving money to panhandlers, and apologizing for crimes committed by ancestors, all of which can be driven by guilt feelings.

Nuclear Power and Genetic Engineering

All humans die. But for some reason, there seems to be survival value in judging the goodness or badness of how someone dies; we think there are good ways and bad ways to die, but that is different for many cultures. Ancient Egyptians shivered at the idea of being eaten by Nile crocodiles, and that resulted in a thriving industry for magic makers who offered protections from that.

In movies, someone who is lying about the death of his or her parents and wants a ho-hum response from a listener says they died peacefully in their sleep. If they want a sympathetic response, they say they died in a car crash. If they want an "Ewww! That's terrible!" response, they tell them they died in a nuclear accident. "And wait!" says the liar with eyes wide open in supposed fear, "Here they come now—as glow-in-the-dark zombies! Ahhh!"

Death due to radioactive fallout has been considered a terrible way to die since it was incorporated in sci-fi in the mid-twentieth century. This fear has spilled over into our perception of the danger of nuclear power and has stunted our ability to take advantage of it; we don't see how much this fear has cost us. We think of nuclear power as good for powering big electrical power stations, but it could also power watches and artificial hearts and be put to many more uses.

A related over-the-top fear is that of genetic engineering in its various forms. The root of this fear seems to be the fear of plague, of uncontrollable disease. Once again, the blind spot is not seeing how much benefit is lost by being over-the-top about the fear.

Further Reading

"Fukushima and the Future of Nuclear Power" by William Tucker is a *Wall Street Journal* editorial (March 6, 2012) that says there's no evidence that low doses of radiation are harmful and are no reason to paralyze our economy out of fear of nuclear power. Tucker wrote,

> This says, quite simply, that because huge doses of radiation— the kind you might get from standing in the same room with a spent fuel rod—can cause illness or cancer, we must assume that even the smallest doses will have the same effect on a smaller scale. It's exactly the same as saying that because jumping off a 10-story building will break every bone in your body, stepping off a one-foot curb will also cause some minor damage.

Health Care

The blind spot here is not seeing the enormous costs associated with decoupling receiving health care from paying for health care. Most things we buy come from a vendor, such as groceries. This direct relation between money and goods and services means the seller pays a lot of attention to what the buyer wants, and the buyer pays a lot of attention to what the seller is offering; that's the heart of shopping.

In the case of health care, the buyer is not the patient (unless the patient is—gasp!—uninsured.) The buyer is the insurance company or the government; they're paying the bill. This means there is great incentive for the health care providers to pay attention to the insurance companies and the government. What is the patient in this system? The patient is a ticket. When the patient is provided a service, a ticket is punched and handed to the insurance company or the government for payment. This is the root of all the wackiness we experience dealing with health care. Patients have handed off their responsibility in health care decisions, and what we now experience are turf wars as health care people, insurance people, government-paying people, and government-regulating people fill that decision-making power vacuum while claiming they have the best interests of the patient in mind.

How did we get into this situation? Part of the root problem is that when people get sick, they don't want to make choices. Historically, when people got sick, their extended families were the first-line caretakers. Think of a mother putting a feverish child to bed with grandma hovering in the background. They would call in advice givers; think of doctors making house calls. These advice givers evolved into the medical profession as we experience it today.

In mainstream America now, the extended family doesn't intervene often in health care, so health care choices are now much more in the hands of the health care infrastructure and patients. This is not so true in East Asia, by the way; there, the extended family is still an active participant and hospitals are filled with supporting family as well as helpful nurses and doctors.

Why is this corrosive? The goal of health care should be to make the patient satisfied and healthy, with satisfied being the much more important of the two. When the patient is not paying—not taking responsibility—wasteful spending occurs and becomes chronic. One group says, "We're doing this for the good of the patients," and another group says, "No, you're not doing it right. We have a better way." This results in extra paperwork and protections and strange ways of deciding what is appropriate treatment and what isn't.

The root problem here is if the patient isn't going to decide what's right for himself or herself, who's to say which other group is right? That's the blind spot we're living with.

Save the Children

We have a blind spot when it comes to our spending too much effort on protecting children. This excess effort is expensive and corrosive as well as misdirected. Growing up is a process that calls for constant enormous changes. We start off as a single fertilized cell, a zygote, and become mature human beings consisting of trillions of cells. We then have to pass the grandchild test; we must have lots of grandchildren. If not, others do and replace our lines.

While all this growing is happening, learning occurs as well, and that's also an enormous process. We learn how to act appropriately in our specific environments. Children learn by trying things many times. Think of a child learning to walk.

At times, children try something that doesn't work, and they fall, for instance, and get hurt. But that's part of the child's learning process, and children who learn to walk in Tahiti will do so differently than children in Siberia will. But in both cases, they learn by trying.

When they are in the learning—the failing and succeeding—process, they can run into their parents' instinct to protect them. That's a good thing, but we have to look at the big picture. In the past, a big number of children died in childhood; those who reached mature ages and could reproduce were the exception. Apples produce many seeds; fish produce many eggs. Kittens and dogs produce litters. In all species but advanced, civilized humans, most offspring are destined to fail the grandchild test, so their mothers bear dozens to hundreds to thousands more children than will reach adulthood.

High rates of infant mortality used to be givens; that prompted parents to protect their children, and that became instinctual. But now, that instinct can be overdone and result in twisted-up adults. We forget that damaging experiences are part of the learning process, not something to be terrified of. For children, damaging experiences are lessons they learn, not something abnormal. Likewise, scars we carry from such lessons are not abnormal; they're part of growing up.

This concern about overprotection is not new. The proverb "Spare the rod, spoil the child" is an expression of concern about overprotecting. But now, how often do you hear this said with any conviction? In this area of thinking, we've changed a lot in the last fifty years. Some current examples of activities trying to combat overprotection are athletic programs, field trips, Boy/Girl Scouts, and summer camps.

Child Overprotection Can Corrode the Community

Overprotection can create adults who haven't learned their limits because they've never tested them; they haven't learned that no pain results in no gain. They have never learned to deal well with adversity, and they tend to get too excited under pressure because they never learned to see things through. This overexcitement is hard on enfranchisement; they worry too much and too quickly and look for cures through applying prescriptive conformity to the whole community.

Those who haven't interacted enough with the rough-and-tumble physical world around them, those who watch too much TV or constantly play video games can become introspective, and this might be the root behind emerging narcissistic lifestyles such as metrosexualism and Japan's "girly men."

Bride-Age Thinking

Children are raised mostly by young women. In pre-civilized environments, young women with young children survived best by cooperating with the rest of the community, which is why they tended to be bride thinkers. Older women who had more experience and older children thought differently; they stood up for their rights and became matron thinkers. But matron thinking is generally not a good strategy for young mothers.

The benefit of bride thinking is that the community instinctively cooperates with and assists young mothers. The dark side of bride thinking is that the community feels empowered to offer lots of advice on how to raise children, and when the government is offering advice, it's called a law. Few things can bring bureaucrats and politicians faster emotional support than shouting, "I'm doing this for the children!"

Consider children's product safety rules, which are not advice; they override parents' ability to decide the right way and wrong way to raise their children. They are the community's forceful way of saying, "We know how to raise your children better than you do." This blind side happens because of the instinct to give advice to young mothers. This is a blind side because the actions supported by this instinctive thinking aren't measured against their consequences; they take away opportunities for children to explore and learn about their worlds and disenfranchise parents from the child-raising process: "Why should I feel responsible? Why should I bother to do this well when everyone around me is telling me how to do this?"

Add Some Sex

The most flagrant waste is associated with protecting children from sexual abuse. This is wasteful for a couple of reasons. First, sex is something children don't comprehend in the way adults do just as one-year-olds don't know how to understand speech because their thinking processes have not developed enough.

I remember the first time I saw a naked girl. I was five, and I was horsing around in the bathtub with my brother, eighteen months younger. We were kicking each other in the balls, but at that age, it didn't hurt much. We had just heard it was a good way to bother other people if you were fighting them, so we were experimenting.

Our upstairs neighbor brought down her daughter, who was six, to join us in the tub. I was going to kick her in the balls, but she didn't have any!

"Why don't you have any balls?" I asked.

31

"Because I'm a girl. I get to have babies instead."

Her explanation left me mystified, but I considered it just another mystery of life, and my brother and I went back to having fun.

Sex has almost no meaning to a child, which means that sexual molestation has almost no meaning. If something is scary or painful, it will have meaning, but not the sexual dimension. Young boys will see some kissing on TV and say, "Ewww! More icky stuff! Let's watch something interesting instead."

Worrying about exposing children to sexual situations makes as much sense as worrying about exposing children to algebra; neither will have much meaning for them.

Even if a child is old enough to be aware of sex, these concepts don't change. Here is an article about a classic "The devil made me do it." "Garn admits paying woman" by Robert Gehrke (March 10, 2012) is about an ambitious thirty-year-old man sharing a hot tub with a fifteen-year-old girl in the 1980s. No sex, no drugs, no drink, no rape. The man regretted his action enough at the time to pay the woman $150,000 in hush money.

Twenty-five years later, the woman claimed that the experience of having a man see her naked when she was fifteen put an evil demon in her that ruined her life, and she was telling all to try to exorcize that demon. There are many lessons to be learned from this tale, but the important one is that many in America believe this woman's explanation. The "sex can put an evil demon in a child and curse him or her for life" superstition is powerful today.

It's so powerful that if you try to explain the problem here, many will worry about your thinking. Consider how sex crimes and child pornography are treated in America—over-the-top situations in which grannies are prosecuted as child pornographers for taking pictures of their naked grandchildren playing in a bathtub and high schoolers being transformed into lifelong registered sex offenders because they were mooning people. That's a result of instinctual thinking, not rational thought. Sex offenders have to register, but murderers, bank robbers, and scam artists don't. Instinctive thinking needs to be mixed with a lot of analytic thinking when creating community policy making. Unadulterated instinctive thinking creates expensive programs that don't protect much but corrode civil liberties and enfranchisement.

In the hot tubbing case above, a man who added a lot of value to his community was about to get deeply disenfranchised and perhaps exiled—thrown in jail—and the fates of other examples aren't any better. A *New York Times* article, "Defiant Judge Takes On Child Pornography Law" by A. G. Sulzberger (May 21, 2010) dealt with the mandatory sentences handed down for receiving child pornography. Just for downloading dirty pictures of kids, 1,600 people were sentenced to an average of more than seven years in jail in 2009.

The original justification for making it illegal to receive child porn, overriding our First Amendment rights, was to protect children from the abuse of the *producers* of child porn. This is pretty convoluted to start with, but now, the viewers are often getting more punishment than are the producers. This is a textbook example of going over the top because of a blind side.

A February 28, 2011 article in *Reason*, "You Can Have Sex With Them; Just Don't Photograph Them," by Radley Balko, illustrates the problem well. A former cop was thrown in the slammer for fifteen years with no parole for having, not distributing, pictures on his computer of a sixteen- and a seventeen-year-old woman he had already had consensual and legal sex with. This wackiness is the consequence of the federal pornography law.

The biggest expense of over-the-top child protecting is the overly hysterical community overprotected children will create as adults. This will be a community that will pursue silly causes just because doing so feels good. The members will not stop to think through the expensive consequences. Intolerant speech policies have been enacted to protect tolerance; think of those people who say, "Yes, of course I'm tolerant. But in this case ..."

Blind spots are important because they result in the waste of time, money, and attention, and they corrode the community by disenfranchising people, promoting crime and corruption, and affecting civil liberties. Some cost us because they convince us not to use a powerful tool that could make our lives much better.

They are hard to see. They are by their very nature blind spots that are the result of instinctual thinking that clashes with the harsh realities of advanced, civilized living. We can combat this by becoming aware of it and training ourselves to avoid such thinking. We can teach our children that not all gut thinking is good thinking. When something is too obvious and looks too good to be true but it causes others a lot of pain, we should learn to back off and do some more analysis to see if the prohibition answer or the hand-money-over-to-someone-suffering answer is just a quick, easy, and simple solution that does nothing.

We must train ourselves to look for blind spots.

Getting the Context Wrong

Not seeing blind spots can keep us from seeing the big picture. Blind-spot thinking happens when people can't understand why something is happening, keeps happening, and isn't solved by their favored solutions.

One of the most common sources of blind-spot thinking is not understanding the context—the circumstances—in which an action is taking place. Imagine someone about to be executed asking for a cigarette and being warned that smoking causes cancer.

Here are some other examples. US church volunteers built a medical clinic in remote Africa, but there were no health care workers to staff it, so it was abandoned. A wet-behind-the-ears soldier salutes an officer in a front-line sniper zone or doesn't salute an officer in a safe, rear area. Either way, he's being wrong for his context and will get called up on it quickly.

A cultural summation of this is the chorus from the 1970s folk song "Walk a Mile in My Shoes" by Joe South.

> Walk a mile in my shoes, walk a mile in my shoes
> Hey, before you abuse, criticize and accuse
> Walk a mile in my shoes

One concept Joe misses in this song beyond abusing, criticizing, and accusing is aiding. Offering help needs to be just as context-sensitive as all other activities. If not, good intentions can produce results as harmful as ignorant intentions can and will be just more ignorant intentions.

Blind-spot thinking can cause problems for those who read history and those who participate in historical events. The latter I call goat sacrificing, and I've written a whole book about it—*Goat Sacrificing in the 21ˢᵗ Century*.

Here is another, more humorous, example of how context matters.

Cow-Human Relations from the Cow's Perspective

Ms. Cow addressed the members of the NAACP (the Nonsense Association for the Advancement of Crawly Protoplasms)

Dear Fellow Members,

It has come to my attention that some of my honored fellows at this assembly have accused my kind, cattle, of selling out to The Man. Nothing could be further from the truth. The truth is humanity serving us, and we cows are proud of it!

Do we spend hours a day looking for our food? Do we have food some days and not others? No siree! Our fine, little, two-footed friends scurry around endlessly looking for our food.

Do you see cows dying of hundreds of unknown fevers? Poisoned by unclean waters? Sickened by mysterious maladies? Hardly ever! Humans check our health continuously. There is nothing short, nasty, or brutish about our health care!

How about breeding? There's nothing hit or miss about that. We have the finest breeding opportunities our little friends can devise. And we have prospered from it. Look at the biomass we command! Who can argue the numbers?

We aren't selling out. This was a tough deal to arrange, and we cows are damn lucky to be here. Before we figured humans out, our ancestors were on the ropes. They hung out in just a small sliver of North Africa and Europe. And those who couldn't figure out how to get humanity working for them? [looks around] I don't see any of them here complaining about our selling out.

So those of you pissing and moaning are just jealous! It's not easy to get humans to work for you, but when you do, the rewards are simply astounding.

I urge you to give humanity a try. Sure, they're a capricious species; we have no idea what they're doing 90 percent of the time. But that last ten percent? Oh my! They do that well, and we have prospered mightily. We cows have no second thoughts about this roller-coaster ride we've jumped on. It's been going our way since day one.

I thank you all for your kind attention.

Conclusion

Understanding the context in which events are happening is vital to understanding why the people of the event are acting the way they are. The more context is not understood, the more mysterious historical events will seem to history enthusiasts.

07

Us vs. Them

One of the most pervasive forms of instinctive thinking is the Us vs. Them instinct. This shows up in obvious and subtle ways. Us vs. Them thinking had benefits in the Stone Age; it encouraged cooperation. It also allowed for defecting when that could bring benefits. The key here is that the defecting should be done with strangers, not friends. Defection or betraying here is in the <u>Prisoners' Dilemma</u> context.

Over the millennia, our brains became hard-wired to foster cooperation but also defect when that was viewed as beneficial. Such cooperation was even more necessary when human beings became agriculturally oriented; that was when the concept of cooperation broadened. This led to hierarchical thinking—the concept of rulers and ruled. This invention has been around just barely long enough that it is also becoming instinctive thinking; monarchical governing is a comfortable form of government for many.

Another social invention was the Chosen People concept. We, a big group, are Us, and outsiders are Them. This was an extension of the family-oriented instinct, and it has proved a useful concept in many circumstances.

Subtle Incarnations of Us vs. Them

Many of the subtle incarnations of Us vs. Them concern whom to betray and how to do it. Examples of subtle versions include corruption in its various forms and using government regulations to raise barriers to entry into an occupation or industry.

Guilds, neoguilds, and unions are Chosen People manifestations.

Another subtle manifestation is something I call Blame Them, a fast and comfortable choice for a leader when something's gone wrong. It's easy for a leader to blame strangers for a problem, and it's easy for followers to believe it. "It's not our problem. Don't ask us to fix it." This tactic often has a lot of conspiracy stories mixed in. Fearing treachery is a powerful part of the Us vs. Them instinct.

Another subtle ritual is Pillars of Faith; those who follow certain rituals or believe certain things are considered members of the Chosen People.

Us vs. Them thinking is pervasive in human thinking on personal and community levels. One of the important elements it controls is whom to cooperate with and whom to betray. This is where it is most important as a fabric of history.

Another place it becomes important is when blame is being placed. When the choice is made to blame others, however, the problem under consideration won't be fixed quickly or well.

08

Panic and Blunder Thinking

- ○ A mother wakes up in the middle of the night and smells smoke. She and the family run out of the house and stand on the front lawn watching their house burn. Then she has a sudden thought. She screams, "My baby!" and runs back in. So far, heroic. But as she was yelling, "My Baby!" her baby was in the arms of her husband standing beside her and crying for her.
- ○ A nation experiences a terrorist attack on a public landmark. In response, it conquers another nation because it fears that other nation has weapons of mass destruction or worse, is harboring terrorists. After the conquest, they figure out there were no weapons of mass destruction or terrorists and the evidence used to justify the attack was flimsy.

Huge blunders are caused by panic thinking, so it's important to realize when you or those around you are engaging in it. This won't help you much on predicting the exact nature of the blunder, but you'll sure know it when you see it being proposed or enacted.

Panic thinking happens when a person or community experiences a situation that is new and threatening and feels it has to act quickly. Because of the strangeness deciding what to do doesn't come easily. The brain goes into a panic mode and focuses on getting one thing done fast. To get into this mode it ignores most of what is going on around it and instead focuses on only those things necessary to get the one thing done. That one thing accomplished, if the scary state is still prevalent, the brain then focuses on Objective Two and, once again, pays attention only to those things needed to accomplish that objective. This thinking style frequently results in huge blunders driven more by emotion than analytical thinking.

Regardless of how stupid an action looks in retrospect or to an objective observer, it can seem very right at the time by those who are panicking. Whole groups as well as individuals can give in to panic thinking, one form of this is Group Think.

Panic thinking occurs when a community is afraid, under stress, is facing a situation it's never handled before, and thinks it has to act quickly. In more normal circumstances action comes after deliberation – a chance to engage in more analytic thinking and to take a look at the bigger picture. In normal times the community can adapt well to change as long as the change comes slowly. This keeps the level of stress in the community low or at least manageable.

But if things change quickly and for the worse, stress goes up. Natural disasters—drought, famine, flood—financial collapse, or a sudden spike in unemployment can make stress levels shoot up dramatically if they haven't been experienced before or if people aren't prepared for them. Stressed communities can fall as easily into panic thinking as individuals can.

Compare these following cases for how much panic they caused.

- Though earthquakes can be sudden and horrifying, they are well known disasters. Still, you'd expect people in San Francisco to better weather such a calamity than would people in Detroit, for whom an earthquake would be a new, unexpected event.
- In 1945, a small military plane flew into the Empire State Building due to fog. Little damage was done, loss of life was minimal, and the excitement generated was short-lived. Compare that to 9/11, which involved big jets, terrorists who were suicidal, many, and well organized, and several collapsed skyscrapers. They caused the deaths of thousands, and the whole country watched it on TV. It's not surprising that in this second case the government and the people engaged in panic thinking.
- Though the North Korea tested nuclear bombs in 2006 and 2009, it had been threatening to do that for a decade, so it didn't surprise

the world when it did. It was a novel but anticipated event. The world reacted with sports thinking—a well-reasoned, practiced, and appropriate response—rather than panic thinking. In such a long anticipated situation, people are less likely to commit blunders.

Blunders

Blunders in this book are defined as big mistakes that leave expensive long-lasting scars on the people or communities which make them. They are usually the result of panic thinking. Ironically, they seem the best response right in the middle of the panic. This is when leaders and followers are yelling, "We have to do something, and this is a good solution! It is the best solution! And anyone who thinks otherwise is badly mistaken!"

Donald Rumsfeld describes this way of thinking in explaining the decision to go into Iraq after 9/11.

> Wed July 9, 2003 11:16 AM ET WASHINGTON (Reuters) - Defense Secretary Donald Rumsfeld said on Wednesday the United States did not go to war with Iraq because of dramatic new evidence of banned weapons but because it saw existing information on Iraqi arms programs in a new light after the Sept. 11, 2001 attacks.
>
> "The coalition did not act in Iraq because we had discovered dramatic new evidence of Iraq's pursuit of weapons of mass destruction," Rumsfeld told the Senate Armed Services Committee. "We acted because we saw the evidence in a dramatic new light—through the prism of our experience on 9/11."

This is a fine example of a novel and scary event changing a person's point of view.

However, to outside observers who aren't caught up in the panic, the course chosen can look like a strange choice or a very bad choice. When they point out the problems with a plan, they get shouted down by those who have panicked.

Blunders can be very expensive; rarely are they well thought out, and rarely is there a fallback plan that isn't also a product of panic. Emotions militate against that.

Chains of Blunders

Blunders can set the stage for other blunders; this is common in history.

The unification of Germany and Italy in the 1860s and '70s were novel events in Europe's history, and diplomats had trouble figuring out how to deal with them. This novelty set the stage for World War I, which turned into a massive, bloody, and long-lasting blunder. That set the stage for worldwide social unrest in the 1920s that resulted in the German, Austrian, Russian, and Turkish revolutions in Europe and prohibition in the United States.

This new kind of unrest set the stage for the Great Depression in the 1930s and the rise of Mussolini's, Hitler's, and Stalin's totalitarianism in the late 1930s that was broadcast over the radio and thus made much more public. This set the stage for World War II, which was more violent than anything humanity had experienced and led to the long and expensive Cold War in the 1950s with yet a different style of confrontation and rulership.

Each blunder fed on the previous one and became a serious, new threat to millions who engaged in panic thinking and created yet another blunder.

Long-Lasting Scars

Blunders change history by leaving huge social scars, lasting changes to how a community feels about certain issues and thus moves through history. Blunders occur when people become scared about new situations they try to solve but fail. But that doesn't stop them from supporting a solution that becomes a blunder for a long time; they do so because they don't want to be afraid again. When people point out the blunder and say, "The solution we have in place now is a rotten fix to the problem, so let's try fixing it," the community says, "Let the sleeping dog lie. We don't want to go through that hell again." Ironically, some blunders fix themselves: Germany, Italy, and Japan fixed their fears by losing wars.

Panic thinking thus can provoke wacky solutions that don't work, and that can lead people to shout down those who don't engage in panic thinking. This sets the stage for the next in a chain of blunders, each of which can leave long-lasting scars. Blunders occur when a community under stress faces a novel and scary threat. The result, unfortunately, will be a blunder of historic proportions.

09

End of the World. Again.

"Repent! It's the end of the world! Again!"

Sigh. Why does this come up so repeatedly, and why is it taken so seriously? Some people become <u>preppers</u>, those preparing for an imminent end to the world, and others become members of extremist groups such as <u>ISIS</u>.

Different people make different End of the World (EOW) pronouncements; the most notorious are religious leaders, but other authority figures and opinion leaders can make them as well. And such pronouncements come out constantly. Ninety-nine percent of them are ignored, but that last 1 percent can generate a lot of attention and action. The high-profile part of the action is highly publicized doom-and-gloom activities, most of which are precautionary, but some of which are celebratory – going out wild party style. At the same time there is lower-profile activity also going on, some people get caught up in taking on risky business speculations.

Then the big day comes. And it passes. And people forget about it. Until the next prediction people pay attention to comes along. A textbook example of gloom-and-doom thinking was the worry about <u>Y2K</u> (year 2000) and the havoc it would cause with computers. A textbook example of the risky investments going sour was the <u>Asian Flu Crash</u> of 1998, which followed the EOW mania surrounding Hong Kong going back to China in 1997.

Seminomadism: The Root of EOW

The instinctive thinking at the root of EOW thinking is seminomadism. Our ancestors would move when resources became scarce in one area. They hauled what they could to the next location and ate or left behind whatever they couldn't take with.

Fast forward to the Industrial Age; what used to be humans' leaving-the-village-behind instinctive thinking shows up as End of the World thinking. As with all instinctive thinking that no longer matches the circumstances well, people say, "It's crazy, but it's comfortable."

Seminomadism and its associated lifestyles were replaced by agricultural societies, which in turn required and developed different patterns of thinking. We have developed new ways of thinking, but we haven't lost the old instincts, and they show up from time to time in strange ways—EOW pronouncements are one of them, and some of us take them seriously.

10

Ambition vs. Fairness

Ambition and fairness are styles of thinking that are often at odds with each other. Some famous examples include unions vs. management, saving vs. partying when it comes to dealing with a windfall, and supply vs. demand battles in the marketplace. Such differing ways of handling situations can create differences in lifestyles.

Patterns of Ambition

Ambitious people work hard to get ahead, and they derive satisfaction from the lifestyle they achieve as well as the status they gain in the community. They're willing to move, to migrate for better opportunities and can bring along their ambition to the betterment of their new community.

Their ambition is based on the hunter instinct, the drive to travel long distances if necessary to better hunting grounds. They are independent in thinking and action and care less about what their peers back in the village—ancient or modern—are thinking than what the game they're stalking is thinking.

Patterns of Fairness

Those who live the fairness lifestyle focus on spreading everything around to community members. Their attitude is, "We're all in this together." Fairness is based on the seminomadic instinct that called on people to migrate at times and help each other do so. "We live together, we move together, and when we get to our new home, we share what we take with us" was the prevailing attitude.

These two thinking styles were necessary and successful in the Stone Age, but where they worked well was quite different. Deciding which was appropriate in a particular circumstance could give rise to disagreement and conflict.

How Merchant Thinking Fits into This Picture

An example of this conflict in the Agricultural and the Industrial Age circumstances is how to treat merchant activities and its close cousin, finance activities.

Merchants engaged (and still do) in hunter-style thinking; they searched for trading opportunities and had to deal with strangers in cooperative ways and risk being cheated. An exciting and different life indeed.

Theirs was a distinctive combination of lifestyle and thinking very unlike that of the average villager or farmer. For this reason, merchants have traditionally been considered distinct from other regular folks and artisans; if times got scary for the community, the merchants would be high on the witch-hunting list.

From merchants evolved financiers. They too dealt with people and money in strange ways, and they kept coming up with even stranger ways as the world became more complex.

Finance is extreme ambition thinking, which puts it solidly at odds with fairness thinking. An example of this difference in thinking is usury laws that try to limit unfair lending practices.

This difference between ambitious thinking and fairness thinking permeates social struggles in all ages of history. As with other thinking styles, the complexities of the Industrial Age amplify this conflict and gives rise to institutions meant to harmonize the lifestyles.

11

Chosen People and Pillars of Faith

The Chosen People mind-set is a thinking invention that allows the Us vs. Them instinct to apply to a larger group. This becomes very handy as a group moves from the Stone Age to the Agricultural Age. This versatile invention is at the core of "We're exceptional" feelings of all sorts.

The Beginning

As humanity discovered the virtues of agriculture, it had to change its traditional lifestyle of cooperating mostly with extended family to cooperating with larger groups. Humanity had to broaden its definition of who were friends when it came to grappling with the necessity of farming large tracts of land and maintaining many villages and a few cities. Their challenge was to transform the Us vs. Them instinct into something that could encompass much larger groups.

The solution was to come up with Chosen People thinking. When people learned this concept (and yes, they had to learn it), they could see larger groups as Us, and when that happened, any betrayal became bad in the eyes of their larger communities.

A handy invention indeed. In large part, this is what the story of Moses in the Bible is about.

How It Evolved

When leaders give pep talks to their followers, they say, "We're exceptional!" That's Chosen People thinking. But the results of that have been astounding. We wouldn't have cities without Chosen People thinking.

Because this is a learned skill, some people have a hard time learning it. In older times, those who didn't or couldn't learn it were relegated to continuing the Neolithic Village lifestyle. They remained on the outskirts of society—think of the "hillbillies" in the eastern United States who said "No, thanks." to the idea of becoming part of any larger groups. These "hill people" didn't mind betraying the "valley people"; they would raid fields and villages and steal horses and women. This is the source of the traditional bad feelings between hill people and valley people.

One of the challenges of sustaining Chosen People thinking is determining who really thinks they are part of the chosen people. One of the surprising ways of doing that is creating Pillars of Faith and seeing who will take them seriously.

"You have to have faith." I've heard this from so many proselytes. For decades, I was a skeptic, but these days, I believe! You have to have faith, lots of it, if you're going to believe in Pillars of Faith because they're so illogical. You believe in them just to demonstrate you're part of this group of Chosen People.

Odd Choices

There are thousands of religions and belief systems thus thousands of Pillars of Faith. Jews don't eat pork. Mormons don't drink stimulating beverages but do embrace polygamy. These seemingly odd choices were once embraced for practical reasons that no longer apply. The leaders and followers had the choice of giving up the practice or sustaining it by embracing it as a Pillar of Faith. When that happens, the practitioners de facto recognize that there is no longer any practical reason for the choice but still embrace it as an emblem of their religion.

The Jews have a practical description of what is happening. This comes from the Wikipedia description of Kashrut.

Philosophical Explanations

Jewish philosophy divides the 613 mitzvot into three groups—laws that have a rational explanation and would probably be enacted by most orderly societies (mishpatim), laws that are understood after being explained, but would not be legislated without the Torah's command, (edot), and laws that do not have a rational explanation (chukim). Some Jewish scholars say that kashrut should be categorized as laws for which there is no particular explanation, since the human mind is not always capable of understanding divine intentions. In this line of thinking, the dietary laws were given as a demonstration of God's authority and man must obey without asking why. However, Maimonides believed that Jews were permitted to seek out reasons for the laws of the Torah.

Not surprisingly, there's emotion involved in transforming something into a Pillar of Faith, and the choice can often split a religion.

Practical Roots

Let's look at the practical roots that started each of these choices, starting with the Jewish prohibition against pork. An anthropology teacher, Robin Chalhoub, introduced me to Marvin Harris and his essay "The Abominable Pig," which talks about pragmatic, ecological explanations for why Israelites gave up on raising pigs. While doing so worked in some circumstances in the Judean part of the Middle East, pigs were usually an expensive alternative to cattle, sheep, and goats, and the Jewish leaders wanted to encourage the latter. As late as the twelfth century AD, the Egyptian Jewish rabbi Moses Maimonides, court physician to the Islamic emperor Saladin, was still dead set against pork eating.

The Mormon prohibition against stimulating beverages comes from Wikipedia's entry about Brigham Young's *Journal of Discourses* about the origins of the *Words of Wisdom*.

When they assembled together in this room after breakfast, the first they did was to light their pipes, and, while smoking,

50

talk about the great things of the kingdom, and spit all over the room, and as soon as the pipe was out of their mouths a large chew of tobacco would then be taken. Often when the Prophet [Joseph Smith] entered the room to give the school instructions he would find himself in a cloud of tobacco smoke. This, and the complaints of his wife at having to clean so filthy a floor, made the Prophet think upon the matter, and he inquired of the Lord relating to the conduct of the Elders in using tobacco, and the revelation known as the Word of Wisdom was the result of his inquiry.

This pillar started as a practical solution to a particular problem. But according to the same article, as late as 1842, there were still questions about what this really meant.

In 1842, Smith's brother Hyrum, who was the Assistant President of the Church and its presiding patriarch, provided an interpretation of the Word of Wisdom's proscription of "hot drinks." And again "hot drinks are not for the body, or belly;" there are many who wonder what this can mean; whether it refers to tea, or coffee, or not. I say it does refer to tea, and coffee.

Fast forward to the 2010s; the question of what to consume now revolves around soft drinks with caffeine. They aren't hot, but …

Polygamy

From a Wikipedia article about <u>Warren Jeffs</u>, we see how FLDS polygamy has evolved into a Pillar of Faith for that community.

In January 2004, Jeffs expelled a group of 20 men from Colorado City, including the mayor, and reassigned their wives and children to other men in the community. Jeffs, like his predecessors, continued the standard FLDS and Mormon fundamentalist tenet that faithful men must follow what is known as the doctrine of "Celestial Marriage" or plural marriage in order to attain the highest degree of Exaltation

51

in the afterlife. Jeffs specifically taught that a devoted church member is expected to have at least three wives in order to get into heaven, and the more wives a man has, the closer he is to heaven. Former church members claim that Jeffs himself has seventy wives.

Jeffs was the 2000s definer of what this Pillar of Faith meant, and he appears to have gone whole hog—the more wives the better. The FLDS experience is an example of how crises revolving around Pillars of Faith can split a community.

Unlike pork eating and consuming hot drinks, polygamy seems to have come into Mormonism by historic accident. Some of the earliest converts to Joseph Smith's new religion were Cochranites, followers of a short-lived religious order founded by Jacob Cochran. His followers practiced a lifestyle comparable to that in 1960s hippie communes and is perhaps where the LDS ideas for United Order—a system in which community members share all the wealth—and plural marriage came from. For the Cochranites this was their practical living style.

I say perhaps because no one knows for sure now, and the leaders and followers may not have known for sure even in their own time. The United States in the 1830s and '40s was an exciting place for many things, including experimenting with new religious ideas; think California in the 1950s and '60s only more so. Mormonism was just one of hundreds of new religious forms being experimented with, and the Cochranites were another; both had chaotic beginnings, so even though there is a lot of documentation from this period, the roots of various ideas that became parts of these religions remain obscure.

When the Mormons settled in Utah in the 1850s (they had moved dozens of times around the Midwest during the 1830s and '40s and made many enemies in the process), they became more open about their polygamy, and it became a Pillar of Faith. In the 1880s, this became a crisis again as the Mormons were torn between keeping that pillar and giving it up so they could become more a part of mainstream US culture. The symbol of this moving mainstream was getting statehood for Utah, something that had been denied many times in previous decades. The mainstream church gave polygamy up, but those who wanted to sustain it split away and became a cluster of fundamentalist groups who were Mormon but no longer mainstream Mormon. The FLDS was one of those breakaway groups.

These are some examples of pillars of faith evolving from practical roots.

The Survival Value

The benefit of having Pillars of Faith is similar to the benefits of having a kinship system. In both cases, the goal is to help people quickly decide whom they can trust and whom they can't.

Believing in a Pillar of Faith demonstrates that a person is willing to sacrifice to become part of a group. When that happens, other members of the group trust this person more—he or she won't betray them as easily as will those who don't embrace the Pillar of Faith.

The system is far from perfect, but perfection has never been an important criterion for evolutionary success. Mother Nature has endorsed this way of thinking. The challenge of the globalized decades is to figure out ways to mesh Pillar of Faith thinking with modern globalized reality, a big challenge.

More Examples of Pillars

While many pillars are associated with religion, many are secular in nature.

Creationism

One of the large and growing pillars of faith in the United States is creationism. It spreads across many Christian religions. From the day that Darwin first proposed it, evolution by natural selection has been a scary concept for those who have faith that humanity has a special place in our universe, that it had been chosen. In modern US culture, this Pillar of Faith has grown strong and widespread and appears to be spreading.

Blame Bush

During President Obama's first term, his administration commonly blamed George W. Bush for why something wasn't working out as expected, saying it was a problem it had inherited from the latter's administration. At first, this was a practical answer, but as the years rolled by, it turned into a Pillar of Faith.

Since Pillars of Faith have become matters no longer based on anything practical, the question of what it really means to follow them comes up constantly and must be decided by opinion makers. The choice is arbitrary, but opinion makers are rarely comfortable with passing on a simple fiat, so they develop stories or construct supposedly logical arguments to support them, but that will vary between opinion makers.

Further Reading about Pillars of Faith

"South Korea Surrenders to Creationist Demands" in *Scientific American* (June 5, 2012) and the *IO9* article "South Korea will remove evolution from its high school textbooks" deal with how South Korean creationist groups are making their influence felt in the Korean educational system.

"It's Official: Coke and Pepsi are OK for Mormons" (*Washington Post*, August 31) 2012) by Peggy Fletcher Stack describes an example of contemporary interpretation of a pillar.

> On Wednesday (Aug. 29), the LDS church posted a statement on its website saying that "the church does not prohibit the use of caffeine" and that the faith's health-code reference to "hot drinks" does not go beyond (tea and coffee).

A day later, the website wording was slightly softened, saying only, "The church revelation spelling out health practices … does not mention the use of caffeine."

Conclusion

Chosen People thinking allowed the Agricultural Age to progress and become so much more than just farming fields. It allowed Us vs. Them thinking to expand and include groups larger than families.

It is a learned skill, and some people have a hard time learning it. Part of what is learned is what group now constitutes Us; Pillars of Faith help people determine that.

This ability to come together in larger groups is the heart of all history based on cultures that have acquired Agricultural Age or Industrial Age technologies and lifestyles.

12

The Variables

Changing Technology

Technology is important because it has such a dramatic effect on how we live and on history as well. If the fastest way to send a message is running and shouting it, what happens over the next hill makes little difference, and two hilltops away is another world.

Our speed of communications now is obvious; the editing of our communications is a more subtle element. Think of the difference between World War II newsreels and the video of the Rodney King police beating.

Technology is a variable part of the fabric that becomes the patterns of history. Which technologies are in place during a historical incident affect how it will evolve. This is why knowing which are in place is important.

Changing Circumstance

People learn from their successes and failures; this is the heart of analytic thinking and why circumstance is so important to how historic events evolve.

We learn from our individual mistakes in childhood, but there are also huge examples of this happening historically. The peace processes engaged in after World War I were huge failures that led to World War

II; those that came into play after the latter war worked out much better. There was peace, though it was scary at times, but the world, including the conquered nations, prospered mightily under those peace processes for the next seventy years and more. This is a fine example of learning from mistakes.

Learning from Successes

We learn from our successes as well; we've learned to adapt free-market systems, finance, capitalism and socialism to the challenge of making Industrial Age technologies work for the good of the community. The fact that this hasn't happened everywhere, and there has been a lot of social unrest and violence mixed in, has shown that the transition to the Industrial Age isn't easy or inevitable.

The rise and then decline of many Industrial Age communities also shows that learning from success is a skill that must be mastered and practiced. The learning is not inevitable, and it must be learned by each generation.

Circumstance affects the course of history. Much of the effect is due to what people of that historic generation have learned. What people have learned affects the actions they will take. Circumstance is very much part of the fabric of history.

13

Enfranchisement

Enfranchisement is the feeling people get when they feel their communities are paying attention to them and when they feel what they do affects the well-being of the community

The more the community members feel enfranchised, the more they will support orderly change and the less they will support crime in all its incarnations.

This makes enfranchisement very important. Because promoting enfranchisement is so important, we should prepare enfranchisement impact statements as frequently as we do environmental impact statements.

Virtues of Feeling Enfranchised

Those who feel enfranchised are more willing to cooperate with other community members and more tolerant when other community members are proposing big, disruptive changes. In the 1880s, railroads changed the nature of many small towns; they were disruptive and inconvenient at first, but they brought prosperity in following years. If community members feel enfranchised, they will support such changes; however, if they feel disenfranchised, they will react with acrimony to changes and say later, "I told you so" rather than, "Okay, let's get this fixed."

Disenfranchised people are less willing to cooperate, and this can allow gangs, crime, and corruption to flourish. A high-profile example of the dangers of disenfranchisement is the protesting and violence that went on in <u>Ferguson, Missouri</u> in 2014 and 2015. An even more extreme example is the feelings of Palestinians in Israel and the surrounding areas since the creation of the Israeli state following World War II. Many of these people have been refugees for three generations now. "Set up a mortar in my backyard. ...Meh."

Conclusion

The level of enfranchisement the people of a community are feeling can explain many things such as the level of toleration and cooperation a community is experiencing. Conversely, strong feelings of disenfranchisement will track the crime and violence rates a community is experiencing.

14

Blame "Them"

Facing a difficult social problem? Here's the quick and comfortable solution: Blame Them. Anyone else. Current events in Venezuela, Russia, and the Middle East revolve around a theme: "Our problems are not our fault. They are caused by our external enemies."

Middle Eastern and Venezuelan leaders claim that enemies are using sneaky tactics to sabotage government giveaway programs. In Russia, Putin is overtly reviving Cold War thinking by taking the position that the United States and NATO are seeking to extend their hegemony over Russia and the former Soviet republics.

In all three cases, blaming others is the governments' answer to the economic and social difficulties they face whether it's the sneaky CIA or the overt Pentagon.

Blaming Them also occurs in US labor relations: "Low-paid foreigners in East Asia are taking away our high paying jobs here in the United States." Unions use this theme routinely when things aren't going well for the workers they represent.

The fifty-year decline of Midwest inner cities is another example; according to those who stay there, someone else is always the cause of the problem.

The alternative, the useful one, is to say, "Ah well, this round of good times is ending. It's time to do the painful research and retraining it's going to take to discover and exploit the next gravy train." This thinking style is useful because it solves problems; it encourages the communities involved to bite the bullet and go through the discovering and retraining hell it takes to master providing the next big thing society is now demanding.

Keep in mind it's not inevitable that a community solves its economic problems. Many once-booming communities around the world are now backwaters and will remain so for a long time.

Blaming others is comfortable thinking but rarely solves problems.

Further Reading

"The revolution at bay: Mismanagement, corruption and the oil slump are fraying Hugo Chávez's regime" (*Economist*, February 14, 2015) went into detail about the 2015 crisis in Venezuela including its blame-them elements. Here's a passage from the article.

> Mr Rondón's rambling remarks over the next 45 minutes belie that claim. Saying Venezuela is faced with an "economic war," he calls on his audience to check food queues for outsiders, who might be profiteers or troublemakers, and to draw up a census of the district to identify opposition activists and government supporters. "We must impose harsh controls," he warns. "This will be a year of struggle."

In the same issue of the *Economist* was "From cold war to hot war: Russia's aggression in Ukraine is part of a broader, and more dangerous, confrontation with the West." It dealt with the current Ukraine confrontation and the blame-them thinking in Russia.

> Russia feels threatened not by any individual European state, but by the European Union and NATO, which it regards as expansionist. It sees them as "occupied" by America, which seeks to exploit Western values to gain influence over the rest of the world. America "wants to freeze the order established after the Soviet collapse and remain an absolute leader, thinking it can do whatever it likes, while others can do only what is in that leader's interests," Mr. Putin said recently. "Maybe some want to live in a semi-occupied state, but we do not."

"Venezuela to sanction U.S. officials, limit diplomatic personnel, require visas for Americans" appeared in the March 15, 2001 issue of *Xinhua* and indicated the blame-others attitude is strong in Venezuela.

> Venezuelan President Nicolas Maduro announced Saturday that his government will deny visas to a number of United States officials whom he called "terrorists," including former president George W. Bush and senators Marco Rubio and Bob Menendez.

Part 2

The Patterns

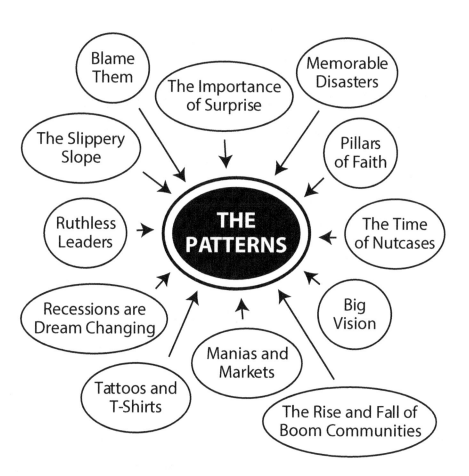

15

Surprise's Part in History

One of the important elements in major historical events is the surprise they were to many of those involved. This element of history is often forgotten—and just as often mistold—especially when the telling was shaped by editorial opinion. But if history is to help us predict the course of current events, we have to take into account the surprise factor.

Surprise is important because it explains why the people of the time didn't respond better to the issue. They hadn't had the time to think about the problem or the ramifications of their solutions. We can look back and call their choices silly, but we're Monday-morning quarterbacking.

World War I

The biggest surprise about World War I was not that it started but how long it lasted and how much social upheaval it caused in terms of deaths and other horrible costs.

Before World War I, countries in Europe had fought regularly. What European wars since 1815 had in common was that they were limited in size and brief—the winners and losers were decided quickly.

World War I was predicted to be like the War of 1870 between France and Prussia, which lasted only three months and resulted in only about 150,000 casualties. World War I lasted four years in Western Europe and six to ten years in Central Europe, Eastern Europe, and the Ottoman

Empire's regions of the Middle East; the casualty count went into the millions.

As it was going on, other surprises occurred, including the violent social revolutions in the Russian, German, Austro-Hungarian, and Ottoman Empires. Another surprise was how badly the Treaty of Versailles worked out as opposed to the treaties that concluded World War II; people had learned.

World War I's length and carnage was such a surprise that it caused historians to spend time and attention on placing the blame for starting the war. Who started it was a small-potatoes issue compared to the issue of why no one could end it sooner, but it was a lot easier to think about.

The '29 Crash and the Great Depression

During the post–World War I era, changes swept across America; Henry Ford's assembly line was iconic of this change. Booms were followed by busts, but the busts were small and recovered from quickly.

Then came the big crash of '29. This one was surprising due to how fast and deep the crash was. It was so surprising that a bank panic followed and a deep economic recession followed that—both surprises.

Many people searched for solutions. Hoover's administration tried to turn things around with some stimulus spending, but nothing worked; Americans were frustrated and scared.

In 1932, Americans elected Franklin Delano Roosevelt (FDR), who, inspired by the then-new theories of John Maynard Keynes, tried even more vigorous government intervention that became known as the New Deal. It didn't work, but FDR became legendary and deeply admired for trying harder and not letting things get worse.

The Great Depression didn't end until America began preparing to fight World War II. And the experience of the 1929 crash helped keep the crash of 2007 becoming as deep and traumatic.

The IC and PC Revolutions of the 1980s

Unlike the wars and market crashes talked about above, the integrated circuit (IC) and personal computer (PC) revolutions were a fun surprise.

Since the end of World War II, computer technology evolved from relying on mechanical relays and vacuum tubes to discrete transistors and ICs. These developments expanded the use of computers and thus the market for them; smaller companies could use minicomputers profitably for many tasks.

ICs made the personal computer possible; that was the surprise use for ICs. Personal computers started being used for not just bookkeeping and spreadsheets but also for word processing and computer games.

Another surprise was open architecture. Because the pioneer PC users were hobbyists who loved to tinker, PCs became even more popular when manufacturers showed their users how the computers were designed and let them participate in the designing by letting them create <u>daughter boards</u> and new kinds of programs. This kind of revealing was unheard of in the minicomputer world; minicomputer companies kept tight control on the developing and designing and maintained software "fortresses." As a result of this market change, minicomputer companies such as <u>DEC</u> declined over the 1980s and 1990s and upstart PC companies such as Apple took their places—very surprising for all those involved.

Not so surprising was that the upstart PC companies matured; Apple became just another niche player after Steve Jobs left in part because it was run by minicomputer company veterans and started embracing the software-fortress mentality. Apple didn't turn around and become legendary again until Jobs came back.

Adding a cherry on top to this decade of surprises was that IBM, an older, mainframe computer company, managed to adapt to the PC computer world quite well and became one of its leaders. One of IBM's managers, <u>Don Estridge</u>, was a company visionary. He figured out this new playing field and got IBM playing successfully on it.

Roger Bourke White Jr.

Conclusion

Surprises are part of history; current events are filled with them. If studying history is to be a useful tool for coping with current events, the surprise elements of the times need to be recognized and be part of the history telling. If not, what people end up doing will very often look foolish in hindsight.

16

The Anatomy of Memorable Disasters

In 1912, the *Titanic* sunk. In 1986, the *Challenger* space shuttle blew up. On September 11, 2001, the World Trade Centers were destroyed by planes. These memorable disasters will never be forgotten.

In 1961, the Agir Hotel in Morocco collapsed in a violent earthquake. But who has heard of that disaster?

Though most disasters involve phenomenal losses of life and property, some aren't remembered as such. Over 20,000 people a year die on our nation's highways, but do we remember that? Over 50,000 died in the battle of Mukden, China, but no one from the West knows much about that battle. Two satellites malfired while being launched from the space shuttle at a cost of $300 million each, but what are the chances you'll tell your kids about that?

Here are my rules involving disasters. There must be loss, but the key to the memorability of a disaster isn't the victims but the survivors. As well, the disaster's time frame has to be short enough to keep people's attention; a year is much too long; an hour to half a day seems ideal. About 1,500 died in the sinking of the *Titanic*; 700 survived. It sunk in about two hours, and the survivors were rescued by other ships in about six.

Next, we must consider who's affected—the richer and more famous the better. The *Titanic* was carrying the cream of Anglo-American society, whereas Korean Air Flight 007 was carrying an average cross section of Koreans and Americans.

Let's consider the condition of the survivors. In the case of the *Titanic*, the weather conditions while the ship went down were ideal. It was cool, about 35 degrees, no wind, and the boat sunk slowly. The ship's lights burned almost to the end, so the view was spectacular. Survivors endured comparatively little physical discomfort; they could concentrate on the significance of the event and remember every detail. They provided so many details that went into the whole story.

On the other hand, of the 400 or so in the Agir hotel, many were rich and famous Europeans. But the shaking came and went, and in seconds, 400 died in a concrete hotel that went from four stories to half a story. It was as visually spectacular as the *Titanic*'s sinking, but it was too fast, and there was no one left to tell any tales of heroism, sacrifice, or cowardice.

Technological hubris is another factor in disasters. The *Titanic* was the biggest and most-advanced transportation system of its day; its engineers and designers were justly proud of it. But its owners never claimed it was unsinkable; that claim was added after the fact and stuck because it resonated with the "hubris of technology" theme.

Let's compare the *Challenger* and the *Titanic* disasters. The former involved technological hubris and billions of dollars of loss and seven lives. But no one survived, only seven famous people were involved, and it took only seventy-five seconds. The *Titanic* disaster will always be more memorable.

The events of 9/11 involved technological hubris—airplanes turned into weapons of mass destruction, massive skyscrapers tumbling, thousands of lives lost, property loss in the billions, and thousands surviving. The terrorists involved became the bogeymen of twenty-first-century American mythology. It took place in about two hours and was watched by millions in real time and later.

These fanatics turned airplane crashes, which usually take short amounts of time and occur usually in remote places, into a long and public event. Thousands of New Yorkers witnessed the memorable event without distraction.

The dust cloud that covered Manhattan following the WTC collapse gave a million spectators a tactile experience that transformed their experience from that of passive spectators into that of active survivors. How much more memorable could a disaster get?

The WTC and the Pentagon were potent symbols filled with potent people. The fanatics couldn't have picked better choices to permanently scare America … as has been shown by the enormous panic Americans have felt since the disaster.

January 2004: 9/11 Update

It took two years, but a poster child for 9/11 emerged—the firefighter, or the first responder. It was surprising how long it took for a human symbol of the disaster to emerge. The *Titanic* had the Astors, the space shuttle had the astronauts and the teacher, and these human-interest symbols were established fairly quickly after the disasters.

Lifeboats on the *Titanic* Thinking

After a high-profile disaster or other spectacularly scary event, many people vow "Never again" and start putting teeth in that vow. The "lifeboat" problem occurs when the teeth aren't thought through and in the end don't accomplish their goals but instead create waste.

After the *Titanic* sank, the hue and cry went up to do something to make transatlantic crossings safer. One of the recommendations was that all passenger liners carry enough lifeboats for all passengers and crew. After the *Columbia* shuttle disaster, NASA decided the shuttles could fly only to places where they could dock so they could be inspected and repaired if damaged, and the only place was International Space Station. NASA abandoned the Hubble telescope because the space shuttles couldn't dock there safely.

"Enough seats for all" sounded like the right response to the sinking, but it failed to take into consideration what happens with shipwrecks. In most shipwrecks, all the lifeboats can't be used if the ship is listing; if the weather is rough enough, the lifeboats can't be launched at all. And any wreck that happens near a coast will allow the lifeboats to ferry people; not all will have to be in the lifeboats at the same time.

The *Titanic*, on the other hand, sunk in clear, calm weather, so lifeboats could be launched. The ship didn't list, so lifeboats could be launched from both sides. Only under such freakish conditions could having enough lifeboats for everyone made a difference, but the *Titanic* accident set the standard for lifeboat capacity for the next hundred years, and the decision to allow the space shuttles to go only where they could dock led to the abandonment of the Hubble telescope. The development of policies based on their intuitive feel rather than formal cost-benefit analysis is the lifeboats-on-the-*Titanic* phenomenon.

In the case of the shuttles, the question revolved around the likelihood that a catastrophic accident could be prevented by something the crew could find and fix in space. If there's only a one-in-a-million chance of such a problem, why did we sacrifice the Hubble?

While comfortable at the time they are made, such decisions are always very expensive. We live in a risky world and should recognize that it isn't cost effective to try to avoid rare scenarios unless we expect that scenario to be repeated at least a thousand times in a reasonable time frame. We would then be spending to prevent something that had a thousandth of a chance of happening again—still a vanishingly small risk.

By the way, cooler heads did prevail; NASA visited the Hubble a final time in 2009.

Further Reading

"How Much Is an Astronaut's Life Worth?" by Robert Zubrin (*Reason* magazine, February 2012) described the alternative to the emotional approach. It offered an analytic, cost/benefit approach to deciding when to risk a Mars mission. The result of using this style of analysis is a much clearer and much quicker decision on when to go ahead.

"The Real Reason for the Tragedy of the *Titanic*" was a *Wall Street Journal* (April 12, 2012) editorial by Chris Berg that summarized the various reasons that have been given over the years for why there weren't more lifeboats: "The disaster is often seen as a tale of hubris, social stratification and capitalist excess. The truth is considerably more sobering." Note how the lifeboats were utilized in the recent shipwreck of the *Costa Concordia* in 2012.

17

The Time of Nutcases

Nutcases have their day when a community gets severely stressed by a problem, usually economic, that continues to plague them. This gives nutcases, those who are usually ignored because of their unconventionality, the opportunity to attract attention they otherwise wouldn't because people become desperate to solve the problem.

Some of what they might advocate will be innovative and beneficial, but their good ideas will be gems in a sea of rehashed urban legends and feel-good/don't-work ideas that will just waste time, money, and effort. People will need logical, not emotional ways of spotting the gems among the garbage. Top on people's minds is, "What's going to work?" And they end up willing to listen to the nutcases because of their panic and frustration.

Examples

Picking Roosevelt and Hitler for leaders

The early 1930s were a scary time around the world. The Great Depression was relentless, and leaders such as <u>Hoover</u> in the United States and <u>Hindenburg</u> in Germany hadn't solved it. People around the world started listening seriously to leaders with unconventional, ideas. During the mid-1930s, many of these unconventional leaders came to power. But the Time of Nutcases didn't stop with the election of these new leaders because these new leaders didn't solve the problem either. It continued into World War II. But then it stopped because the war changed the world problem set (my term) dramatically. For every nation and every people fighting in the war, winning the war became top priority.

The rise of the Tea Party and Occupy Wall Street in 2010

The financial crash in 2007 brought on the Great Recession, which lingered for years. Conventional wisdom and the conventional solutions enacted by the Fed and the Obama administration weren't solving the problem. Three years into the recession, the Time of Nutcases started flowering; the Tea Party and Occupy Wall Street were examples. In the run-up to the election of 2016, the Time of the Nutcases was still in bloom with Donald Trump and Bernie Sanders being the high-profile icons.

This 2007 financial downturn and subsequent frustration were not just US problems, and the Time of Nutcases was not just a US phenomenon. One spectacular example of the overseas version was the Arab Spring of 2012.

Conclusion

The Time of Nutcases comes around when a community is stressed for much longer than it thinks should have been necessary; people feel conventional leaders and conventional solutions have failed. They open their ears to alternative leaders who, along with their wild and wooly ideas, get their day in the sun.

18

The Importance of a Community Dreaming Big

The pyramids, the early Mormon temples in Utah, and the Great Wall of China are just a few examples of what can be accomplished when communities dream big. Even while most of the people were living in mud huts, they were able to produce marvelous works because everyone thought spending their resources on something grand would produce more value than spending those resources on better roads, housing, and food.

In these cases, the importance of unifying the community was valued. Each of these projects gave community members the opportunity to learn about cooperating with many other people, especially strangers. They learned the value of cooperation and tolerance instead of just standing around watching others or taking cheap shots at these projects, and that was learned rather than instinctual behavior that turned out to be a vital lesson in civilized living.

As vital as the lesson they learned was, it was underappreciated more often than not because most people pay attention to divisive rather than unifying issues. When people don't learn the cooperator lesson, they become acrimonious, and that spells death to progress.

Big dreams can help a community better itself rather than letting itself disintegrate. I saw this happen in Detroit and Cleveland (where I grew up in the 1960s); read <u>Midwest Disease</u> (my term, covered elsewhere).

Picking the Vision

Picking and promoting a big vision is vital but tough to do. Kennedy got it right with landing a man on the moon, Bush Jr. got it wrong with the war on terror. FDR caused one surprise turnabout during the Great Depression. When he decided that fighting fascism in Europe was more important than fighting class warfare in the United States, he came up with a hugely successful series of big visions, which started with creating the Arsenal of Democracy. After the acrimonious 1930s, Americans learned to cooperate again during the harsh times of World War II and were rewarded with fifty years of prosperity.

For a more recent example of picking first wrong then right dreams, check out my book *Surfing the High Tech Wave*; it's about the Novell Corporation in the 1980s, which first got the dream wrong but then got it spectacularly right and became a billion-dollar company at the heart of a new, multibillion-dollar industry.

It isn't easy, but if you get the dream right and promote it right, some will grumble from the sidelines and say, "I told you so" when any blunders occur, but many others will get onboard and love the result.

Communities need periodic big visions; they teach people to cooperate, and this can result in innovation and rapid and exciting growth. So be a leader with a big vision.

Some places which got the big vision right: consider the Meiji Restoration in Japan starting in the 1870s, the United States starting in the 1780s, and Singapore starting in the 1960s as shining examples. Many more do not: Midwest America starting in the 1960s, the post–Ottoman Empire Middle Eastern States starting in the 1920s, and most of the world starting in 1930 (the Great Depression) are examples of trying and not getting it right. Instead of getting successful big visions launched, the people involved in these failures end up staying distracted and doing a lot of squabbling.

One of the differences between success and failure is how threatened a community feels. If a community doesn't feel threatened by something outside the community, it will be complacent and feel that engaging in acrimony instead of cooperation is not a big cost. Conversely, when a community feels deeply threatened by outsiders, it will put aside internal differences and mutually cooperate, and one form of that cooperating is seeing the community's big vision come to life.

Inspiration

The inspiration for this section on big visions came to me from a Special Report on Singapore (*Economist*, July 18, 2015). One of the themes in these articles was how threatened Singapore felt after it had been cast out of the newly formed nation of Malaysia in 1965, two years after Malaysia gained independence from the British Empire. Over the fifty years since, Singapore has responded very successfully and has become a shining example of successful economic development in the Far East.

The Cost of Acrimony

Acrimony—arguing instead of cooperating—results in missed opportunities. Acrimony often follows complacency—many people think things are going just fine in their communities even if there's no growth or a little decline. When ambitious folk call for improvement, that's viewed as disruptive; arguing ensues, nothing gets done, and acrimony reigns. People's feelings get hurt, the ambitious leave, and cooperation and progress become harder to achieve.

Overcoming Acrimony

Responding to external threat is one way of overcoming acrimony, and getting behind a big vision is another. An ancient example of this happening is the pyramids. These big visions started when the Nile Valley unified under a single pharaoh rather than many. The unification was violent—wars were fought and won—and after the final victory, many people were unhappy with the outcome; revolt became likely.

The unifying pharaoh solved the acrimony problem by ordering the people to contribute to his big vision, a pyramid. Pride was built up, and acrimony declined. It proved so successful that pyramid building became a common element in Egyptian culture. We see and admire the result today.

The Mormons did the same with the temple in Salt Lake City, just as medieval builders did with cathedrals in Europe. Today, we can look to hosting Olympic Games and World Cups as examples of thinking big and unifying a community.

External Threats Conquering Acrimony

In Japan, the Meiji Restoration mentioned above was an example of an external threat prompting cooperation. In the early 1800s, Japan was in an isolationist swing of its cultural pendulum and ruled by a shogun— originally an assistant to the emperor but then the chief decision maker. Its ports were mostly closed to international trade, and its feudal leadership was mostly self-contained and comparable to what China and Korea were experiencing.

Then came a dramatic change. In 1854, the US naval commander Commodore Perry visited Tokyo with a fleet of high-tech warships, an early example of gunboat diplomacy. He wanted a trade treaty and got the Convention of Kanagawa, which established trade between the United States and Japan.

His warship display convinced many important Japanese leaders to end their complacency; they realized if they didn't embrace what it took to make these high-tech warships themselves, someone who did would come knocking on their door in a much less peaceful way than Perry had and kick their butts.

Far from everyone was convinced that these warships were a meaningful threat, but enough were that the shogunate government was overthrown and replaced with the Meiji Restoration government. In China and Korea, complacency won out, and both got their butts kicked.

The leaders of this Meiji Restoration used the threat to keep the Japanese focused on transforming the country from an agricultural and feudal society into a modern, industrialized society. These new leaders were good at what they did; they completed this big-vision task in about fifty years, and by 1900, Japan was ready to become an industrialized, colonial power. First on its list for colonizing was Korea, which continued as a colony of Japan until the latter lost World War II.

The Singapore Experience

In 1965, Singapore was the Beirut of Southeast Asia. It was a cosmopolitan world trader with a mix of Chinese, Malaysian, and Indian inhabitants. It could have easily ended up as Beirut did, experiencing a fifteen-year civil war fought by its different inhabitants, but these people came together and worked together for a big vision. Fifty years later, Singapore emerged as one of the most prosperous cities in the world.

Part of what caused this was the constant threat that if Singaporeans became acrimonious, its neighbors would take advantage of their discord. Instead of being acrimonious, the people of Singapore cooperated. It's now famous as a dictatorship that worked well, and it's considered a model for other communities who think they need a dictatorship.

The US Experience

In the early 1800s, the United States faced external threats comparable to those facing Japan and Singapore. The big external threat was the British, a much smaller one was the wilderness, where Native Americans were supported by the French, British, or Spanish. The wilderness was a small threat but a huge opportunity. Taming it was seen as an opportunity to show how the world should be run!

Cooperating to exploit the wilderness was a big vision, and the benefits of cooperating rather than being complacent or acrimonious were much clearer than in most other circumstances around the world. Being able to see the benefits of cooperation is at the root of American exceptionalism. The Americans took advantage, and the results of many versions were new farms, new cities, new factories, and new technologies. America did indeed become exceptional.

Big Vision vs. Harmonious Paradise

Any community pursuing a big vision will argue over it, but a successful big vision will ultimately unite them in spite of the disruption and arguing that will occur. An example of some serious arguing that didn't stop progress was the Civil War, though it was tragic. Disruptive changes continued to happen, and the vigorous arguing continued right along with it, but the level of cooperation in the United States remained exceptionally high.

Conclusion

Vigorous cooperation can result in making big visions reality. Leaders of a community need to convince people that cooperating is necessary to create magnificent works such as the pyramids or host events such as the Olympics. Or they can convince people that an external threat is serious and can be faced successfully only if they cooperate. Making a big vision happen isn't easy, but it makes for big history.

19

Big-Vision Killers: NIMBY and Acrimony

Big visions are the heart of a community growing and prospering, but there's nothing inevitable about communities embracing big visions; history is filled with examples of more failures than successes. Two ways of thinking that poison big visions are NIMBY and acrimony.

NIMBY

<u>NIMBY</u>, Not In My Backyard, is the feeling a community will indulge in when it is faced with changes that will affect it adversely, particularly its property values. "A Walmart? That's nice, but not on my street. It would kill the value of my home." This is why Walmarts and other large retailers spread rapidly through new suburbs during the last half of the twentieth century but very slowly through long-established urban areas. The big vision such commercial establishments represented was nothing that established urban neighborhoods embraced.

Acrimony

When people disagree but not acrimoniously, they will usually come to an agreement, a compromise, and forge ahead. But when feelings of acrimony are high, coming to an agreement can take a long time and still garner just half-hearted support, a recipe for slow and poor progress.

America argued a lot about the New Deal during the Great Depression, and the slow progress lasted ten years.

Conclusion

When communities are enjoying Industrial Age lifestyles, they will at times have to undergo disruptive change to keep up the pace and prosper. Large changes—big visions such as new roads, ports, and factories—require much cooperation. When the cooperation happens, the progress happens. But the progress doesn't always happen. Some people will hold onto their NIMBY mind-sets and respond with acrimony. If they do this vigorously enough, the big visions won't become reality.

20

Entrepreneurship vs. Instinct

Prostitution may be humanity's oldest profession, but commerce surely started only days later. People love the benefits of trading but are envious of the wealthy and fear being cheated. The story of Jesus casting out the moneylenders is an example of a community's populist response when it perceives that a small group of the community is profiting too much from commerce.

Today, salaries, spending (taxes and infrastructure), and sharing wealth (entitlements) are hot-button issues everywhere. Over millennia, people have developed successful instinctual thinking about many activities, but commerce isn't one of them. Commerce doesn't lend itself to instinctual thinking because there are so many ways it can work well, and that variety requires analytical thinking to master.

Old-Fashioned Commerce

Commerce started as barter with strangers. In the Stone Age and Agricultural Age, contact with strangers was rare enough that the Us vs. Them thinking predominated; it wasn't considered okay to cheat family and friends, but strangers were fair game. So commerce was risky; caravans had guards, merchant ships carried marines, and ports were fortified. The rule was caveat emptor—let the buyer beware—merchant and their customers had to be on their toes.

Those who indulged in intervillage trading had to be exceptional in their thinking as they navigated alien environments, something few in the community did often. The result was that for much of commerce's history, merchants were considered as being outside mainstream communities. When times were good, they were tolerated; when times were bad, they and other outsiders were considered targets for witch hunts, thus their need for security.

Merchants tended to be free thinkers; they traveled more, they had to deal with alien situations more often, and they didn't gain a lot from being conformists. Their world was gray from day one, and new ideas could bring new opportunities, so they listened more intently. It's not surprising that finance was spawned by commerce and that the two have always remained closely related.

Social Justice and Commerce

The question of who should get what has been with us since well before we became Homo Sapiens. Most animals have dominance disputes about who should get what, and even plants do so in subtle ways.

In Neolithic times, the total amount of goods that could be disputed over was small; people could take only a limited amount of resources along when they migrated. Communal sharing arrangements worked well with what was taken from place to place. This environment is what human instinctive thinking is well designed to work with.

But in the Agriculture Age, when people tended to stay put for longer, the "goody" count rose astronomically and who got what becomes a big issue. We're talking permanent farms and cities, not seminomadic villages. Our instinctive thinking is beginning to adapt to this, but that adaptation is far from complete.

Neolithic people's instinct revolved around fairness; communal sharing helped them survive. This thinking also works in some Industrial/Information Age environments, but not always, though it's still a powerful concept. The more prosperous a person gets, the more easily they can let their hearts be their guides and consider the fairness aspect.

But fairness and commerce often butt heads; the latter focuses on winning in any exchange. A trade can be a win-win event, it should be, but fairness is not important here. Fairness thinking prompts certain attitudes: "There's one right way to handle this situation, and we all should handle it the same way. That's fair." Commercial thinking sees many ways of handling different situations, it is a many shades of gray situation rather than a black-or-white one.

Life, however, has become so much more complex and has resulted in the development of an even bigger resource pie (my term)—all the goodies that constitute a community's wealth and assets. This difference between being fair thinking and growing the resource pie thinking is at the root of a lot of Industrial Age social history.

Conclusion

Commerce, finance, and entrepreneurship have been going head-to-head with instinctive fairness thinking ever since long-range commerce came to be. These are two different mind-sets, and there is a lot of history made in expressing these two mind-sets and then in deciding how communities should take actions that will combine them.

21

Differences in Hunting and Gathering Thinking

Hunters and gatherers both helped their villages prosper, and we have inherited thinking well suited to both. But the thinking styles that make them work well are different, and today, people can be predominately hunter thinkers or gatherer thinkers.

Hunting and Gathering Differences

Gathering tended to be more of a communal activity. While hunters cooperated with each other, their activities included a lot more solo activity. And gathering didn't take as much analytic thought as did hunting.

Hunters were more ambitious, more willing to migrate, just as those in the Industrial Age were more willing to leave villages for cities. Those who stayed behind and said, "I don't want to leave home and my friends"; they were gatherer thinkers.

Conclusion

In the Industrial Age, the hunter style of thinking leads to ambition, investing, and migration, while the gatherer style of thinking leads to considering the fairness involved.

22

Growing the Resource Pie

Neolithic people lived in a world of limited resources and threats to those limited resources, including drought, fire, flood, and predatory neighbors. Human thinking came to expect limited, not growing resource pies. They could discover new places to gather more resources elsewhere through migration, but the idea of growing a resource pie didn't occur to them.

In the Agriculture Age, people could clear and farm fields and actually create a yearly excess if they were lucky, but still, they were limited by what any one field could produce yearly, and that could decline if the field declined in fertility; their pie, even if it expanded, still had harsh limits.

But in the Industrial Age, technology resulted in a great expansion of the resource pie. The hope for a bigger and better pie was expressed indirectly as early as the late 1700s. The Marquis de Condorcet, William Godwin and Jean-Jacques Rousseau indirectly expressed hopes for the possibility of a bigger pie, though the latter was scoffed at in the next generation by Thomas Malthus.

But throughout the 1800s, the pie grew—railroads and mechanized ways of textile manufacturing were two icons of the period. This was when the Protestant work ethic started to match real-world possibilities.

In the 1920s, the first big, real-world game changer was Henry Ford's successful concept of the assembly line, which spread around the world. (Interestingly, Ford played the fairness card prominently by paying workers above-average wages, but he didn't play the innovation card as much as he could have; he said that buyers could have whatever color Model T they wanted as long as it was black.)

Writers and thinkers in the first half of the twentieth century considered it miraculous that the size of the pie could change and marveled at what that would mean to human living. (This by the way is an example of our ability to adapt our thinking; nowadays, we take this miracle for granted.)

But instinctual thinking is not based on our current experiences, so it hasn't caught up, and it's still sure there are limits. Consider the warnings about our having reached a peak in oil reserves that will now be declining and the Club of Rome's reports on limits to growth. These tell us, "We must beware! In spite of how good things look now, things *will* run out!"

Fairness vs. Growth

Entrepreneurship has chiefly been responsible for our growing productivity. We have built new organizations that offer things and services in new, more-efficient ways. Though entrepreneurship produces exciting results, it can step on the toes of powerful instinctive thinking about harsh limits, fairness, and its buddy, prescriptive thinking—"There's one right way to do this."

As a result, entrepreneurship makes many people uncomfortable; only a few people—entrepreneurs and others able to adapt to commercial thinking—can get around their instinctive thinking, which can be strong. Consider the Luddites, who were violently opposed to mechanized looms replacing human weavers in nineteenth-century England, and the Socialist, Communist, and Unionist movements that had more pro-fair concerns. Average community thinking was caught in the middle.

On one hand, the benefits of growing the pie are immense and obvious. The desire to grow pies encouraged western European nations to become colonizers and industrializers on a grand scale during the 1800s. On the other hand was the outrage about poverty amid this growing wealth. An example of this are the Charles Dickens–style stories of the wealthy stepping over sick and starving children on the new avenues lined with smoke-belching factories. Walmart puts small, inefficient, but neighbor-friendly stores out of business. This is an issue that seesaws communities and their governments. This seesawing makes for good history.

Laissez-Faire vs. Legislation

Commerce enthusiasts often cry out for a <u>laissez-faire</u> environment in which transactions between private parties are free of tariffs, government subsidies, and enforced monopolies; they want only enough government regulations to protect property rights against theft, fraud, and aggression.

No community has ever granted that much liberty to its commerce people. The Curse of Being Important and the instinctive thinking fears mentioned above combine to always produce lots of government involvement in how commerce is conducted. But from time to time and place to place, this involvement has taken many forms and has produced dramatic differences in communities' lifestyles. Many of these differences become lessons of history. Here are some examples.

- Ancient Egypt compared to Ancient Greece
- Medieval western Europe compared to Renaissance Italy
- Asia and Africa compared to nineteenth-century western Europe
- Soviet Russia compared to United States during the Cold War

In these pairs, the first held fairness as more important in the community legal and moral framework while the second respected commerce more. In all these cases, though, these times were golden ages for the second. In spite of their brilliance in the historical record, in all these cases, the balance shifted with time and the frameworks of the two became more similar and more oriented toward fairness. Instinctive thinking is powerful.

Immigration: A Pillar-Supporting Enterprise

New styles of enterprise thrive where new styles of thinking are tolerated. Those willing to pull up roots, travel, and learn new ways of doing things take giant steps toward tolerating new thinking styles.

Mix in the ability of Industrial Age technologies to grow the pie and you have one reason why America and other immigrant nations of the 1800s became the developed nations of the 1900s. They had a steady stream of newcomers willing to tolerate new ideas and learn to exploit them;

they found themselves among others who weren't fettered by instinctual thinking; they all had it, but they didn't let it dominate their thinking.

Finance and Commerce: Always Something New

The essence of business financing is, "Trust me … but be very careful when you do." It's all about giving resources to someone on the promise of great returns.

In the past, we bartered for goods; in the present, we pay for them using our smartphones. We have so many more ways to transact business, but we still worry about being cheated. Thus, the need for regulation.

Further Reading

In The Self-Destruction of the 1 Percent (*New York Times*, October 13, 2012), Chrystia Freeland reviewed the book *Why Nations Fail: The Origins of Power, Prosperity, and Poverty* by Daron Acemoglu and James A. Robinson. The book described in fair detail how the golden age of Venice in the early 1300s came and went. The thesis was that the plutocrats of Venice cut off their own continued growth by overcontrolling the disruptive economy at the heart of their growth and prosperity—the winners made up a list of winners and gave that list legal teeth.

I like this article's analysis, but I think their thesis is half the answer, not the whole answer. Average Venetians wanted their fair share of this new wealth. I think what closed off the prosperity was that the plutocrats offered the average citizen bread and circuses to stabilize their system and that average citizens bought into that.

Golden ages seem to end consistently by declining into a mediocrity that supports a rigid hierarchical social structure; instead of supporting growth, the community ends up happy to simply get by with what it has.

This article mentions that Venetians could see this problem coming— they were writing about it, but they couldn't stop it. This was also the case for Cleveland as it suffered from the Midwest disease.

Conclusion

Though commerce and finance have been around a long time, they are outliers to the average human experience because they often run counter to human instinctive thinking and the concepts of prescriptive conformity and communal fairness and give rise to deep fears of being cheated that the Us vs. Them instinctive thinking resonates with.

When the Industrial Age resulted in a much bigger pie, average humans had a hard time figuring out how to live harmoniously with the new commerce and finance innovations that came with the bigger pie, making for interesting history.

Expanding the pie requires outside-the-box thinking and a community willing to tolerate scary disruption and potential unfairness. When the pie contracts, it's generally because of wet blankets thrown on progress by those uncomfortable with or afraid of it.

23

Rise and Fall of Boom Communities

History records the rise and fall of countless communities; from the ancient Mesopotamian city of Ur through the modern Rust Belt in the Midwest, communities have boomed and then busted.

Why does every boom seem to carry the seeds of its own return to mediocrity? The people who create these booms are clever enough to create the boom in the first place but can't seem to pass on the magic.

Consider how different history would be if teaching booming were well understood and able to be passed on. We'd be reading about the many centuries of consistent glories that have sprung from Mesopotamia, the Indus Valley, and the Yellow River Valley because those were places where booms started and would have never gone bust. They would be the New Yorks, Londons, Singapores and Shanghais of today. But this isn't the case. Booming isn't easy to teach.

Declines and Falls

This subject has enthralled historians for a long time. One of the more enduringly famous is Edward Gibbon, who wrote <u>Decline and Fall of the Roman Empire</u>. We read in the Wiki article,

> According to Gibbon, the Roman Empire succumbed to barbarian invasions in large part due to the gradual loss of civic virtue among its citizens. They had become weak,

outsourcing their duties to defend their Empire to barbarian mercenaries, who then became so numerous and ingrained that they were able to take over the Empire. Romans, he believed, had become effeminate, unwilling to live a tougher, "manly" military lifestyle.

Gibbon argued that Christianity created a belief that a better life existed after death, which fostered an indifference to the present among Roman citizens, thus sapping their desire to sacrifice for the empire, Gibbon believed its comparative pacifism hampered the traditional Roman martial spirit. Gibbon held in contempt the Middle Ages as a priest-ridden, superstitious, dark age. It was not until his own age of reason and rational thought, it was believed, that human history could resume its progress.

Rises and falls come in varieties of time and size. The Roman rise and decline took ten centuries; the Venetian rise and decline took one. Apple's first rise took ten years, as did that of many other leading high-tech companies of the 1980s all the way to the 2000s. Cleveland, my favorite example, boomed from its founding in 1814 through the 1950s; in 1920, it was America's fifth largest city. They go through growth, peaks, and busts.

Anatomy of a Boom

In the beginning, a booming community is just one of many; the Romans were just one of many competing tribes in Italy, Cleveland was just one of many thriving cities west of the Appalachians in frontier America, and Apple was just one of many hopeful start-ups in Silicon Valley in the 1970s.

All these communities experience growth, but then weeding out occurs; some communities falter, and those that don't grow even more due to their abilities to use their resources better and to acquire the resources those that falter can no longer pay for. They grow in stature; people start asking them, "What's your secret?"

Anatomy of a Peak

While a community is booming, it has to make many tough, scary, and expensive choices to do things new ways, but that's the lifeblood of a booming community. It will make mistakes, but it will make fewer of them and recover more quickly from them than its competitors do.

But at the peak, things change; fewer tough choices are taken up. This can happen when a new generation of decision makers emerges and tries less hard to change things. When what the community thinks is important changes, the leadership will change as well. Historians tend to attribute such changes to the leaders, but leaders are much closer to their community's feelings than that—they make choices compatible with what the numerous but less-visible second-tier decision makers in the community want.

In many high-tech companies, top management stops being made up of visionaries and starts being made up of seasoned managers as they grow from small- to medium-sized companies. My book *Surfing the High Tech Wave* dealt with how this happened at Novell in 1989, nine years after its start-up. The change at Novell precipitated an "organizational phase shift" (my term—think of water changing to ice) that changed Novell's direction of development.

The second example is a common business truism that when a company grows to the point that it can move into its own building, the company culture will tend to become more complacent. To prevent this, managers must be on their toes.

Changing top management and moving to new buildings can be peak times for companies, times when the boom ends. Peaks are reached when many members of the community decide the constant, tough choices it took to make the boom happen and to sustain it are no longer worth the effort. This leads to the post-peak era.

Anatomy of a Post-Peak

Historians bemoan them, but post-peak times are actually fairly comfortable times for most community members. At first, they're relieved that the times of change and uncertainty experienced during the boom time

94

are lessening; they become complacent. Rules and regulations are enacted, and life becomes much more predictable—people know their places. The article about Venice mentioned above dealt at length about this happening in Venetian society; I witnessed it as I was growing up in Cleveland, when in the 1960s, being fair became a much more important part of day-to-day business decision making than making things work better. Being fair in Cleveland meant enacting many zoning laws, combating pollution, and electing Carl Stokes, one of the nation's first black mayors.

When the peak comes, many people support the harmony that comes with it, but the ambitious ones chafe and leave for better opportunities. In the case of Novell, Eric Schmidt was brought onboard from 1997 to 2001 to get the company booming again. It didn't happen, so he moved to Google, where a big-time boom occurred.

Some companies return to their boom roots. Apple did when Jobs came back; New York and London have rebounded as well. A famous historic example of moving on and looking elsewhere to support a boom is Italian Christopher Columbus finding investors for his crazy idea of finding a direct route to India in Spain rather than in Italy.

In most cases, those who stay in post-peak communities don't mind that glory is passing them by; they're comfortable where they are. The glory and the ambitious migrate to another community that's still competing and willing to support the tough choices that come with booming change. This seems to be very much the human way.

Further Reading

"NASA-funded study: industrial civilization headed for 'irreversible collapse'?" is an article in the *Guardian* (March 14, 2014) popular in social-media circles. It was posted by Nafeez Ahmed, who lumps blame on the one percenters, which is easy, from-the-heart thinking, but is incorrect. I lump this in with the Club of Rome doom-and-gloom thinking popular in the 1970s.

"Japan's Economic Dilemma: Comfortable Decline or Painful Revival? With Abenomics at a Crossroads, Our Correspondent Writes on the Difficult Choices Facing Japan" by Jacob M. Schlesinger (*Wall Street Journal*, December 3, 2014), describes the comfortable, post-peak conditions going on in Japan in the mid-2010s and the resulting hard choice between continuing, comfortable decline and jarring, uncertain growth.

> TOKYO—"Recession," "stagnation," "slump," were the ominous labels I constantly read describing Japan before I moved here in late 2009. After I'd settled in, a better word seemed "kaiteki," which means "comfort," and conveys a wide range of virtues like convenience, reliability, safety, even charm. I was struck by the disparity between the world's perception of Japan and the remarkable feeling of prosperity here—compared not just with the bubble-era Japan I saw when last living here 20 years earlier, but with the America I experienced in the interim, during its own boom times.

Conclusion

Booming is exciting and rewarding, but it isn't easy, and the rewards aren't necessarily those the community values the most. Famous booms happen when a community supports tough, disruptive choices that turn out more frequently good than bad.

Boom times are scary and full of change. When a decision-making generation that doesn't like all the tough choices and changes takes over, a peak occurs. The way things are done changes to a more predictable style, and this style becomes a comfortable one for many community members.

If the community doesn't reverse course and support tough choices again, the ambitious move on along with their ambition to find communities that are supporting booms, and the community they leave will comfortably move into the obscurity of being average again.

24

Mania and Markets

End of the World instinctive thinking can influence financial marketplaces in distinctive and dramatic ways.

- In 1997, Hong Kong transferred from British to Chinese control, an End of the World moment for Hong Kong and the East Asia region.
- In 1998, we had the financial crisis called the Asian Flu in America and the IMF crisis in Korea.
- In 2000, we had the end of the twentieth century accompanied by End of the World pronouncements.
- In 2001, we had the dot-com and the telecom busts that later sucked in Enron, Arthur Anderson, and Worldcom.

These are examples of markets succumbing to End of the World mania that first booms the marketplace and then busts it when the morning-after reality sinks in.

Mania

Manias cause people to become so excited that they react impulsively and drop their customary ways of thinking rationally. The new-economy concept that surfaced in 1998 and '99 tried to explain the stratospheric dot-com stock valuations—the stratospheric price-to-earnings ratios—of that era as rational.

Manias take time to develop. They become most pronounced and easily identified when the mania is linked to an end or a beginning clearly seen in the future. Everyone knew Hong Kong would revert to Chinese control at the end of the century. Negotiations for the fate of Hong Kong took place in the '70s and were resolved fairly quickly; real estate developers needed some certainty, and the British government obliged them by addressing the subject with China.

Even the possibility of a city hosting, say, the Olympics or World Cup events can produce local manias in the cities under consideration and those finally selected.

Not all manias are tightly linked to a beginning or ending event. I think the '29 stock market bubble came at the tail end of post–World War I euphoria. The habit of cooperating mixed with the euphoria of the revolution in domestic lifestyles due to the proliferation of cars, refrigerators, and washing machines among other innovations. The timing of the peak of such a nonevent-driven mania is hard to predict, whereas event-driven manias have an easily foreseeable pattern.

Mania Evolution: Noisy "Doom and Gloom" and Quiet Investing

In the case of End of the World, event-linked mania, as the community approaches the exciting event, certain people in a community will pronounce doom-and-gloom pronouncements. In modern times, they show up as worst-case scenarios the media and pundits trumpet in lurid detail. But quietly, underneath the noise, some people will identify and jump on opportunities for investment.

People worried about how China's Communist regime would treat Hong Kong after the turnover of 1997. Some were afraid the Red Army would march in holding copies of the *Little Red Book* (the Western name for Mao Tse-tung's *Quotations from Chairman Mao*), nationalize everything, and "reeducate" the entrepreneurs who had built up Hong Kong. Meanwhile, quiet investors were buying into building office buildings elsewhere around the Pacific Rim, thinking the best and brightest in Hong Kong would leave and set up shop close by.

In the five years leading up to the Hong Kong turnover, a building boom occurred in Calcutta, Vancouver, and many places in between in anticipation of a Hong Kong diaspora. Banks were willing to lend, and property values soared. But when the Hong Kong turnover happened, there was no mass exodus, leaving South and East Asia overbuilt with offices and construction companies and banks holding the bag. That was the start of the Asian Flu of 1998.

The mania brought on by the end of the millennium in America was known as the Y2K crisis, fears surrounding how computers would handle switching from 99 (as in 1999) to 00 (as in 2000). The doom-and-gloom pundits predicted planes falling from the skies, ships crashing into docks, and infrastructure everywhere grinding to a halt.

While the doom and gloomers were getting all the talk-show attention, others were investing in the Internet and telecommunications start-ups. During 1999, there was talk of two economies, an old economy tied to the traditional business rules and a new economy that would play by different rules.

When the millennia passed without terrifying incident, it took a few months for investors to snap out of it and realize the old rules applied to the new-economy companies too. As that realization hit, the stock market and the economy tanked—The Dot-Com Bust.

When the Bubble Bursts, You Can't Go Back

Noisy naysayers and quiet investors notwithstanding, post-bubble environments are always different from the pre-bubble environments; the good old days aren't coming back soon. The 1989 Japan stock bubble that burst became Japan's lost decade, and Japanese thinking and lifestyles changed.

Whatever crashed in the old bubble will stay that way for at least a decade. The next mania will prey on a different concern, and the next bubble will form in some other sector of the economy.

What Can We Learn from These Examples?

Lesson one is that we should watch for a mania. An event-linked mania will be brought about by an exciting event coming in the future. The intensity of the mania will be proportional to the significance of the event and the time the mania has to grow, up to about thirty years.

Actions based on the mania can show up from a few months to about five years before the event, but these mania actions are based on mania thinking that has been maturing for a longer time. Hong Kong and Y2K allowed plenty of time for mania thinking and actions to establish themselves, whereas Pearl Harbor and 9/11 were equally exciting events that allowed no time for mania to develop even though plenty of mania followed these events.

Lesson two is that mania will latch on to an incipient bubble of some nature and inflame it into a real bubble. The mania-related actions will be investments in something that looks good that prompt even more investing; the mania obscures the risk as prices rise and seem to promise great returns, but all can come crashing down for an unrelated reason; this is particularly the case with investments in real estate.

Lesson three is that whatever was swept up in the old bubble will stay crashed for at least a decade until another mania develops for another reason in another sector of the economy. That is the mania and markets model.

Conclusion

Manias and markets can explain many bank panics and bubbles that frequently occur at the end of manias. If a community is experiencing End of the World excitement, part of that excitement will channel into risky investing.

When the End of the World comes and goes, that's hangover time when the riskiness of the investments becomes obvious and results in a bust that will be in proportion to the mania that preceded or caused it.

This is the difference between a blunder and a bubble; the former might not be acknowledged for generations while the latter is recognized very quickly.

25

Recessions are Dream Changers

A recession marks the end of a boom and says the good times are over for a specific industry. Once a sector stops growing fast, it's unlikely to start growing fast again right away. The magic is gone for the time being and moves to another sector of the economy.

A recession following a boom is a time of searching for the next boom sector. Businesses and technologies experiment to find out what sector will grow fast next. When a recession is mild and ends quickly, that's because replacement boom sectors were easy to discover and exploit quickly.

If the recession is deep and long, it means that boom sectors took some time to discover and exploiting them wasn't quick or easy. The Japan recession of the 1990s is a good example of not finding a quick replacement; that economy searched and searched for its next boom sector.

The Importance of Positive Feedback

A boom is a time of positive feedback. In 1800s America building railroads was at the heart of many boom cycles. Railroads are labor and capital intensive; that makes it a "heavy" industry. The costs involved in developing an extensive railroad system were more than compensated for by the fact it made many kinds of manufacturing so much easier, cheaper, and more profitable. When a railroad came to town, all sorts of things got easier to do there, and business grew—positive feedback.

In the 1900s, the automobile replaced the railroad as the center of positive feedback in transportation, and the auto industry replaced the railroad industry as America's chronic center of boom.

Pop Quiz: What Had Positive Feedback after the Telecoms in the 2000s? (Hint: Not Housing)

As America came out of the dot-com recession housing remained strong. That was a mystery to me then. Housing usually tanks when the economy does. I couldn't figure out what US demographic was powering the powerful demand for housing? But because of the robust housing market, this boom of the mid-2000s looked like it was a housing boom. The bust of 2008, however, revealed that it wasn't demand for housing that was powering the boom but the demand for a new style of finance that included collateralized debt obligations, CDOs, groups of mortgages bundled to sell to investors. This 2000s boom could be more properly labeled the structured finance boom.

Finance was half of the root of this boom. The other half was the War on Terror mania that flowed fast and furiously around the United States and the world following 9/11. The bust of 2008 was the hangover from the 9/11 panic-and-blunder cycle.

The structured finance boom and 9/11 mania was a double whammy and the result a boom that didn't run out of steam until 2008. What followed was a deep bust, the Great Recession. Structured finance didn't power the next boom, but it did become another tool, like stocks, to enable some other sector's boom growth.

The Great Recession was about searching to find out what the next boom—the next positive feedback mix of industries—would be based on.

What Was the Next Boom?

What boom followed the Great Recession? This one took a lot of searching to discover. What was discovered was high tech devices such as smartphones, biotech, and a boom in infrastructure building in China which powered a commodities boom around the Pacific Rim and Africa. That boom lasted until 2015. Then the dream changed again.

Once again, in 2015, the world was facing the question, what will the next positive feedback mix of industries be? What will be the positive feedback foundation for the next boom cycle? Big Data was coming along, but there still weren't good ways to predict booms yet. Boom predicting is a whole lot like creating start-up enterprises. There are usually many good possibilities. As one or a few get worked out and prove themselves, the boom gets under way. Finding the positive feedback choices is the first step.

The second step is there will be new twists—a new market, a new finance method, or a new technology. This will let businesses provide new services and get new kinds of money. The popularity of structured investments in the mid-2000s boom was due in part to the reduced popularity of stocks that came about because of the increased regulatory burden of the Sarbanes-Oxley Law, which was designed to protect Americans from the Enron-style excesses of the dot-com bust. A similar panic response was the Dodd-Frank Bill, the US legislature's response to the subprime meltdown. This added a lot more hoop-jumping to being a big bank. Likewise, the Affordable Care Act added a lot of hoop-jumping to health care providing.

Further Reading

The concluding paragraphs of "Six Steps Toward Financial Reform," an editorial by Maurice R. Greenberg (*Wall Street Journal*, March 4, 2010), dealt with recession dream changing in America's financial world.

In "We're Governed by Callous Children" (*Wall Street Journal*, October 29, 2009), Peggy Noonan reflected on recession thinking.

In "The Robot Roughnecks: Out Of The Oil Bust Comes A Golden Age Of Drilling Technology" (*Forbes*, August 19, 2015), Christopher Helman gave a 2010 example of dream changing in oil drilling.

> But where others see disaster, Clay Williams, CEO of NOV, sees opportunity. Busts have a bright side: Oil companies get interested in learning new tricks. "In the $100-per-barrel world there's not much incentive to do things differently, because

everybody's making money," he says. "But in a $50-per-barrel world, reality sets in and our customers say, 'How can we do things differently? How can we make the economics work?'"

Conclusion

Booms occur when a community latches onto a positive feedback industry and grows by exploiting all the opportunities it is creating. But at some point, the law of diminishing returns kicks in and the positive feedback declines. The community heads into a recession, a time of dream changing, searching for the next big dream, a new mix of positive feedback industries to invest in. When it finds them, the next boom gets underway.

There's nothing certain about discovering the next boom; there's no guarantee it will be long lasting or wildly successful; that makes recessions very scary and frustrating.

The one certainty is that what comes out the far side will be very different from what the previous boom mix was.

26

The Sequel to Recessions: The Next Big Thing

The next big thing (NBT) is my term for an industry or other activity in which a community invests that gives positive feedback to the community in terms of its growth. Think here of railroads and labor-saving appliances to smartphones and biotech.

Positive feedback sustains a boom until the law of diminishing returns kicks in, then the economy dips into recession, and business slows down. In an otherwise robust economy, one in which people don't daydream about the good old days, business and government interests hustle to find at least one NBT and often more.

New Technology and Social Disruption

As a new technology becomes widely accepted, it changes how people do things. Refrigerators, an industrial commodity developed to transport food before it spoiled, became household appliances and replaced ice boxes. As well, the whole concept of refrigeration spawned a new industry: home air conditioners.

Home refrigerators alone changed what grocery stores offered: all kinds of things from ice cream to TV dinners. But this had an effect on family life; moms may have been the winners in that TV dinners cut down time they spent cooking, but family time as a whole could become a loser in that everyone could eat whenever they wanted and sit-together family dinners became rarer.

The moral here is that new technology can bring benefits but it can also be scary; consider a widow forced to leave her home because a railroad needs her property.

Those who come up with what they think will be the NBT will say, "This change is going to be profitable. It's going to bring well-paying jobs to the community. Let's get at it. If we don't, someone else will take our place!" Pressure to change can be immense and cause social unrest. The steel, auto, and railroad industries were pushed hard and created such intense controversy that whole new political philosophies evolved to deal with the changes they caused. Coping with the social stress caused by the positive feedback of these industries (rapid industrialization) spawned the popularity of liberalism, capitalism, progressivism, socialism, communism, and fascism.

NBTs Are Different

Heavy industry was a stressor in the first half of the twentieth century; it sucked up capital, land, and other resources. The stressors of the second half of the century—electronics and software—were different in that they were medium or light industries. They sucked up intellectual talent much more than anything else, which is why the term Information Age was coined in the 1990s. That made a big difference in how much and what social stress they caused—much lower and milder. In terms of dealing with disruptive positive feedback technologies, the gens and millennials have gotten off a lot easier than their ancestors did.

"What Am I Here to Do?"

Disruptive booms cause people to answer this question differently. When they have to change their answer this can be scary. In the Agricultural Age people said, "I'm a farmer," but the Industrial Age caused people to answer the question, "What do you do?" in a thousand ways, and some would even say, "I'm not sure." That promotes stress even if prosperity comes along with it.

What's coming next in your lifestyle?

Conclusion

The NBT replaces a recession; it's an answer to changes in dreams, but finding the NBT isn't easy; it's stressful, and there's no guarantee of success. Many communities never find one and become backwaters whose residents dream about the good old days.

27

Full Employment: Equilibrium or a Brick Wall?

"I want to work, but I can't."

This sentiment can be felt for many reasons that shift depending on the lifestyle the person is living. Stone Age people wouldn't have work if they were disabled or if their environments had been picked clean of the resources they needed; they would had to move. Agricultural Age people faced the same problem if they were disabled or their crops failed.

In the Industrial Age, things became more complex. Work is something offered mostly by companies or governments, and how much they offer depends on their success and the success of the economies they are part of. Regardless, businesses and governments aspire to what they call full employment. This is such a powerful aspiration that it is often equated with equilibrium, the condition the economy is always striving to settle into. Full employment: the economists love it, governments love it, and communities love it.

But aspiration and equilibrium are not the same. Governments regulate finance and business to dampen the volatility of business cycles, which they want to be orderly and predictable as they grow. Most people cringe whenever a business cycle goes through a contracting phase because of the results: less money being spread around, lower wages, lower tax revenues, fewer jobs, less manufacturing and service business being done, and less goods and services being bought. People end up wondering how they'll make ends meet and often turn on the politicians they've elected or the autocracy that rules them.

Growing economies are highly desirable, but reaching equilibrium is not the same thing. A pendulum offers a good example of a system that reverts to equilibrium after energy is applied to it and it swings back and forth a number of times. Friction and gravity reduce it to a state of equilibrium.

But employment is not a pendulum. There may be an equilibrium point, but it isn't necessary full employment—a condition when work available matches workers to do it. The equilibrium here varies with the financial and business aspects of a culture and is often something quite different from full employment.

A chronic example of this is the unemployment of black teenagers in inner cities; such neighborhoods rarely if ever have enough work for the workers available. But no politician is voted in for acknowledging this reality, and no economist gets high-profile support from politicians or fellow academics for doing so either. (An example of getting high-profile support is Keynes being acclaimed by the Roosevelt administration in the mid-1930s.)

The economists who get support and continue in their jobs are those who argue that anything but full employment is a temporary aberration and that the government should be spending money to wipe out the aberration.

But full employment is a brick wall, not an equilibrium point; it's the point at which no more people can be employed. If the market wants to hire more people when all the people are employed, this demand forces something else to give in its place—inflation, immigration, interest rates, or a downturn in the business cycle are some examples of something else giving.

Full employment is not an equilibrium point but a goal, but because of political and academic realities, it isn't convenient for economists to point out this difference.

The Softness of Macroeconomics

The root of this difference in definition is the softness of the macroeconomics field. I've studied economics; I've heard various professors talk about economic issues. They were expressing opinions and backing them up with cherry-picked data; that's a "soft" method that isn't practiced in physics or other "hard" sciences.

Sociology and anthropology professors can justifiably argue, "What I am talking about is complex and we don't have enough data to sort through the complexity. So here is my opinion." Economics, on the other hand, thanks to business managers wanting to know what condition their companies are in, involves much data. So why does it rely so heavily on opinion, conjecture, guesses, and editorializing? Why do economics professors sound more like religious leaders or politicians than physics professors?

Because economics as a field of study is swept up with The Curse of Being Important (my term).

Many people in the community are interested in the economic well-being of their community, but because of this curse, their interest is dominated by instinctive rather than analytical thinking. People know what answers they want to receive to their questions and won't pay attention to whomever or whatever doesn't answer them that way.

Such soft answers are comforting but aren't based on harsh reality and thus won't reveal effective solutions to problems. The solutions that make sense to instincts will be irrelevant in the face of harsh reality of modern times, which means much time, money and effort will be wasted in pursuing them.

Further Reading

"Reality cheque: Angus Deaton wins the Nobel prize for bringing economics back to the real world" (*Economist*, October 17, 2015) dealt with Angus Deaton getting a Nobel Prize for adding some "hardness" to economics.

The Nobel committee had awarded him the Sveriges Riksbank Prize in Economic Sciences, "for his analysis of consumption, poverty, and welfare." The prize celebrated a whole career, in which he has used data to overturn sloppy assumptions, reimagined how we measure the world, and intertwined microeconomics and macroeconomics. He even has a paradox named after him.

Conclusion

Economics is an interesting field of study, but because it is so complex and at the same time important, it's conducted as a soft science. This is sad because it means that economics research is not coming up with effective solutions to economic problems; rather, it is offering comforting solutions that help people sleep better at night but don't solve the problem. This waste of time and effort is why economics needs to harden up. Thanks to new tools such as Big Data, it can, but the decision makers in the field need to recognize the influence of The Curse of Being Important and deliberately avoid it.

28

Tattoos and T-Shirts: How High Tech Replaces Low Tech

It was a lazy Saturday afternoon; I was slumped in my easy chair, my mind idling after some hard writing. I was watching a PBS documentary on aboriginal peoples. In my relaxed haze, I heard the interviewer ask the explorer, "Of all the treasures of modern technology, which do these Stone Age tribes want first?"

It felt like a *Jeopardy* question, so I jammed my imaginary button and yelled, "Guns or firewater!"

"They want T-shirts," the explorer answered. "T-shirts with gaudy designs. They have no idea what the designs mean, but they want them."

"What?" I sat up. "What sort of crazy answer is that?"

Sigh. It was the kind of crazy answer that gets me thinking. And out of that thinking came an inspiration about how an older technology is displaced by a newer, better technology.

A New, High-Tech Solution

Perhaps the aborigines consider T-shirts emblazoned with this or that as high-tech substitutes for tattoos, the oldest of which was found on Oetzi the iceman, a Stone Age hunter from 5,300 years ago whose body was uncovered in the Alps in the 1980s.

Tattoos and T-shirts can decorate a body, but T-shirts can be brighter, more elaborate, easier to change, and less painful to acquire for those who value such adornment. This relationship between tattoos and T-shirts is an example of a general phenomenon: the replacement of one technology with another.

The Substitution Cycle

As T-shirts replace tattoos, the latter decline in demand and use as the former advance. In addition, T-shirts are of interest to a larger segment of the market than are tattoos; women and children start wearing T-shirts though they didn't submit to tattoos, leaving that to men.

But you can still find tattoo parlors; T-shirts haven't completely taken over the personal-adornment market. Indeed, tattooing has improved in terms of design, safety, and comfort (less painful than in the past). The one technology (silk-screened T-shirts) has not completely displaced the other (needle-and-ink tattooing). Because of the T-shirt's ability to adorn more easily than tattoos, simple economic theory suggests that T-shirts should have displaced tattoos entirely. In reality, high-tech substitutes will displace a lot but not all the uses of low-tech alternatives; the remaining devotees to low-tech alternatives become more skilled on average than when the old technology was the only choice.

Here are some other examples of low tech surviving high-tech replacements.

- Horse use survived cars and trucks
- Sailboats survived motorboats
- Handwritten letters survived typewritten letters
- Typewriters survived word processors.
- Mechanical wristwatches survived the digital era.

In each case, the high-tech alternative opened a much wider market than the low-tech alternative could ever reach, but the low-tech survived because it offered something the high-tech couldn't, a mode of personal expression. Horses survive as racehorses; sailboats survive as yachts.

Handwritten letters survive as indulgences and thank-you notes. Vacuum-tube stereos survived transistors and such in the high-end audiophile market.

If you just want a design on your chest, a T-shirt will do. If you want to get from point A to point B, a car will do. If you want to do these things in an extravagant or exotic way, high-quality, low-tech alternatives can be attractive: think tattoos and horses.

Pianos have displaced harpsichords almost entirely, but harpsichordists survive. They survive because harpsichord playing is a form of personal expression. And today, I guess, the average harpsichordist of today plays better than did past harpsichordists. And now pianos are losing ground to electronic keyboards. But lower-tech musical instruments, in this case, have not disappeared; the high end of the low-tech market retains its appeal to accomplished old players and dedicated new players.

Forecasts

Where else will we see this substitution of high-tech for low-tech, but the low-tech survives? Not in handheld calculating devices; electronic calculators have displaced slide rules pretty completely, and Bessemer-process steel is hard to find these days. In both cases, there is little artistic component to the product's use, so the displacement is complete or nearly so. On the other hand, there is still some hand-processed paper available these days, and musical instruments will always have low-tech survivors because of the high artistic content in their use.

Photography also involves a lot of art, so don't expect film cameras to disappear completely in the face of digital cameras. Film-based photography won't be used to take assessment pictures of real estate or passport photos, but it will be used for a long time for formal portraiture and for distinctive special effects such as long-exposure pictures. Fine art–style painting lost most of its commodity value when photography and TV appeared, but it is almost pure art these days, so what's left won't be affected by digital cameras.

Sports equipment has a lot of personal expression but very few artistic components. In some areas, old designs will survive, but the competitive nature of sports keeps that sort of low-tech survival to a minimum.

Cars, surprisingly, have a lot of art; consider the number of classic car shows. Art-oriented shows are by definition expressions of art which means that technology is likely to linger on.

Handwriting started as a communications commodity. The commodity use has been steadily diminished by newspapers, phones, television and now texting. What is left is the artistic uses.

Typing still thrives; not with typewriters but with word processing and texting. Information storage techniques vanish as quickly as their replacements become standards—think of eight-tracks and floppy disks, these have no artistic components.

Likewise, there is little art in paperwork, red tape, forms—electronic transfers handle those tasks so much more efficiently, so they should vanish as soon as their utility vanishes.

Driverless Cars

Driverless cars will soon be practical, widespread, faster, cheaper, and better at their tasks than human-driven cars can be; they will take over most of the heavy lifting when it comes to getting people from A to B. They will become more like taxis than personal vehicles and will become more like furniture than anything special. But there is a lot of personal expression involved in car owning and driving. For this reason, it's likely to endure as much as horses and sailboats have.

And in story telling cars will symbolize the 20th century, much as horses symbolized the 19th century. For this reason movies of the *Fast and Furious* style will endure much as Westerns have done for so long.

Memory Aids Becoming Art

As teaching became a more and more valuable human skill, memory aids also became more valuable. One of the powerful pre-writing memory aids was poetry. If you want to cross index weight and volume, "A pint is a pound the world around" gets you started. Rhyme and meter, chapter and verse, and parallel and chiasmic structures are all ways of error checking what is memorized.

> Roses are red, violets are blue
> Sugar is sweet and so is Uncle Ozmo.

That just doesn't pass the rhyme and meter test.

Australian aborigines used songlines to preserve their cultural memory. The songs were keyed to local geography. Periodically, an aborigine would walk a songline to check if he or she had remembered the song correctly and to make changes to the song to update it as necessary. Many of these songs were top secret, but these walkabouts looked rather aimless to the early European settlers who first witnessed them, hence the name.

Both poetry and songlines are inefficient and hard to use as information storage devices when compared to writing. But writing takes elaborate infrastructure to make it useful—a written language and accessible writing instruments. When these are developed it displaces poetry, songlines, and such for literate people doing routine memorizing tasks. They could record rather than memorize names, dates, and taxes and bride prices paid.

Poetry survives today not as a memory enhancer but as artistic expression. Its divorce from commodity memorizing is what has allowed it to evolve into so many different forms over the centuries.

Who Will Be the Best Practitioner?

The samurai culture developed in Japan during the 150-year period of unrest before Japan was unified by Toyotomi Hideyoshi. During this time, samurai had a demanding, commodity-level job to perform: protecting their masters from unrest.

The most famous samurai came from the period immediately following the unification. With unification, the commodity use for samurais declined, and they had a chance to "perfect" their art, unfettered by the day-to-day demands of actually doing commodity samurai work. Likewise, horse people and horses of today perform at much higher standards than did those of the pre-automobile era. Another Roger rule: The golden-age craftspeople and practitioners of a technology will flourish after the commodity aspect of using the technology is displaced.

Commodity Will Wither; Art Will Survive, Quality Will Improve Dramatically

As one technology replaces another, the commodity uses of the older technology will disappear first. If the old technology survives, it will be because of an element of personal or artistic expression involved in using the old technology that the new technology doesn't have. That surviving part will be the highest quality part, and the practice and practitioners will be of higher quality than the average practice and practitioners during the old technology's heyday, when it had to service a commodity as well as a quality market.

Wide application

It is surprising how widely this phenomenon can be applied.

For example it can explain the current evolution of marriage and weddings. The commodity use for marriage and weddings was to strengthen cooperation between families (arranged marriage) and create lots of children. Lots of children were needed because the child mortality rate was so high. These days there are many other ways of arranging cooperation between people and only 2.1 children per family are needed to sustain the population, and there are many single mothers. The commodity uses of marriage are being diminished. What is becoming central are the personal expression uses. This is why weddings are getting more elaborate and being in love is so much more important than it used to be. And the practitioners are getting better at it.

Further Reading

"Only the digital dies" (*Economist*, January 26, 2013) is about technology extinction. What it doesn't bring up is the importance of personal expression to an obsolete technology's survival.

"Second wind: Some traditional businesses are thriving in an age of disruptive innovation" (*Economist*, June 14, 2014) dealt with companies and industries that are surviving on what I call personal expression. One of the more striking in its size and profitability is mechanical wristwatches.

29

Technological Revolutions

When a new technology or technique is first discovered, the first question is, "What's it good for? How are people going to use this?" The first answer is usually, "We will replace an existing product or service and do it faster, better, and cheaper." I call this the "commodity use" of a technology. If that first use succeeds, the new technology will attract attention.

If a new technology is revolutionary, what follows is discovering other surprising uses for the technology: "You can do that with it too? That's neat!" If this surprising use is world-shaking the result is a history-making technology.

Commodity Use

The commodity use of a new technology is the first use it's adapted to. Most of the time, it replaces what an older technology did by doing it faster, better, and cheaper. Doctors were early adapters of cars because they were quicker than horse and carriage for making late night house calls. Those whose responsibility it was to keep track of agreements, taxes, bride prices, and contracts adopted writing because it was more efficient than memory.

If no commodity use is found for a new technology, it dies. Nikola Tesla had an idea for the wireless transmission of electricity, but it wasn't faster, better, or cheaper than existing electrical transmitting technologies, so it never spread widely. The Tesla coil is a scientific curiosity, not a useful product.

The Surprise Uses

The commodity use of a technology is valuable in that it gets it being used widely and raises awareness of it, which cuts production costs and convinces more people to use it. Cars allowed not only doctors to respond quicker to house calls, it also allowed people to live in suburbs and while holding down jobs in cities. Think also about writing giving rise to skywriting, computers of first relieving people of having to make mind-numbing calculations, then letting them play games, and plastic first replacing ivory in the manufacture of pool balls, and then becoming phonograph records, and then so much more.

Even evolution provides an example: birds can tweet "Danger!" but one human can now tell another, "Tomorrow, about 5:00 p.m., behind that tree over there will be a tall man with a big club. Watch out for him! He's trouble!" That's a better danger warning, a commodity use done better.

The surprise use of this strong language skill is teaching: humans can pass on what they have learned and that helps the species survive generation to generation.

The second surprising element is that strong language skill, through the surprise use of teaching, affected our brain evolution. Our bigger brains became valuable because we developed strong language skills, not vice versa.

Conclusion

New technologies are at the heart of what makes humans human. Since the Agricultural Age, humans have changed their lives by incorporating new inventions and techniques into their daily routines. New technology replaces older technology by doing what the older technology did faster, cheaper, and better. If it succeeds at that, it becomes widespread. If it is a history-making technology, it will also develop surprisingly valuable other uses. This is an exciting process that has become much more rapid as our societies evolve.

30

Communications Revolutions

Changes in the technologies we use for communication are important because they change how we live; they can even revolutionize it. Back in the good old days, the Stone Age, people would communicate by waving, fighting, kissing, and spanking but mostly by talking.

When writing evolved, it was in response to the need for an accounting tool more accurate than memory; that was its "commodity" use. The oldest forms of writing archeologists have discovered were connected with the earliest cities and recorded important trading transactions such as bride prices and taxes. Writing was later used to record history, memorials, government decrees, and religious texts.

Writing brought two major enhancements to communication: it could "remember" better than the human mind could, and it could move information much farther and more easily than moving a person who had the information in his or her memory.

Writing has been around long enough that it has begun to influence human instinctive thinking. People around the world respect what has been written. The archetypical Hollywood version is a misquote from the movie _Ten Commandments_, "So it is written, so it shall be."

In Agricultural Age societies, reading and writing were specialty occupations for scribes because the medium of paper or alternatives were scarce. What was written ended up in libraries. The result: there wasn't much to read, so there wasn't much demand for readers.

Printing

Printing, a game changer, has gone through many stages. One of the earliest forms of printing involved wood blocks with drawings or writings being inked and then pressed on a medium—cloth or paper.

The famous revolution came in the 1440s, when German <u>Johannes Gutenberg</u> invented a printing press system that used moveable type and a faster way of pressing pages to the print blocks. The commodity use of this invention was printing a holy text: the Gutenberg Bible.

This new printing system made a big difference because many words could be printed quickly. This made a difference because with lots more words to read, the skill of reading became valuable to many more people; by the 1800s, Europeans and North Americans were seeing the advantages of universal education to promote literacy, and this wide literacy promoted the Industrial Age.

Because printing became easier, many more books were published on many more topics, one of the first being how-to books. Many inventors learned to read and write books about their neat inventions, and many others started taking advantage of these neat inventions. New discoveries moved around the literate world much more quickly than they did around the illiterate world, so discovering new things became more valuable. And one of the surprise fallouts of this growing interest in inventing was inventing patents and copyrights.

Printing's efficiency gave rise to magazines, newspapers, bulletins—all sorts of new formats directed at new audiences for all sorts of different reasons. This was a far cry from having a handful of monks laboriously copying a handful of manuscripts between prayers.

People got used to the idea of moving more and different ideas more rapidly, and printing's limited use in the Agricultural Age boomed mightily as the Industrial Age took hold. This fulmination of new ideas was the source of much inspiration and vexation, the social revolutions of the 1800s being examples of both.

Telegraph

The value of fast communication over long distances was well known even in Stone Age times. The constant question was how to do it faster, better, and cheaper.

During the Agricultural Age, horse-mounted messengers were relatively fast but expensive, so only the well-to-do or the governments could utilize that method, and the bandwidth—the capacity—of this form of communication was limited.

Beacons and smoke signals were even faster than horses but even more limited in bandwidth and once again expensive. Typically, only the military found these networks worth the cost.

A huge cost and usefulness breakthrough came in the 1830s when electricity started to be used to transmit messages over the telegraph. Three of the people involved in commercializing this idea were Englishmen Cooke and Wheatstone and American Samuel Morse of Morse code fame. The speed element made a big difference in what was useful to transmit. Instead of how-to manuals or religious texts, the hot item for this revolution was scheduling information; the commodity use for telegraphs was helping railroads communicate train scheduling information faster, better, and cheaper.

The surprise uses developed as the telegraph networks proliferated. In 1861, the telegraph connected the East and West Coasts, which put the Pony Express Company, which had started just eighteen months earlier, out of business.

Another surprise use for the telegraph was transmitting news; the Crimean War in 1850 was one of the first wars documented with telegraphic information. The military and news services both used it.

The communication revolution continued with the invention of the telephone; people could talk long distances in real time. But telephoning was expensive, and it was just a one-to-one style of talking, not broadcasting the way printing was.

Radio

Radio systems developed slowly starting around 1900 as a wireless offshoot of telegraphy. Commercial voice broadcast radio began in the United States, England, Canada, and other parts of the world in 1920. The big holdup was not transmitters but receivers; radios weren't common then, which limited the utility of broadcasting.

In these early years, there was no advertising sustaining these efforts, which meant no commercial involvement, so they were very experimental. When marketplace uses for broadcasting developed, the industry boomed.

The commodity use for broadcast radio was sending out news, educational, and entertainment information. The surprise use was how popular entertainment became. It became steadily more popular and came to dominate the medium.

Another surprise use was how valuable radio became as a political tool. One of the early examples of this was Franklin Roosevelt's fireside chats in the 1930s. But radio was audio only. The next revolution involved the addition of video.

Television

As had radio, television developed slowly starting in the 1920s but became widely popular in the United States and Britain in the 1950s, and it continues to evolve in format to today. The revolution was the combination of audio and video, an impressive improvement over just listening. The commodity use for TV, as was the case with radio, was news, education, and entertainment. And like radio, the surprise use became entertainment. The famous expression of the day (1961) was, "TV has become a vast wasteland."

High-Tech Relatives

One of the surprises of the TV revolution was creating high-tech relatives (my term). It created people known to (and trusted or distrusted by) many though they were seen only on screen (movie celebrities fall into

123

this category); nonetheless, they became high-tech relatives who were also opinion influencers.

But because TV cameras were bulky, huge, and expensive; the subjects of TV had to go to the studios, not the other way around. The next revolution solved that drawback.

Handheld Video and Other Personalizing of Communication

When the subjects of TV had to come to the camera, governments and others of influence could exert control over what the camera sees; this is a form of censorship. One nongovernment official with a lot of control over TV in the 1960s was Ed Sullivan, the host of the popular *Ed Sullivan Show.*

As the cost and size of cameras declined and TV's popularity grew, this made it possible to conduct man-on-the-street interviews, the commodity use. The surprise outcome of this was reducing the violence associated with social protesting. Neither the protesters nor the government cracking down on them could be as violent as they were before handheld video equipment became widespread for fear of social backlash.

The Rodney King video in 1991 showed him being beaten by police. Larger-scale examples of this change happening were the breakup of the Soviet Union and the Tiananmen Square protests in China in 1989. In both these cases, the violence was ten times less than what occurred in their predecessor unrests, the Russian Revolution in 1918 and the Cultural Revolution in 1966.

Conclusion

How we communicate makes a big difference in how we live in many ways. We can move ideas around more easily, and as a result, we think differently and about many more topics and are more outraged at violence. This means we are living lives that are much more mellow than those of our forbearers. All in all, some really good changes.

31

Gunboat Diplomacy

The fossil-fuel revolution started in England in 1712 with steam engines pumping wastewater out of mines (Newcomen atmospheric engine). As they were improved, these engines did this pumping faster, better, and cheaper than human or horsepower, and inventors started developing other applications.

One of the pioneers who improved steam engines was James Watt. As this Wikipedia steamboat article describes, many European and American inventors in the 1700s worked hard to adapt the steam engine concept to boats and ships. The first commercial success was created by Robert Fulton on the Hudson River in 1807, which fired a revolution in transportation. Steamboats could go places sailing ships couldn't such as small and shallow rivers. This revolution opened up the Great Lakes and the Mississippi River watersheds to commerce in the United States. "Go West, young man, go West," made a lot more practical sense when that West could be serviced by the iconic riverboats of the mid-1800s.

Waging war changed as well; steamships could transport and supply armies. Think of the pictures of Civil War cannon (here is the twelve-pounder Napoleon) that could be transported long distances over water much faster than they could be transported over land dragged by horses.

Steam-powered ships became offensive weapons with the advent of the Civil War _Monitor_ of Battle of Hampton Roads fame: "The use of a small number of very heavy guns, mounted so that they could fire in all directions was first demonstrated by Monitor but soon became standard in warships of all types." This first *Monitor* could mount a pair of fifteen-inch guns that could fire 130-pound rounds—ten times the punch of horse-drawn cannon. Steam-powered ships got bigger and better rapidly from there. The HMS *Dreadnought* (1906) and the *Bismarck* (1940) are famous icons of the improvement.

This ability to bring firepower to bear on an enemy as well as support ground troops wherever there was navigable water was the root of gunboat diplomacy. One war where this made a notable difference was the First Opium War between Britain and China (1839–42). Another case was the liberation of Panama in 1903 which concluded bloodlessly because American ships supporting the rebels showed up.

While the western European and North American powers had an edge in these technologies, this ability was decisive in many disputes between nations and cultures. And the diplomats of the times recognized this, hence the name.

32

Ruthless Leaders

In 2002, George W. Bush faced off against Saddam Hussein. In the process, a lot of "dirt" about Saddam Hussein received media attention in the United States. The dirt included stories about frequent and arbitrary imprisonment and murders, secret police and death squads, and many other terror-inducing activities on the part of the Iraqi leadership.

Why did the Iraqis permit this kind of leadership? The Middle East has had long experience with governments, and the Iraqis pride themselves on being civilized, so why did they let a gangster such as Saddam Hussein run their country?

This question presumes the Iraqis could change leaders on fairly short notice (within a couple of years). If that presumption is correct, Hussein's regime was actively supported by important Iraqis who considered him not as bad as the alternatives.

In the same vein, why did the Russians permit Stalin to rule, the Chinese permit Mao to rule, the Serbs permit Milosevic to rule, and the North Koreans permit Kim Il-sung to rule? Why have countless other communities submitted to ruthless leaders who imprisoned and killed large segments of their populations?

A friend of mine and fellow reflector on weighty matters such as these, Richard Block, offered this insight into this phenomenon of ruthless leadership: "The only problem a ruthless leader can get into is not being ruthless enough." His insight is hard to dispute, but I wasn't satisfied with it. It was so ruthless! I gave this phenomenon some more thought.

Basic Definitions and Presumptions

Ruthless leaders are those who enact policies based neither on law, tradition, or consensus, so they don't mind stepping on many toes. They get away with being violent because they're actively supported by an influential minority that believes this kind of leadership is necessary considering their circumstances and passively supported by a majority of the populace that agree or feel there's no better alternative.

These leaders are leading as people expect them to lead and enacting policies that people expect them to enact. Even the most seemly arbitrary and powerful ruler is acting within limits prescribed by his important followers and within the mores of the community he leads. This means important segments of the community support ruthless leaders in their ruthlessness. It's likely that early in their regimes, the ruthless leaders' support is more widespread, but even late in their reigns, important (but historically nameless) community members still support the leaders. Leaders cannot ignore their important followers but can change who they are; that's what purging and power shuffling are all about.

As well, ruthless leaders are selected by the community at the time of their rise to power as the best choice. There are always other aspirants for the leading position, but these others are either not chosen or cast aside quickly after being chosen. This casting-aside process is most obvious during a social revolution. Moderates are usually the first to take power when a regime is toppled, but ruthless faction leaders topple them as the revolution evolves.

And not all leaders are ruthless; some invoke consensus or divine right to achieve and hold onto power. When a community chooses a ruthless leader, it's an active choice on the part of the community.

Examples of Ruthless Leaders

I offer examples of the ruthless leaders of World War II because they are numerous and well known: Roosevelt, Churchill, Stalin, Hitler, Mussolini, Chiang Kai-shek (Jiang Jeishi), and Mao Tse-tung (Mao Zedong). There were others at this time, and most were ruthless.

Hitler killed millions of Jews and other dissidents. Stalin killed millions of kulaks and military officers before and after the war. Mao killed millions of dissidents during his crackdowns as well as farmers in avoidable famines. Chiang killed millions of dissidents labeled as Communists or bandits. But there are other ways to be ruthless. Churchill ran roughshod over unions and workers' rights. Roosevelt ran for a third term and set up social systems such as Social Security.

Nonruthless leaders tend to be rather colorless compared to ruthless leaders, so they aren't as memorable, but here are some to consider. Eisenhower kept the Allied military cooperating, and Neville Chamberlain tried to build consensus in Europe while Hitler gored him. Edouard Daladier, the French premier in 1939, was similar to Chamberlain.

Ruthless Rulers and Crises

Ruthless leaders go hand in hand with crises, which worry communities if they aren't solved quickly. If crises linger, people get frustrated as well as worried and begin casting about for any solution to the crises.

The potential leaders who benefit most from a sustained crisis are the nutcases, those who have long aspired to put their unconventional policies and philosophies into practice, but before this crisis have been ignored. They'll say, "We have to crack some heads to get through this," and they're paid more respect and attention than during business-as-usual times. This becomes the Time of Nutcases.

Ruthless leaders emerge during long, drawn-out crises with promises to solve the problems even though their solutions are radical. Once in power, they will immediately begin suppressing rivals for fear of being suppressed themselves. If the crisis ends quickly after they gain power, they will be replaced by conventional leadership. But if the crisis lingers they will too, or they may be replaced by even more ruthless leaders who are even more effective at suppressing rivals.

Another characteristic of ruthless leaders, particularly infamous ones, is that they tend to lie a lot—even for politicians. They do so to justify their actions and to perpetuate a crisis atmosphere.

Ruthless Leaders Can Perpetuate Crises

Once in power, ruthless leaders will attempt to solve the crises that led them to power, but they will also attempt much more. If they solve their crises, they might be asked to step down and let conventional governments take their places. Pathologic ruthless leaders doesn't relish that prospect, so they search for more crises to sustain their mandates.

The most enduring ruthless leaders convince their communities that the root of the crisis is betrayal by a subset of the community, an internal enemy who is supported by powerful external friends. Together they have caused the crises, and are working to bring about an even bigger but currently hidden crises, and these foes must be combated vigorously.

If the community buys into this larger- and more-subtle crises concept, it gives its leader a blank check; Richard's insight into ruthless leadership kicks in with full force, and a vicious cycle of escalating, extreme behavior begins. The ruthless leader begins a reign of terror.

Ruthless but Stable Leaders

Because ruthless leaders always generate opposition, they will try to muzzle it by implementing an internal reign of terror. They will point to this as necessary because of the conspiracies they claim to be fighting. By doing so, they smear dissidents whether they are still around or have fled the country. The existence of an opposition in exile is pointed to as evidence of external support for the resistance.

Reigns of terror suppress opposition voices and make the crises even more real to the communities, which rally around the leaders, whom they see as protecting them. And ruthless leaders will confiscate the property of the opposition to support their reigns and lower taxes. A leader who can conjure economic miracles without raising taxes always gains community respect.

Once the reign of terror is well established and institutionalized, there seem to be only two ways of ending the leader's rule: the leader's death or a massive external intervention.

Ruthless Leaders' Successors

Hitler was succeeded by German chancellors, while Stalin, after a few Stalin wannabees, was succeeded by Khrushchev. And after some wannabees, Mao was succeeded by Deng. Chiang was followed by a bland KMT party official, while Churchill was succeeded by rule of the Labor Party. Amazingly, Truman, and less amazingly, Eisenhower, followed Roosevelt, and Mussolini was followed by a long string of Italian premiers.

Ruthless leaders' successors are rarely other ruthless leaders even when one is available. Stalin's immediate successor was his former head of security who wanted to be as ruthless as Stalin had been and had the Communist security apparatus at his disposal to sustain the crisis, but he was short-lived. The stable successor was Khrushchev, a much more moderate leader.

What seems to happen is the community grows tired of a ruthless leader's reign of terror and some see that the crisis by which the leader sustains power is a pseudo-crisis fabricated by the ruthless leader. And the community members come to realize they could be next in an upcoming purge.

Mao's Cultural Revolution is one of the best-described examples of a pseudo-crisis. If the successor to a ruthless leader attempts to be a ruthless leader using this same technique of thriving on crisis, the community rejects the successor and opts for a more conventional leader.

Churchill led his country to victory in World War II but was voted out of office shortly after. The British appreciated his efforts during the crisis but didn't think his style was at all appropriate once the crisis had been resolved. Churchill hadn't muzzled his opposition, so they were able to bring an end to his power.

Truman wasn't expected to win in the first postwar election in the United States. But during his four years in office as a fill-in for Roosevelt, he proved to be such a popular conventional leader that he dispelled enough of the nation's distaste with Roosevelt's ruthlessness to win on his own merits.

Conversely, Stalin handled the postwar adjustment by keeping crises fresh in the minds of the Soviet people. He started purging the military again as soon as the fighting stopped, and he fomented crises in the neighboring Central European countries and Korea, which demonstrated to Soviet people the need for continued vigilance.

The crisis of China's underdevelopment was still full in the face of the Chinese community when Mao finally drove Chiang off the mainland. External threats had loomed over China since the Opium War of 1840, but Mao kept it fresh by participating in the Korean War, and Chiang helped by threatening to come back to the mainland from Taiwan, supported by his "American imperialist lackeys."

Mao invoked crises several times during his reign—the Thousand Flowers, the Great Leap Forward, and the Cultural Revolution. His first successors, the Gang of Four, tried to do the same, but they were quickly vilified by the post-Mao leadership decision makers, and his stable successors such as Deng Xiaoping (Deng Shiao-ping) were much quieter rulers. An example of this quieter rule is that Tiananmen Square–like crackdowns on protesters brought about no significant outrage in the Mao era, but in the post-Mao era, they were considered quite distasteful and embarrassing.

The exception to the no-ruthless-successor rule is Kim Jong-il succeeding Kim Il-sung in North Korea. But there is a mitigating circumstance in that succession: from the point of view of the North Koreans, the crisis that brought Kim Il-sung to power has not ended. Kim Il-sung came to power after a forty-year occupation of Korea by Japan. During those forty years, the Japanese had tried very hard to convince the Koreans that underneath their Korean facade they were really Japanese.

When Kim died in 1994, the North Koreans still felt they were surrounded by dangerous, aggressive enemies and their economic livelihood was still in great peril. They supported continuing ruthlessness and supported it yet again when Kim Jong-un replaced Kim Jong-il. All in all, a very unusual circumstance.

The Hazard of Ruthless Leadership

The hazard of allowing ruthless leaders to stay in power is that they will continually create crises to justify their rule or face being deposed in favor of traditional governance. Because ruthless leaders tend to lie more than do their nonruthless counterparts, those lies are subject to exposure and could affect their chances of sheer survival.

Because of this, ruthless leaders are continually tempted to take their followers down the path of adventurism to bigger and riskier projects.

But when that fails, the whole structure can come down like a house of cards. Hitler was an adventurist, and Stalin took full advantage of it, and then picked up most of the pieces when the Thousand Year Reich came tumbling down. Stalin was also an adventurist, but until the end of World War II, Hitler provided all the adventure Stalin needed.

Not all ruthless leaders are adventurist, and some will survive after they are out of power. The South Korean generals who ruled between the Korean War (in the '50s) and Kim Young-sam's ascendancy (in the '90s) were ruthless. But they were not particularly adventurist, and most survived as members of the Korean community into the 2000s—which was controversial for the Koreans. Chile's Pinochet survived for long after he retired—which was controversial for the Chileans.

Hypocrisy and Delusion in Ruthless Leadership

When I talked about this issue with my brother, Toby White, he made the comment, "Ruthless leaders such as Hitler and Stalin are lying hypocrites." I thought about that hard. I thought about the battle for Berlin at the end of World War II, which lasted about ten days and killed about half a million German and Russian soldiers—a bloodfest that didn't have to be fought! It was fought only because both Hitler and Stalin wanted to fight it.

First, the Russians, English, and Americans had already split Germany when Berlin was encircled by Russians. The Germans weren't going to win the war; they wouldn't be able to fight more than a few weeks no matter what happened in Berlin. There were no German troops near enough to Berlin to break the encirclement. Hitler couldn't win, and that was clear to the Germans. If Hitler had been rational, if his important followers had been rational, he would have surrendered Berlin.

Second, only Russian troops surrounded Berlin—the American and English armies had stopped at the Elbe River, miles away, by prior agreement. There was no risk the Americans would steal a march on the Russians and occupy Berlin. Stalin could have waited, but he and his military chose to attack. Hitler and his leadership chose to defend vigorously. The result was a bloody but militarily meaningless battle. There were delusional people on both sides of this massacre.

Here is my explanation for this mystery.

My brother pointed out that these leaders and their confidants talked openly about their hypocrisy in their early writings. Ruthless leaders start as hypocrites. Early in their rises to power, they make statements based on what will gain them tactical advantage in any battle for power. But hypocrisy is an uncomfortable state of mind, few people like living a lie. Instead of living the lie the mind adapts by becoming delusional, it changes its memories, and creates a more comfortable state of mind.

A more recent minor example of this moving from hypocrisy into delusion comes from George W. Bush and the 9/11 events. This comes from a *Wall Street Journal* article that came out in the spring of 2004 (part of their reporting on the 9/11 committee work).

> President Bush likes to recount that on the morning of September 11, while he was waiting to make an address to a class of school children, he was watching TV and saw the first plane crash into the WTC. He thought *[he relates]* "That's one terrible pilot!" It was only after he got news of the second plane that he thought, "America is under attack!"
>
> The problem with this memory is that no pictures of the first plane crashing into the WTC showed up on TV until late in the afternoon, after the broadcasters got a hold of amateur video footage.

I believe that by 2004, Bush believed his story to be true. I believe that the first few times he told it, he was being hypocritical; ruthless leaders will fabricate their big lies as hypocrites, but their minds will steadily transform from hypocritical to delusional as their big lies seem to be believed. This phenomenon may be the inspiration for the proverb, "Power corrupts."

Another Writer on Ruthless Leadership

In his book *1984*, George Orwell castigated totalitarianism, but the atmosphere he described was more general than just totalitarianism; he described the world of mature, ruthless leaders of any persuasion.

In that book as in real life, a mature, ruthless leader's reign can look hopeless and unassailable, but the system vitally depends on the leader himself. When the leader is gone, the harsh rule will fade like winter into spring provided the community leaders at the time of the leader's death feel the crisis is over. This tight linkage between a reign of terror and a specific ruthless leader was something Orwell chose not to explore in his book. He linked reigns of terror to the party, the leader's influential followers, rather than the leader, although in his book, the leader was portrayed as a vitally important symbol in maintaining the reign of terror.

Orwell and I agree in effect that a reign of terror is tightly tied to a specific leader. But he worried that modern technology would allow community leaders to sustain a reign of terror without tight linkage to a specific, real leader. On that we disagree.

How Does Saddam Fit into This Picture?

The Iraqis have long experience with government, but they also have long experience with crisis. The Iraqi state was carved out of the Ottoman Empire that disintegrated in 1918, at the end of World War I. The Fertile Crescent, the heart of Iraq, is populated by people of many cultures: Iraqis, Kurds, Sunni Arabs, Shiite Arabs, Jews, and others. It's like the Balkan Peninsula, another chronic crisis area.

Iraq is a relatively new state; none of the groups living there has any great loyalty to this new creation—these groups are all watching to see who will run this new entity and if this new nation will be worth staying a part of. Iraq could easily Balkanize and become many smaller states that could be swallowed up by powerful neighbors. Living with that kind of uncertainty is a crisis in itself.

The people of the Middle East remember acutely that three hundred years earlier, before the Industrial Revolution, the Middle East, not western Europe, was the center of civilization. They all face the crisis of determining how they lost ground relative to the West and how do they get it back.

Saddam came to power as Iraq's influential community leaders searched for someone to save Iraq and restore the Middle East's former standing vis-à-vis the West. He was brought in as a modernizer, someone who would kick ass and take names while he got Iraq and the Middle East straightened out. What the Iraqi community got instead was a pathological, ruthless leader who has been a model totalitarian. In Saddam's case, oil rather than disenfranchising a community was the major way of keeping the cost of government low.

Further Reading

"The dread of the other: The leading role played by anti-Americanism in today's Russia" (*Economist*, February 16, 2013) described how Putin was using Us vs. Them thinking to sustain crisis thinking about America in Russia and maintain his power base.

Conclusion

Ruthless leaders are creations of their communities who seek ruthless rulers because they face protracted, serious crises and no previous, less-ruthless leaders has been able to handle their crises.

Once in power, ruthless leaders may turn pathological and try to perpetuate their leadership by suppressing dissidents and by revealing or even creating new crises, whether external or internal, to scare their communities. If such leaders succeed in institutionalizing their reigns of terror, only their deaths or massive outside intervention will end their rule.

One sign that a ruthless leader is going for a long rule is the growth of a vocal dissident community in exile, which prompts these leaders to play the conspiracy card as a way to sustain the crisis.

Ruthless leaders tend to be adventurists. It wasn't World War II that brought World War II's leaders into leadership positions; the worldwide Great Depression had done that already. It is possible that World War II wasn't inevitable. It was, instead, a manufactured crisis brought on by depression-era ruthless leaders so they could extend their rulerships. Adventurism started the war.

33

The Slippery Slope

As communities prosper and become more industrialized, they face the challenge of how their newfound wealth should be distributed. The serious temptation is to divorce wealth distribution from wealth creation for many reasons ranging from noble to crass. But this is serious because the more the divorce happens, the slower further wealth creation happens and the communities stay poor.

Even worse, a community with a big split between wealth creating and distributing gets strongly tempted to live beyond its means. This happens because the political leaders are tempted to borrow money in one form or another, which is followed by over borrowing that leads to a day of reckoning—a crash.

Even worse than that, when the crash happens, serious <u>Blame Them</u> thinking ensues and the root cause of the crash is not recognized by many community members—*denial* is the word here. That means that recovery and progress to more prosperity are very slow and difficult—instead of living and learning, it's easier to keep living the good old, pre-boom days or even return to Agricultural Age conditions.

Background

This chapter was inspired by watching the Greek bailout crisis of 2015 unfold, in particular, the reaction to the referendum in July in which the

Greeks voted against the austerity the Eurozone members were calling for to continue their bailout of Greece.

What these anti-austerity groups didn't seem to take into account was that the Greeks had been living a lifestyle since they had joined the Eurozone in 2000 that relied too heavily on government borrowing and was thus unsustainable.

Why did the Greeks choose to live this unsustainable lifestyle? And why is it so popular in many other areas of Europe and the world? Venezuela was also facing its day of reckoning with government money running out and lots of Blame Them sentiment spreading through the country's communities that couldn't keep basic goods on store shelves. In Russia, oil wealth has gone into sustaining Putinism, aggressive nationalism, kleptocracy, and a reluctance to diversify the economy to avoid so much dependence on oil.

Many US cities found themselves on this slippery slope—the most spectacular being Detroit. Puerto Rico and Illinois are following close behind.

Why is the Slippery Slope of populism plus growing debt so attractive to so many people in emerging and declining communities around the world?

Ignorance, Social Justice, and System Gaming

The Slippery Slope shows up so often because of an interaction between three factors that play strong roles in emerging communities: widespread ignorance in the community, the aspirations of social justice crusaders inside and outside the community to "help" the poor, and the emergence of many new ways of gaming the system as the community's prosperity grows.

Ignorance

The biggest cause of slippery slope attractiveness is ignorance. The people of a newly emerging community have been dirt-poor for generations and are still steeped in inherited Agricultural Age thinking. These farmers must respect the artisans, warriors, priests, and nobility who run everything but the farms because though few, they have great knowledge of things beyond farming and can cause the farmers much grief.

As a community starts to transition into a post–Agricultural Age lifestyle, as it becomes an emerging community, it starts to get more prosperous. It still deals with changes in the physical world—bad weather, fires, floods and famines—but the social order starts changing in new and startling ways.

The artisan and merchant classes grow in number, variety, wealth, and influence. As industries develop, many new things are made and sold in new ways, which gives rise to a middle class (which actually comprises many classes—accountants are not in the same class as factory managers).

Children start wondering what they will be when they grow up, but their parents cannot advise them. That's confusing and scary, particularly because family ties are so important in emerging societies.

And what this means is that trust becomes even more important in the decision-making process; trust is the meat-and-potatoes of image-oriented politicians who are members of this developing middle class.

The community muddles through these new issues and make mistakes; that's part of the learning process. But Slippery Slope mistakes happen because this ignorance mixes nicely with the aspirations of another breed of this newly emerging middle class—the social justice crusaders.

Social justice

Social justice crusaders are those who are trying to "help" the poor, a form of instinctive thinking that can be satisfied in many ways—giving to charities, organizing protests, or directly assisting the poor by teaching them or building schools for them.

Many of these crusaders and much of the money they contribute come from people outside the community who are prosperous and have social justice aspirations. This noble intention can easily become distracted and corrupted, but those who have it are often oblivious to the real good or harm that results. They don't monitor the results of their efforts; they just want to think they're helping the poor. This is why charity scams are so easy to perpetrate.

In the Slippery Slope context, the damage they cause is raising poor people's aspirations without also cautioning them to respect harsh reality. The social justice warriors are training them to dream big but not to make sure their dreams are achievable. This causes a disconnect that charismatic, populist politicians take advantage of. They promise the world and deliver it for a while—with borrowed money. People say, "He made it happen once. He can do it again!" and the leader gets even more ambitious.

System gaming

When people take advantages of loopholes in a system for personal gain, they're gaming the system. They can do so in many ways, and laws and regulations can't always prevent that. Those who successfully game systems can feel good about it instinctively—it's Us vs. Them thinking.

Businesspeople can pad expense accounts, and others give into the lures of corruption. They hire family members or friends even though they're not needed. Some juggle the books and skim off the top or accept bribes for doing so. There are plenty of ways to game the system—to extract wealth without contributing to making more of it. This can all be aggravated greatly if borrowed money is used to fund ways of gaming the system.

Pluses and Minuses of the Slippery Slope

The benefit of being on a Slippery Slope is that it can raise community enthusiasm especially in communities in decline. Leaders can drum up enthusiasm for their next big thing, their next big idea, and that can pump people up and make them feel enfranchised in the short run.

When the next big thing doesn't happen it's because of ignorance—people don't know how to make the next big thing a reality, and that can lead to waste and confusion as they experiment. The social justice types contribute by applauding these efforts to help the poor, but they are usually just as ignorant of good ways to accomplish the vision as the locals are. They help raise aspirations but don't help meet them.

The system gamers in the community take advantage of the mix of ignorance and enthusiasm to exploit loopholes unless the community is quick enough to find and close those loopholes.

Big Cost

The big problem with the Slippery Slope is the big cost in terms of not just money but also time, effort, and attention that could have made the community more profitable, more educated, and wealthier.

This cost grows when little return comes from the envisioned project, or when it comes late, or when cost overruns diminish the expected return. One of the chronic cases of this is hosting an Olympics—these always overrun their budgets. When the project was being financed with borrowed money, and the borrowed money comes due, a crisis ensues.

The Alternative to the Slippery Slope

The alternative to the Slippery Slope is staying focused on wealth creation by being diligent about keeping the community climate favorable to wealth creating. This can be achieved by taking a few steps.

Keeping things simple and fair

Don't add rules and regulations just so there are more jobs for regulators and enforcers, but be vigilant about keeping the wealth-creating playing fields level and transparent. Don't let system gamers or corrupters have their day by allowing murky backroom deals to be acceptable.

Being tolerant

When an idea that created a current boom stops working—that's the time to search for new ideas that will foster the next boom. That requires tolerance for those who are ambitious and trying new things. Otherwise, those who are ambitious and can think outside the box will move on to better opportunities. This brain drain is why complacent communities can revert to ignorance.

This also means being tolerant of change, even disruptive change—new roads, new buildings, new kinds of activities taking place, new people engaging in these new activities. NIMBY thinking is hard on progress.

Leaving enough wealth in the hands of its creators to encourage them to do more wealth creation

Coming up with good boom ideas is not easy, and turning them into real, tangible successes requires talent. Reward your idea and talent people to encourage them to keep it up. You want to reward your new business makers, not the sports stadium makers.

These are ways of staying off the Slippery Slope; some might consider them counterintuitive, but they can result in a boom rather than a slide down the slippery slope.

Further Reading

"Greek Political Contagion: Parties of the left across Europe are looking to Syriza as an anti-reform model" (*Wall Street Journal*, July 6, 2015) talked about how happy the various anti-austerity parties were around Europe when the results of the Greek vote on austerity measures were announced. Here's a passage from this article.

> And sure enough, parties of the left across Europe are emerging as the Syriza Party's most vociferous allies. Consider Spain, where the Syriza-like Podemos ("We Can") party supported a "no" vote and in a statement last week praised Mr. Tsipras for reacting to the "ultimatum and blackmail" of Greece's creditors "in an exemplary manner."
>
> Podemos added that "today in Europe there are two opposing camps: austerity and democracy, the government of the people or the government of markets and non-elected powers. We are with democracy. We are with the Greek people."

"<u>A Grecian Formula for Courting Disaster</u>: Greece's position is now much worse. Voters seem not to have realized how much pain Europe's help averted" by Jeremy Bulow and Kenneth Rogoff pointed out how delusional the anti-austerity types were. They write,

> Following their charismatic prime minister and a pied piper parade of left-leaning economic pundits, the Greek people have voted resoundingly to "reject creditor demands for more austerity." That's nice, but who exactly is going to pay for less austerity?

Conclusion

The Slippery Slope is a chronic and powerful temptation that starts when a charismatic, populist leader touts a grand vision, wins, and tries to implement his or her vision. Unless the leader is exceptional, the grand vision will end up being beyond what community members are capable of, and the community will figure that out soon enough. The blame game that follows is disappointing, discouraging, and distracting.

The loss is greater if borrowed money implemented the vision and cannot be paid back.

The resulting crash may simply leave a sour taste in the community's mouth, but the damage can be much larger; it may wreck the community's government, bring violence to the streets, and bring on social revolutions.

In spite of these hazards, the Slippery Slope remains popular.

34

Getting the Right Government

One of the assumptions Americans have about government is that vibrant, multiparty democracy is a good idea and we Americans should do our best to spread this form around the world. But as good as it has been for the United States and Western Europe, much of the rest of the world has had a hard time making democracy work.

Why does vibrant, multiparty democracy seem to be so closely linked to American—and the developed world, actually—exceptionalism?

Many Possible Solutions vs. Many Possible Betrayals

One characteristic of regions and cultures where democracy doesn't work is the high rates of betrayal in dealing with the Thems—those who aren't part of the trusted circle. Such thinking was common in Stone Age and Agricultural Age thinking and became instinctual, but it doesn't work as well during the Industrial Age and sure doesn't work in the Information Age.

Today, we need widespread and diverse cooperation to function effectively. Think of barter, then coins, then smartphones as ways of paying for anything; the trust involved had to go way up with each step. Betrayal can bring down any enterprise, particularly those that are complex.

When betrayal occurs in a modern organization, it's called conflict of interest at best; when organized crime is involved, it's called criminal activity. The betrayal can easily lead to violence, feuds, and vendettas. Once again, these forms are hard on Industrial Age progress because they make building larger and diverse kinds of organizations more difficult.

Today, we need lots of cooperation, but we also need the loyal opposition, those who can propose new or better ways of doing things; this can lead to disagreements, but they can be healthy and beneficial if the resulting decision is a better way of doing things. To do this, however, people have to cooperate and trust, not pull knives at the first sign of dissent.

Widespread cooperation is a learned skill, so teaching it has to be inherent in the community on all levels—from the classroom to the boardroom.

If You Can't Make Democracy Work ...

If a community cannot or will not cooperate widely, is democracy the best governing choice? Probably not. Not at least for a few generations. In the meantime, that community will have to deal with the "I've got the biggest stick so we're doing it my way" mentality.

If this big-stick governing style is producing rising material prosperity and helping the community learn how to cooperate in Industrial Age ways, then it's doing a good job. Consider Singapore under the ruler Lee Kuan Yew (1959–1990). His rule was dictatorial, but Singapore evolved from Third World to First World status in a single generation. Many modern Chinese rulers have openly admired his success.

But his example is not an easy one to follow. Contemporary failures at following his example include Hugo Chávez and Nicolás Maduro in Venezuela and Vladimir Putin in Russia. They are spending their countries' resources but not building diverse and thriving Industrial Age communities with it.

The Virtues of Other Governing Forms

There are many stable alternatives to the democratic nation-state that America is. Here are some and their virtues.

Monarchy

A monarch is a sole ruler who administers the resources of a community with the advice of a council. Monarchies are generally hereditary.

The virtue of this style is strong instinctive support—most people understand the concept of a king and accept it as a stable ruling form particularly in agricultural communities.

Imperialism

Imperialism works when a community is too diverse to create a monarch; this is the case in many communities in the Middle East. In such a case, an outsider with a big outsider army to back him can bring monarchy-style peace to a diverse community. That's what the Ottoman Empire did in the Middle East in the 17th and 18th centuries.

Warlordism/Tribalism

If a community is diverse and no imperialist is available, local rulers will fill the vacuum. This governing style brings diversity in ruling style to a region and often much violence. For this reason, it's usually a transitional form of government that will be replaced fairly quickly with some other form, usually a monarchy or an imperialist rule.

China proved an interesting exception. The warlordism of the early 1900s was replaced with communism in the 1950s, not monarchy or imperialism.

Editorial: The Hazard of the Trigger-Warning Mentality in the United States

America in the 2010s is not without its threats to democracy, its form of government that has served it quite well for two hundred years. But there have always been threats to it such as cultural trends that might make other forms seem better. Ironically, what those threats were has always been the subject of much debate.

One of the threats of the 2010s is thin-skinnedness—the trigger-warning mentality. If issues can't be debated rationally, they won't be solved well. If people can't or won't listen to unpleasant talk about harsh realities, coming up with and implementing good solutions devolves into simple wishful thinking.

Looking harsh reality square in the face has long been a virtue of the American way, but in the 2010s, it looks as if this virtue is on the brink of extinction. If it goes over that brink, democracy will stop working well. Democracy depends on well-informed voters who can talk about issues in a straightforward manner; that kind of tolerance supports democracy.

35

Central Planning vs. Free Markets

One of the chronic questions in the twentieth and twenty-first centuries is which works better, central planning or free markets?

Places such as the United States and post-Thatcher Britain have chosen free markets most often, and places as diverse as China, Cuba, and Soviet Russia have chosen central planning most often. This is not a black-and-white issue—most nations are shades of gray here.

Another tough choice is spending and working for short-term returns vs. doing the same for longer-term benefit.

The Big Question: What to Invest In?

Industrialized and industrializing nations always wonder what to invest in. There are so many more opportunities to invest in than there are funds and other resources (such as skilled people) available to spend on them. Hard choices must be made. What should we build or create? How do we borrow money for that? How much? Who will benefit?

Someone who decides to build a road from Town A to Town B has to decide

- What type of road will it be?
- What will be its route?
- What property has to be acquired for it?
- How will it be financed?

- How will the financing be repaid?
- Who will build it?
- What companies or governmental organizations are going to be doing the heavy lifting?
- Who should benefit from this? (This is an arm-long list of choices that includes who gets the fruits of any corruption.)
- What's not being built because the resources are being used for this road?
- Is putting these other projects off a good choice? (This is called the opportunity cost.)

Such a project can be easy to envision but hard to execute. When does a free market handle tasks such as this better, and when does central planning do so?

Central Planning Shines

Central planning shines when a project is big, well understood, and doesn't change much with time. When constructing steel mills became well understood in the mid-twentieth century, the USSR's central planning could build them as effectively as the free-market steel companies in the United States did. Likewise, after the Suez Canal was up and running, the Egyptian government could handle it as well as British- or French-based free-market companies could.

Mature heavy industry and road and railroad building are examples of these kinds of big, stable, and well understood projects, and this is why governments have taken over many of these projects.

Another area where central planning shines is when fairness in handling a project is considered more important than rapid progress. Central planners are good at coming up with schemes such as subsidizes that distributes wealth in what the community considers a fair way.

Free Markets Shine

The free-market system is at its strongest when a project involves much uncertainty, complexity, and change; for moving targets, free markets work better because they can quickly adapt. Plan A gives way to plan B and plan C if and as necessary.

The bottom-line mentality of the free-market system is often criticized as narrow minded and misguided, but it has a powerful virtue. Having a bottom-line mentality means that results are constantly being monitored. If things aren't working well, this is discovered quickly because the bottom line suffers, a powerful incentive to change the way of proceeding.

Designing an incentive system to monitor results that is as effective as bottom-line thinking is always a big challenge for central planning systems.

A Level Playing Field

One key element to making free markets work well is a level playing field—fair laws, fair courts and lots of transparency. Free marketers observe the system they're working in actively and carefully and respond to it quickly and flexibly. Backroom deals and "You can't do that" thinking work against the free-market concept.

The transparency part is also critical for good functioning in central planning systems—good choices can be made only when lots of good information is available, and transparency allows corruption to be spotted more easily.

Progress vs. Fairness

As I cover in my book *Goat Sacrificing in the 21*[st] *Century*, debate rages over whether progress or fairness is more important. Fairness advocates promote spending for short-term gains, while progress advocates are willing to sacrifice now for greater gains later on. "A rising tide lifts all boats" is a progress truism, while "The rich get richer while the poor get poorer" is a fairness truism.

The drawback of investing too much in progress is not spreading enough of the wealth to alleviate the suffering of poor people. The occupational hazard of investing too much in fairness is borrowing money that can't be paid back. The suffering is alleviated only temporarily and is followed by a crash, or repression, or both.

The pendulum swings back and forth; suffering exists at the extremes. The fairness mentality can encourage borrowing that can lead to a crash and no progress at all.

Part 3a

Case Studies: Patterns in Action

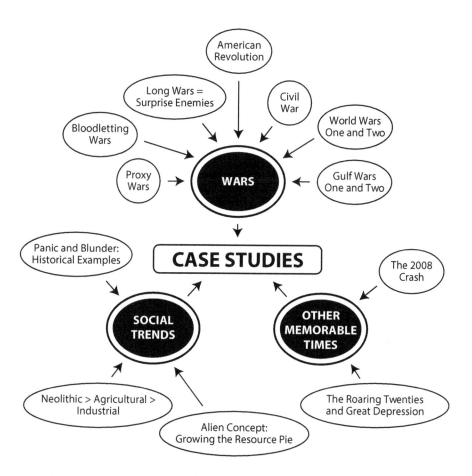

36

The Biggest Picture: Neolithic -> Agricultural -> Industrial Ages

The biggest picture of human history is the progress we've made technologically over the ages as we've moved from the Stone Age to the Agricultural Age and then to the Industrial Age.

The Time Scales

The first thing to keep in mind about these various ages is the difference in time scales, which are enormous. The Neolithic Age has been around since the beginning of modern humanity and is still the living style practiced in some places today such as in remote areas of the Amazon River basin and the Indonesian archipelago. It has been around for tens of thousands of generations. This means that the human body and human thinking are well adapted to survival in this environment.

The Agricultural Age began in a handful of places roughly five thousand years ago, 250 generations ago for those who have been living in the Agricultural Age the longest (and more like 150 for the median human). This is long enough to do a lot of learning and weed out inefficient body and thinking traits but not long enough for evolution to come up with adaptations to add to the mix—there has been some sorting out but little sorting in.

The Industrial Age began in western Europe roughly three hundred years ago, fifteen generations (five generations for the median). This is long enough to do some serious learning but not long enough to make much change to DNA. The instinctive thinking that served well in the Stone Age and was modified a bit during the Agricultural Age is still very much with Industrial Age inhabitants even where the fit is poor.

This change (and lack of it) in thinking patterns is why keeping time scales in mind is important.

The Neolithic Age

The neolithic village environment incorporated enormous variety. Prior to the wide spreading of agricultural practices, people were living from the tropics to the arctic in neolithic villages. The range of foods they had was as large as the number and types of catastrophes they had to deal with.

Within all this variety were some constants that shaped the instinctive thinking we have today.[1] Here are some of the constants.

Village size was small.

They contained up to three extended families who could trust each other; people outside the village couldn't be. They might cooperate, but they might betray. The Us vs. Them instinct developed to deal with this social environment.

Foods and other essentials changed in quality and quantity constantly.

What was available to eat, what was still pure and not tainted, and what could be transformed into edibles were matters that required constant attention. This is the root of the constant interest in food we experience today.

---

[1] I write about this mix of instinctive and analytical thinking styles in all my *Business and Insight Series* books. If you want more details, look through them.

When something vital ran out, such as food, shelter, water, tolerable weather, the village moved.

These were seminomadic people, and that affected their ideas about property. You could "own" only what you could carry from one location to the next, but you would probably share that too.

The world was dangerous.

Lots of nasty surprises lurked inside and around the village; vicious animals were understandable, but diseases were mysterious. Some threats were small, such as mosquitoes, but some were big, such as storms and floods. The world was uncertain and surprising and could be lethal. This is the root of the instinct to protect children and other instincts that thrive on fear.

The world was a varied place.

It was hot during the day and cold at night. It could be wet, dry, windy, calm, sun-baked, or shady. They had to deal with different conditions wherever they moved.

How This Helps Prediction

People lived with these variables and more for thousands of generations, and that shaped our bodies and our thinking. We still use instinctive thinking with day-to-day living and novel events alike. But knowing what instinctive thinking is telling a person or a community can make his or her or their actions more predictable. The most dramatic example of this is panic thinking followed by blunders. (See the Cyreenik Says section on my website.)

The Agricultural Age

The shift to the Agricultural Age was dramatic for humanity though it started in just a handful of places (in warm valleys with rivers that flooded regularly) and spread slowly. Inventive humans there developed farming technologies and lifestyles different from those still in the Stone Age.[2]

During the Agricultural Age, people began embracing new technologies and techniques and became more comfortable with them, and the concepts spread far and wide.

Here are some major differences that agricultural-style living brings to humanity.

Switching from Seminomadic to Sedentary Living

This one makes a surprisingly big difference because of its effect on the concept of property. If you live in one place most of your life, you can accumulate lots more stuff and become protective of it. Your village can grow to the size of a town and then a city. You'll also embrace writing rather than relying on your memory to keep track of who owns what—animals, land, and so on.

Larger groups pay off

When farming large fields year after year, having groups larger than extended families work together pays handsome dividends and it cuts down on the Us vs. Them instinct of the neolithic village and leads to the development of a hierarchy—the rulers and the ruled. Kings, supported by warriors, scribes, and priests, ruled farmers and a few artisans and merchants. This hierarchical system led to larger farms that could support those in the towns and the cities as well as armies.

---

[2] Humans and society: "Beads suggest hunter-gatherers resisted farming in Northern Europe: Culture clash may have delayed arrival of agriculture" (*Science News*, May 16, 2015) by Bruce Bower dealt with this.

Labor becomes specialized.

Stone Age people were generalists; Agricultural Age people started specializing in their work, and this led to the creations that only specialists could come up with, and they developed into social organizations.

Us vs. Them thinking didn't go away; during the transition, there were still seminomadic people around—hill people and valley people didn't mix easily.

How This Helps Prediction

People in Agricultural Age communities will utilize appropriate social styles and thinking; they will develop hierarchies and be ruled by warlords in small communities and imperial-style rulers in larger communities. Under stress, they might revert to Stone Age instincts and individual families or a small group of families will circle the wagons—mafia-style rule.

The concept of nationhood will come into play when various communities are ready to cooperate, not betray, on a national scale. That won't happen until the Industrial Age lifestyle becomes established for several generations, until most everyone is comfortable with the concept because they've witnessed the benefits of wider, much wider cooperation. Until then monarchy, imperialism or tribalism will be the comfortable and enduring governing styles.

The Industrial Age

The Industrial Age was another dramatic shift of orders of magnitude in how people thought, worked, and cooperated.

Enormous variety of work

While neolithic villagers engaged perhaps in dozens of kinds of jobs and everyone in the village could handle most, and Agricultural Age folks engaged in maybe hundreds of kinds of jobs, those in the Industrial Age worked tens of thousands of kinds of jobs—labor specialization was in full force.

Enormous variety in kinds of cooperation

Because of the proliferation of jobs, people had to develop new styles of cooperation if they wanted their communities to thrive. Businesses are all about widespread cooperation, which means learning how to use more analytic thinking and how to keep the Us versus Them instinct under control.

Advances in the understanding of the world

While the inner workings of plants and animals could remain mysteries prior to the Industrial Age, solving those mysteries in the Industrial Age environment has been at the root of many dramatic advances in agriculture and health care. Solving the mysteries of the universe is one of the big benefits of using lots of analytic thinking.

Enormous certainty in the living environment

One pleasant irony of the Industrial Age was the dramatic reduction in the variety of environmental conditions humans needed to adapt to. If you're living in a warm place with heating and indoor plumbing, you don't worry about the cold weather as much. If you're living in an area that has a grocery store you don't need to worry as much about going hungry and thirsty and having to move on. For those in the Agricultural Age, many elements in life became more predictable, and even more so in the Industrial Age.

But these shifts from one age to another took a long time and weren't easy. Just as some Stone Age people didn't make the shift to the Agricultural Age, and became Hill People, some people in the latter age were reluctant to make the shift to the Industrial Age and stayed being peasants. "Thank you, but we'll keep living our lives our way."

It was only after the benefits of the next age's productivity and inventions (including advanced weapons) became obvious that the neighbors took a second look. And those second looks usually caused a lot of civil unrest when the decision was made to attempt the transformation. It wasn't easy.

How This Helps Prediction

Communities that started industrializing traveled rocky roads for at least three generations. The rate limiter—the slowest part of the process—was the pace at which community members learned thinking styles compatible with industrialized activities. Critical mass was reached when the majority of them were able to think analytically and cooperate on much larger scales.

But even then, success wasn't guaranteed. The communities of the post-Ottoman Empire have tried to industrialize many times and in many ways since the beginning of the twentieth century. Successful industrializing is not inevitable. And the social and cultural differences between industrialized countries can be vast—think of the differences between the United States and Russia.

Conclusion

These three are the big ages—the biggest-picture transitions. The transition from one to the next is always a big task for a community, and it sometimes fails and the community reverts to the good old ways but with some changes.

Technology and thinking change with each transition, and each one brings surprises. As a result, the outcome of a transition will be unique for every person and community that undergoes one. This uncertainty makes history exciting and current events unpredictable.

37

Panic and Blunder: Historical Examples

Here are some famous events that are examples of panic thinking and blunder responses.

9/11 Disaster

The 9/11 disaster is the most vivid example of panic thinking; it started me down this line of thought. America's response to 9/11 was a textbook example of community panic thinking and then blundering in response.

The base stress

In 2001, America was attempting a soft landing after the dot-com bust and the post-Enron accounting scandals. These economic and technological stresses followed the fear of the Y2K end-of-the world event.

The novel event

Never before had anyone witnessed jet planes being flown into skyscrapers by suicidal terrorists. This will be the most famous disaster of the twenty-first century, and it will still be memorialized in 2101.

The blunder

Over the next decade, Americans enthusiastically trashed their legal protections and the airline industry, started wars with two countries, and spent billions on wars and seriously inconvenienced themselves in day-to-day life with various procedures and agencies designed to improve homeland security. All this in response to the novel scare of the century that started America's blunder chain of the century.

The Blunder Chain

America's blunders threatened other communities and created more panic thinking and more blunders.

- The Iraq War destabilized the Middle East and ironically made it more violence- and terror-friendly.
- The discarding of Rule of Law in favor of "These terrorists are a special case" thinking added to the threat of government-sponsored violence worldwide. It also disenfranchised communities, which added to violence and terrorism.
- The Iraq situation of the 2010s was the result of a blunder chain that started with too little thinking about what post-Saddam Iraq would be like in 2002.
- The novelty of Homeland Security produced blunders ranging from new security procedure gaffs to the 2007 Boston bomb scare overreactions discussed below.

The Long-Lasting Scars

The long-lasting scars from the post-9/11 blunders are deep and numerous. They have affected America and the rest of the world. America's 9/11 response brought terrorism to center stage in America's culture. After 9/11, America could have treated Al-Qaeda as a crank terrorist cult that had gotten lucky, but instead, America chose to treat it as a major symbol of evil and likely to produce more damage on a similar scale. America also chose to treat terrorism as a major evil to be battled with direct and righteous effort instead of choosing to treat it as just another kind of criminal activity that should be combated as part of comprehensive anticrime activities.

The Abu Ghraib photos scarred America's image as a right-doing culture and cost America a lot of high moral ground. And starting the war with Iraq scarred America's image of doing things for good cause. More high moral ground was lost; America looked prone to doing stupid things.

Not being able to make Iraq into a shining example of democracy in the Middle East in just a few years scarred America's reputation as an able problem solver. (America had succeeded doing this in the case of Germany, Italy, and Japan after World War II.) Instead, America looked stupid and its government looked like an imperial storm trooper rather than a shining light of democracy, a huge loss of goodwill and respect.

And America beefed up a state-sponsored neoreligion: all must pray at the altar of the holy metal detector so the plane will fly better. America looked insane and cowardly as well as stupid.

Airline trashing altered America's transportation network; the airlines didn't fill the transportation role projected for them before 9/11. Alternatives such as trucking, autos, private aviation, and the Internet prospered in its place.

These are all textbook examples of unadulterated community panic thinking and blundering that will be with us for a long time.

Example: The American Civil War Era (1850s–1870s)

The Civil War gets its own chapter as a case study. This chapter looks at it through the panic and blunder prism.

Underlying stress

The regional differences between the North and the South in America date to colonial times. As the North became more industrialized and the South prospered on a cotton-growing boom, those differences became sharper. This led to big differences in desirable economic, social, and legal policies between the North and the South. There had been disputes for decades before the Civil War and many successful solutions to the disputes. The problem was not new, and solving the problem was not new.

Novel event

The Whig Party dissolved in the 1850s, and the power vacuum it left behind was filled suddenly and aggressively in the late 1850s by the newly founded Republican Party (founded 1854). The surge to power of the Republicans was a novel event in the politics of America, and the Southern leaders saw it as deeply threatening.

The threat was made even more scary by a worldwide bank panic in 1857. Bank failures were taking money out of everyone's pockets, North and South, and everyone was getting scared. The Republican platform for how to handle the economics—things such as protective tariffs—were promising to take even more money out of Southern pocketbooks.

Blunder

The Southern leaders responded to the Republican threat by declaring that they would secede from the Union if a Republican were elected president. That happened in 1860 with the election of Abraham Lincoln, and the Southern leaders made good on their threat.

Blunder chain

Secession was something new to America, and so it was not responded to well either. Lincoln and the Republicans saw it as a threat, and the Civil War ensued. That was far from the end of this blunder chain. Other elements include the surprisingly long and damaging Civil War itself (1860–65), the Reconstruction Era (1860s through the 1870s) and Jim Crow South (which lasted into the 1920s).

Long-lasting scars

- the strong federal government of the United States (compared to that of Canada, Australia, and New Zealand)
- America's high concern with race relations
- the South always voting Democratic from the 1890s through the 1970s
- the South being an economic laggard in the United States until the 1960s
- Northerners' economic, social, and cultural perceptions of Southerners and vice versa.

Example: The Winter 2007 Cartoon Sign Scare in Boston

Though this was an example of panic and blunder on a smaller scale, the unnecessary expense was just as real.

Underlying stress

Along with many other issues facing cities of the Northeast United States in the 2000s, Boston's government was in the throes of dealing with the Big Dig, an automobile tunnel under downtown Boston that became a controversial public works issue. It had cost billions and was late and over budget. In 2006, it became a high-profile scandal because parts of the inner wall fell and killed a driver. The event was stressful enough to the city government that it called in outside help to do damage control.

Novel event

On the night of Sunday January 30, 2007, two young marketers put up about twenty battery-powered, odd-looking plastic signs in high-traffic areas of downtown Boston. It was part of a low-budget guerrilla marketing campaign for an upcoming movie based on a cable TV cartoon show.

Blunder

In twelve other major US cities, the signs were looked upon as curiosities and no unusual action was taken. But in Boston, the first reaction of city officials was that these novel signs could be a terrorist bomb threat. Traffic was shut down in many high-volume parts of the city for half a day as bomb squads checked out the signs.

Blunder chain

Boston arrested two men who had been paid to put up the signs, the cartoon producer paid Boston $2 million to cover emergency expenses, and a VP of the cartoon company was fired.

Long-lasting scars

Boston gained a reputation as a city with a touchy, provincial-minded government that would hurt people who did strange things in their town. The people of Boston started living with a lot less novelty in their lives and a lot more paperwork. Those planning on doing something "strange" in Boston started having to look for some government official to give them an okay. As is usual with such things, this would affect low-budget experimental projects much more than high-budget, low-risk projects.

As of April 2007, Boston's mayor was still standing solidly behind the blunder. He urged the people of Boston to boycott the movie. Other Boston officials responded with "No comment" to media questions about this.

This became a warm-up for the Boston Marathon bombing panic and blunder in 2013. Sadly, Boston had learned to overreact to these kinds of crisis. Overreaction became the sports thinking for the region.

Example: the War on Drugs

In 1969, President Nixon started what he called the war on drug abuse. It still hasn't passed the English-French Hundred Years' War in length, but it's a long-running US social blunder.

Underlying stress

In 1969, President Nixon was still trying to extricate America from the Vietnam War. Inflation from Johnson's "We'll have both guns and butter" fiscal policies was rising and worrisome. This was also the time when the Generation Gap was in full flower: the baby boomers were coming of voting age, and through choices in music, movies, and protesting, they were already demonstrating they were going change America's social mores. One of the slogans of the era was "Don't trust anyone over thirty-five."

Novel event

Long hair and new styles of music, sexual mores and drug use were some things baby boomers were experimenting with that upset the older generations.

Blunder

The Nixon administration decided that drug abuse was at the root of the generation gap–related social unrest in the nation and wanted to stop it. Drug abuse as perceived by the Nixon administration was entirely different from the way baby boomers perceived it, so the laws and programs established were bad matches with boomer reality; they saw the laws as disenfranchising persecution made worse by "the narcs"—narcotics agents.

Blunder chain

The drug program is something of an oddity because it was a blunder chain that continues even though the novelty of the threat wore off long ago. The drug program didn't solve the drug problem, but it's still supported. Even stranger from an outsider's perspective is that the once-persecuted boomers are now the ones supporting the blunder.

Long-lasting scars

The disenfranchisement of large parts of American society over drug issues has progressed into the 2010s. This disenfranchisement is the source of much of the violence America experiences in the twenty-first century, and the programs feed the disenfranchisement; putting so many people in prison is one way.

The police's role in America has become much more violence oriented instead of community-mediator oriented. This is a form of disenfranchisement that has spread to other countries that supply drugs to the United States, such as Colombia, now home to an essentially permanent countryside insurrection financed by the disenfranchisement that creates the illicit drug market. This insurrection leads to chronic disenfranchisement.

A program such as the War on Drugs—one that deals with lots of dollars of product demand and disenfranchises people for years and years—becomes a spawning ground for corruption, violence, and arbitrary trampling of civil liberties by government officials. The corruption is a government credibility killer.

These are some historic examples of panic thinking and blunders that show how expensive this cycle of thinking and responding can be and how the waste and damage can go on for decades.

38

Panic, Blunder, and Terrorism

This case study shows how seeing a pattern, a bad pattern in this case, can help us avoid expensive mistakes when deciding what to do when a scary crisis strikes.

I will be editorializing here about the 9/11 disaster, America's response to it, and what would have been a better response—carrying on and conducting business as usual.

Background

Few things have been as painful for me to watch as America's response to the 9/11 disaster. In the words of Kurtz in Joseph Conrad's short story "Heart of Darkness," "The horror! The horror!" I'm referring to the response, not the incident.

The response, which is sometimes called the war on terror, was a decade-long distraction from America's real problems such as adapting the economy to post–dot-com crash conditions and foreseeing an upcoming financial crisis and thus cost America dearly.

Watching the response was what sparked my thinking on panic and blunders. There had to have been a better response, and there had to have been a way for people to see it. This is a huge issue, and if we can avoid a repeat of a blunder of this magnitude, the world will be better for that.

Key Topics

Terrorism should be considered a criminal rather than a military concern.

The first and biggest mistake the Bush administration made in response to the 9/11 disaster was deciding that terrorism was a military rather than a criminal problem. Many bad solutions cascaded out of this choice, the biggest of which became the Iraq War and the following decades-long widespread unrest in the Middle East. This was not just a Bush administration problem; the American public was solidly behind these choices. But this Middle East quagmire was only the most visible problem; there were many others.

Terrorism is a criminal problem because terrorists are first and foremost criminals. They are a very small group of people with very little firepower; they count heavily on surprise and shock. They hide in a large population that is mostly against what they do but is not enfranchised enough to stop them. This is a situation that calls for police officers, not soldiers. Police officers have enough firepower to stop terrorists once they are found— terrorists don't succeed because police can't outshoot them; they succeed because they can't be found before they cause trouble.

This means that finding terrorists is the key to solving the terrorism problem, and since terrorists hide in civilian populations, this means that getting good intelligence on civilian populations is the most critical step.

Civilians produce the best intelligence on other civilians. Who hasn't been watched by a neighbor? Terrorism can happen when a neighbor sees something but doesn't feel motivated enough to report it. Palestine is a hotbed of terrorism because terrorists' neighbors feel little motivation to report their suspicions to a police force that will take action. The best cure for terrorism is changing the perception of neighborhoods concerning the appropriateness of terrorists. The more neighbors think terrorists are a bad idea and are worth reporting, the less terrorism there will be.

If a neighborhood can't be convinced to report terrorists, the next best line of defense is the police force and lawyers. Police are very much involved in gathering intelligence on the day-to-day activities of neighborhoods. To have police add antiterrorism activities to their normal anticriminal activities is very easy and cost effective because it involves almost no change in their activities. Terrorists are criminals just like drug dealers are. If police are trying to find drug dealers, they can also try to find terrorists almost as easily.

Another very important reason to keep antiterrorist measures as a neighborhood and police activity is that doing so supports the rule of law, the foundation of good government in general.

Dealing with the novelty

What makes terrorists different from other criminals is the novelty of their acts. Timothy McVeigh and Terry Nichols were the first people to use a truck bomb on a US building in the American heartland. The 9/11 people were the first to suicide hijack an airplane. This novelty element is very important; once it has happened, average people know what to look for to keep it from happening again and can watch vigilantly for it. Few if any additional precautions are needed. Expensive elaborate precautions usually don't work. The way to deal with a novel terrorist attack is to recognize that it is novel and then get back to business as usual.

The best way to fight terrorism is to build communities that won't support it. This means stable and prosperous communities in which the members feel they have a stake in their own well-being and strong faith in the justness of their government—they feel enfranchised. One element in building enfranchisement is promoting the rule of law.

If communities believe what terrorists are doing is wrong, they will do something about it when they see terrorist acts being prepared. Note again that this form of antiterrorism is identical to anticriminalism; every effort to fight crime becomes an effort to fight terrorism.

The problems with using soldiers to fight terrorists

Soldiers don't fight terrorists well because they are trained to fight other soldiers, not criminals, and second, the military will use military rather than civilian intelligence to find terrorists.

In the Second Iraq War, US military intervention produced large numbers of guerrillas where there were formerly small (perhaps vanishingly small) numbers of terrorists. The military can deal with armed insurrections, but that's not the road the United States wanted Iraq to go down when it started the war. Using the military to fight terrorists in Iraq changed the mission in Iraq from stopping terrorism to putting down insurrection. The American troops found themselves fighting alligators instead of draining swamps.

Compared to civilian intelligence, military intelligence is very limited in quantity. The latter is designed to find out things about other militaries: bases, supply lines, depots, troop movements, and troop capabilities. Other militaries will have these things in fairly distinct organizations and places—military units operating out of military bases—so the resources needed to keep track of another nation's military capabilities are limited.

Terrorists are vanishingly small in number compared to another nation's military; they hide in a huge sea of civilians, not in distinct, isolated places. They don't need much infrastructure, so terrorist bases are also vanishingly small when compared to military bases. Using military intelligence techniques to uncover terrorist groups is a matter of using the wrong tool. Instead use police forces, lawyers, and enfranchised neighbors, who are much better equipped to find and deal with dangerous malcontents among benign civilians.

A problem that confronts all intelligence gathering is separating fact from fantasy. The number of people who have fantasized about committing terrorist acts is staggering compared to the number of terrorist acts committed. One of the tasks of a police force is distinguishing harmless cranks from truly dangerous people. This kind of distinguishing is much harder for military intelligence people to do at the neighborhood level because it takes knowing the territory.

The military can't easily use civilians to find terrorists, so it uses captured or betrayed terrorists to find other terrorists through interrogation. When community research is used, the military tends to kick in doors rather than knocking on them, which undermines the rule of law and can alienate whole communities and turn them into terrorist hotbeds, which exacerbates the problem.

Military intelligence interrogations are usually conducted in secret, outside the bounds of the rule of law, and results in the abuses depicted in the <u>Abu Ghraib prison photos</u>, which verified rumors of prisoner abuse.

Building communities that reject terrorism requires respecting the rule of law or some other kind of legitimate rule; that will prompt communities to view terrorist activities as they should be viewed and report them to improve their lives and not bring the military down on them.

Big Media and Big Government Feed Big Terrorism

Big Media loves a good story, a stream of them, particularly if they include catchy sound bites, so it has no problem with playing up the terrorist angle in news.

This has been good for news, but it has also been good for Big Terrorism. Terrorists are advertising a cause and want value for their advertising dollar. Whenever terrorism is big news, the terrorists get huge returns from their "advertising" efforts, which encourages more of the same. Sadly, terrorism is a booming entertainment segment today.

This vicious cycle can be stopped if the media and their audiences realize that playing up the terrorist angle of a news story promotes more terrorism by promoting or advertising the terrorist angle when they dig into the whys of an act. Such coverage also lets terrorists learn the value of different targets.

Big Media should break its habit of sensationalizing terrorism by introducing negative feedback. It will require self-regulation for Big Media to decide promoting terrorism is in poor taste. Here is Roger's modest proposal on how to do it: Each month, the terror percentage of a media outlet could be calculated (terrorist-related material as a percent of total material), and when the percentage is high enough, a discount is given back to advertisers. This would be easy for the media to calculate, and it would make their advertisers happy. Hot news would still be covered, but broadcasts of terrorists' angles would drop, and that could help cool the current terrorist hysteria.

The Government's Key Antiterrorist Tactic

The best antiterrorist tactic every government and community can support is the concept of business as usual. Because terrorism tries to change the actions of the community, it fails if the community doesn't change its actions.

When the Bush administration changed the way billions of federal dollars were spent and encouraged local governments to change how more billions of dollars were spent, these people were not unbowed by terrorists, they were succumbing hook, line, and sinker to the terrorists' message and giving them a great return on their investment. When Big Media whips up antiterrorist frenzy daily, that will hand another win to the terrorists and prompt their further efforts.

This cycle could be broken if business were conducted as usual in spite of terrorist events. They should be reported but not advertised. The Bush administration's creation of the Homeland Security Department was a wonderful example of what the government shouldn't be doing; instead it should fight crime, poverty, and other factors that cause people to not buy into the system. General, common forms of crime, not rare terrorist acts, should be the justification for security-improving expenditures.

The concept of the rule of law was diminished by Prohibition, the War on Drugs, and the War on Terror. If rule of law is promoted in spite of the crisis de jour, the community will feel that it benefits and will be more willing to battle crime and terrorism and will be less likely to feel isolated and resist the police's efforts to fight these problems.

The Curse of the Patronizing Habit: "I'll be pilloried if something happens on my watch."

One of the deadliest deterrents to the rule of law occurs when a TV reporter demands of a government official at the scene of a disaster, "What will you do to prevent this from happening again?" The official feels obliged to respond with some action rather than promoting the concept of business as usual. Sometimes, things just happen. And sometimes, things should just be allowed to happen.

In 2003, after the *Columbia* disaster, NASA announced it would no longer use the space shuttle to repair the Hubble telescope because it couldn't be inspected for problems there. This was an example of when NASA should have allowed whatever was going to happen to happen. Launching the space shuttle was an inherently risky business that should have just been allowed. NASA was patronizing the public by refusing to tell the news networks, "That question is not in good taste at this time."

This curse of being overpatronizing is aggravated by the current American legal system. I have lived in New Zealand and seen how New Zealanders operate. This is a place where people take more responsibility for their actions. I've seen people there rappelling down hotel buildings in big cities, something that isn't allowed in the United States because hotels here can't count on the courts deciding that someone who rappels down a building is fully responsible for his or her own actions. This is a sad loss for America.

Antiterrorism Has Redefined What It Means to be American

Homeland Security, the Bush administration's War on Terrorism, and Big Media's constant yammering about the terrorist angle has changed Americans. We have become cowardly and have institutionalized seeing a terrorist behind every bush.

Our fear is replacing our can-do attitude; we're closing our borders to new people and new ideas. Fear is replacing the high moral ground we once had in our foreign relations. Our government has become a fertile ground for Kafkaesque regulations. One that affected Sen. Edward Kennedy when he tried to fly was reported in the *Washington Post* on August 20, 2004. When he went to purchase a ticket, the airline representative said, "I can't sell you one."

"Why not?" asked the senator.

"I can't tell you that," said the airline person.

"Who can tell me?"

"I can't tell you that either."

"What should I do now?"

"I can't tell you."

The senator had the misfortune of having the same name as someone being watched by Homeland Security. You'd think the airlines and the government would want to clear up a mistake such as that one. But the thinking goes, if Homeland Security revealed who had made that decision, that would reveal the sources used for making the decision, and that would compromise Homeland Security. So in the name of antiterrorism, the public has to live with a decision made by a person who will never know the harmful results of the decisions he or she makes. And by law, this deciding person can't know the results. This kind of thinking has been condoned by the executive, legislative, and judicial branches of the government.

This Kennedy incident came from the Clinton years, not the post-9/11 years, this thinking style has been around a long time. And to this day no one in government or the media seems to recognize that this puts the decision maker outside an accountability loop, so we should expect heaps of abuses as a result. This accountability problem produced the prison abuse that was the recorded in photos.

This Kafkaesque-style of fighting terrorism has poisoned the American way of thinking and has diminished the concept of the rule of law. It was a huge step toward developing a secret police system because the next step in government logic is, "If the citizens won't protect their government, we'll establish an institution that does."

This could spell death to our concept of informed democracy, the heart of our governing system. How can voters make good choices about government when the government conceals relevant information from them?

Here is another example of the problems this leads to. If we know our government has secret rules and someone with an official-looking ID tells us, "I want something from you, and there's a secret rule that says you have to give it to me," what are we supposed to do? How could we possibly check this out? This spells a-b-u-s-e. Secret rules are bad ideas; they poison democracy.

America Needs to Get beyond 9/11

We need to get back to business as usual by considering 9/11 as a unique incident, not the basis for a new way of thinking. We need to view terrorism as crime to be handled by the police, not the military. We need to accept that the world is a risky place; not to do so costs us terribly in terms of our personal freedoms and in the strength of the rule of law. This won't be easy, but when we succeed, America will be a safer and more comfortable place that will be closer to the American ideal.

More on the Media's Role in Sustaining Terrorism

On July 22, 2004, a large commercial building in Suwon, Korea, caught fire and burned for about twelve hours. I saw flames gush out of the top two floors while fire engines with huge hoses were trying to knock the flames down. I watched and photographed it from my office window a few blocks away.

No lives were lost, but tens of millions were lost in the destruction, the cleanup, and forgone revenue. Spectacular as this fire had been, I couldn't find an article about it in the *Korea Herald* (Korea's largest English-language newspaper), the Asian *Wall Street Journal*, or on the Internet.

On July 25, 2004, a United Boeing 747 turned around ninety minutes after taking off from Sydney and returned to the airport. Someone had written "BOB" on a barf bag and dropped it near a toilet. Instead of assuming this meant "Bob," or "Best of Breed," or "Best on Board," or "Boobs on Bounce," or something else innocuous, the pilot assumed this meant "Bomb on Board" and succumbed to antiterrorist panic. Aborting the flight was an expensive response, but no one was hurt. Nonetheless, it was covered by the Asian *Wall Street Journal*, and I found mentions of it on the Internet. It was hot news for two days, as opposed to the building fire, which had sufficient visual interest as well as financial impact.

Terrorism and the war on terrorism are alive and booming in the 2010s; they're being subsidized by Big Media.

Covert Financing of Terrorism

The biggest source of financial support for terrorism is American and world media. Terrorists are taking page one from the Marketing 101 textbook: as much as possible, get someone else to pay for your advertising. If you frame your advertising as a news event, the media will advertise you and make it look much more credible.

Big Media is wholeheartedly behind the terrorists in this marketing strategy. Long after the 9/11 disaster, the media filled up news holes with stories that had terrorist-related hooks; in essence, they subsidized terrorism.

The Good News of Good News

We are allowing fear to cause more fear, which is becoming institutionalized. We need to break this cycle and get back to living optimistically. This is not impossible or naïve; FDR said, "The only thing we have to fear is fear itself." A key element in regaining optimism and dismantling the institutions of fear is changing how media report on terrorism. Media people must live up to their own words about how they run their industry and become truly responsible in their reporting on terror; this means being brave enough not to do hysterical reporting at every opportunity. The terrorism advertising discount I proposed above is a way of adding courage to the media people so it will be easier for them to do the right thing.

When we break the cycle of fear, we can get beyond our obsession with 9/11 and go back to being optimistic Americans—the kind of Americans we all like the best, the kind who will do the best things for the world.

Civilians Can't Try Terrorists? What Hooey!

This thought came to me when I read "Civilian Courts Are No Place to Try Terrorists: We tried the first World Trade Center bombers in civilian courts. In return we got 9/11 and the murder of nearly 3,000 innocents" (*Wall Street Journal*, October 19, 2009) by Michael Mukasey, US attorney general from 2007 to 2009. In it, he claimed the rule of law couldn't handle terrorists.

> The Justice Department claims that our courts are well suited to the task. Based on my experience trying such cases, and what I saw as attorney general, they aren't. That is not to say that civilian courts cannot ever handle terrorist prosecutions, but rather that their role in a war on terror—to use an unfashionably harsh phrase—should be, as the term "war" would suggest, a supporting and not a principal role.

Grrrr. There's no quicker way to bring my blood to boil than by suggesting that terrorism is so special that the rule of law can't handle it. Such thinking brought on the 9/11 decade of terror. The war on terror was America's biggest blunder in this decade, and perhaps bigger than the blunder the Vietnam War was part of.

Mukasey wrote that trying terrorists was expensive and … well … *scary* would be the way I'd paraphrase it. He seemed to think of a terrorist trial as a mob boss trial on steroids. I agree that it has some things in common with a mob boss trial, but the on-steroids part I question. If I were a Manhattan resident who could either be on a jury trying a Jersey mob boss or a Kabul terrorist, no question about which one would cause me more worry.

Mr. Mukasey's opinion that terrorists were a special case was an example of the scar that 9/11 created in America's thinking, particularly in the thinking of those in New York and working in the Pentagon, those who were more than distant spectators if not participants in the greatest terrorist act of the century.

Mr. Mukasey needs to rise above his fear and recognize that if civilian courts can't handle this problem, he is disenfranchising civilians from being part of the solution to terrorism, and that disenfranchising is a big part of the recipe for more decades of terrorist disaster.

Terrorism must be considered a crime, not a cause for war. As long as terrorism is considered and handled as a war, only warriors can fight it. If terrorism is viewed as a crime again, people will be enfranchised and this problem will be solved by community action. People can spot terrorists a hundred times more effectively than can government workers because there are millions more civilians than government workers hired to look for terrorists. If these people feel enfranchised, they will report suspicious activity. And trusting in the rule of law is a big part of feeling enfranchised.

The Evolving Image of a Terrorist

Terrorists and their historical equivalents have scared people throughout history. The image of what a terrorist is evolves to match the worry circumstances of the contemporary culture and time. This evolution is interesting because it's a mix of instinctive thinking and current events.

What these images have in common (the instinctive thinking side) is that terrorists are sneaky and betray the community in very dangerous ways and have many sneaky and dangerous friends inside and outside the community. As a result, the majority of the community agrees it must discover and stop them even if that means trampling on civil liberties and the rule of law and conducting witch hunts.

In the 2010s, the ISIS atrocities created the image of the black-masked iconoclasts waving black flags and beheading enemies. When ISIS displaced Al-Qaeda as the high-profile Islamic terrorist group, they turned out to be much more photogenic and adroit in using social media. Because of their skills in this area, I suspect they will displace Nazis as the generic photogenic movie villains for Hollywood action movies.

The underlying stress was worldwide slow economic recovery from the 2007 crash and years of chaotic violence in the Iraq-Syria region of the Middle East.

In 2001, Al-Qaeda and Osama bin Laden burst on the terrorism scene with what is likely to be the most memorable terrorist act of the twenty-first century—the 9/11 disaster.

The underlying stress was the United States recovering from the dot-com crash on the economic side. In the Middle East, there were many unresolved issues swirling around the futures of Iraq, Iran, and Afghanistan.

The 1890s were the Gilded Age, a time of rapid industrial growth and immigration in the northern United States. There was also a lot of heated dispute about how workers should be treated and how wealth should be spread around. A hot spot that had just erupted was at the McCormick Steelworks in Chicago. A memorable, historic bomb was thrown at one of the demonstrations. What evolved from that was the image of the bomb-throwing anarchist. One interesting element here is that prior to this incident, anarchists were just another Socialist-style group with what-are-now-called libertarian ideals mixed in. Following this incident, they became the Al-Qaeda of their day.

In the 1880s, getting the South reorganized after the Civil War turned out to be a difficult task that didn't go well. It was hard to figure out how to organize a society that mixed freed men with former slave owners. The good news was that the cotton market remained large and thriving. The archterrorist in this time of stress became the crazed black man chasing after white women. Fear of that resulted in lynchings. In a surprise twist, it was the vigilante counterterrorists of this era, the KKK, that became legendary, not the terrorist image itself.

In the early 1800s, the newly formed United States had many issues and stresses to face due to the tension between England and France as the French went through their revolution. The archterrorist for this era became French revolutionists bringing dangerous ideas to the United States. The answer President John Adams came up with in 1798 was the Alien and Sedition Acts. The good news about this one was that American thinking quickly moved on to other issues and these acts were allowed to expire.

In the 1930s in Germany, the Nazis and Communists were bitter rivals. In 1933, a newly arrived Communist was found at the scene of a fire that burned down the Reichstag and admitted to starting it. This terrorist act let Hitler and the Nazis sweep the Communists out of the legislature; this let him consolidate his power and become a de facto dictator.

This happened during the desperate times of the Great Depression. These times were even scarier in Germany than they were in the United States.

In the 1950s, the United States and Russia became bitter rivals in spite of their having been allies during World War II. With the revelations about Julius and Ethel Rosenberg selling atomic bomb secrets to the Soviets, an archterrorist came on stage—the closet Communist—and led to the McCarthy-era fear that the US government was infested by secret Communists.

Conclusion

Terrorists in one form or another have always been a part of history; the forms they take depend on what the community's worries are. The root emotion terrorism plays off is the worry of secret betrayal.

Terrorist acts can vary greatly, but if they happen in the right place at the right time, they can cause big social change that results in restricting civil rights and the instigation of witch hunts. Both of these activities can get quite memorable and quite expensive.

39

The Postwar Decline of Detroit

All cities in Midwest America experienced booms that started in 1800s. Curiously, all the booms peaked at the same time, in the 1950s, as the Cold War issues evolved into the Generation Gap issues of the 1960s. Detroit was the icon of what was happening during the transformation from boom to decline.

Thomas J. Sugrue's *The Origins of the Urban Crisis*, which I read for a history class at Salt Lake Community College, inspired this chapter. Sugrue took what is in the 2010s a mainstream premise as the cause of the postwar decline. I disagree with his premise. I think there was a different cause.

The Sugrue Premise

Sugrue's thesis was that racial discrimination in Detroit led to a housing and job crisis. The collusion of federal and state regulators, bankers, real estate agents, and white-based community organizations kept blacks segregated in small, poor neighborhoods. The job issues were the result of racially insensitive employers and unions; only a few Detroit companies hired black people, and that was for low-paying, dirty service jobs such as janitorial work with little chance for advancement.

Sugrue considered this the situation in Detroit and surrounding black areas from the '30s to the '60s. But he gave no feeling of what was different between the booming Detroit of the '40s and '50s, the city that was peaking in the '60s and '70s, and the city that was then in steady decline from the '80s through the 2010s. He described job opportunities and housing for blacks as being pretty much the same through all these decades.

When he dealt with Detroit's deindustrialization, the first item in his rogues' gallery was automation, which he argued sucked jobs out of Detroit and thus the unions' power. The reduction in earning power of the city's inhabitants was at the root of the crisis.

What he didn't talk about was the harsh reality that overall, automation made production faster, better, and cheaper. He actually implied in some places that this was not the case; the big benefit to management was not faster, cheaper, and better but union busting, the hot topic on their minds. His book gave in to classic Blame Them thinking.

My Premise

Detroit's crisis was not that automation happened but that Detroit's environment was so toxic for it. The city leaders and its people didn't accept the challenge of making Detroit automation friendly to keep jobs in the area.

Sugrue and many Detroiters had a common blind spot in their thinking that led them to believe businesses owed them jobs and those businesses that left betrayed Detroit. I think businesses are grief sensitive—if you give owners and managers lots of grief, they'll look for places that cause them less grief. This is what happened in Detroit and other Midwest inner cities. The city leaders, unions, and residential neighbors made conducting business in Detroit a grief-filled process, so they left. This is a race issue only where race affects the grief level.

Available technology makes a big difference in where businesses set themselves up, another concept Sugrue didn't grasp. Detroit and the huge River Rouge auto plant boomed when it was difficult and expensive to move raw materials and finished goods over roads or to distant places as was the case in the '40s and '50s and earlier. In such an environment, centralization and localized vertical integration paid big benefits. Raw materials, coal, steel, and fresh water were easily shipped to River Rouge on the Great Lakes, and finished automobiles were easily moved out using railroads. Detroit and its neighborhoods supported the numerous smaller factories and services that supported this flow and transformation of raw materials into finished goods.

When global transportation got quicker and more reliable thanks to better ships, ports, and airports and local trucking got faster and cheaper thanks to freeways and interstates, companies could decentralize and take advantage of local specialties and lower grief levels in other locations. In the '50s and '60s, this killed the River Rouge advantage and threatened all the relatively high-paying black jobs that existed there.

Detroit could have reinvented itself as New York did in the '70s, but the people and communities of Detroit chose not to. They liked the status quo and stuck with steel and auto making until the factories shut their doors because they couldn't make money. When that happened, Detroiters blamed all sorts of external problems for it happening—again, classic Blame Them thinking on the part of those who stayed.

The ambitious people became frustrated, voted with their feet, and set up thriving businesses elsewhere. By the 1980s, there were a whole lot of Detroiters who exited.

This technological and business practice crisis killed the Detroit boom, not race or housing, but Sugrue downplayed this. He wrote about the strong correlation between Detroit's decline and the growing percentage of blacks living there but didn't give any reason not to presume causation, as in the decline in industry was caused by the increase in blacks. This leads to another implication, that blacks there couldn't handle the challenge of assimilating into a US urban environment as well as could other ethnic and immigrant groups. Not an encouraging suite of implications. I don't think that was Sugrue's intention, but it's not a great leap to make this inference based on his book. If this wasn't what he intended, he should have widened what he talked about so that, as I have pointed out, this crisis could be viewed in a wider context and the correlation didn't look as prominent.

New Insight

As I read, I gained an insight about home owning, an aspiration of many Americans since the mid-twentieth century, part of the American dream. The dark side, not seen by these enthusiasts, is that home ownership strongly supports the status quo and prescriptionism—those who own homes become deeply concerned about property values and whatever can negatively affect them, neighbors included. Top of the don't-do-it-here list is experimenting, doing things differently. This is a surprise dark side to the aspiration for widespread home ownership. It stifles innovation and entrepreneurship, and without them, growth is stifled as well. This was one of the roots of the urban crisis the Midwest cities have experienced.

The Dan Gilbert solution

These cities try to solve this problem, but they don't understand it well and think about it the wrong way. The most common wrong way is to build a high-profile edifice that increases city pride in hopes of attracting businesses back. The high-profile person who did this in the 2010s in Detroit (and Cleveland, my hometown) is Dan Gilbert, billionaire head of Quicken Loans. He is supporting professional sports teams, buying up distressed inner-city real estate, and getting various governments to finance high-profile edifices such as sports arenas, convention centers, and casinos. He's also trying to get gentrifying going strong.

Such activity makes for good news items but doesn't solve the underlying problem, the high grief level experienced by many nameless but aspiring businesspeople. To make them more interested in setting up shop in a city's center, things such as restrictive zoning laws, status quo–loving neighborhood associations, capricious city officials and union leaders have to be dealt with. They all need to have less power over how business is conducted so the business environment is flexible, transparent, and simple.

Dan Gilbert's solutions are grand works of urban art which city leaders can take pride in but they don't solve the root problems.

Further Reading

"The Maestro of Midwest Revival: The billionaire who brought LeBron James back to Cleveland talks about his business bet on the big cities of the former Rust Belt" (*Wall Street Journal*, October 31, 2014) by Matthew Kaminski dealt with what Gilbert has accomplished.

At 52, Mr. Gilbert has accomplished a few things beyond reeling in LeBron. The son of a Detroit bar owner, Mr. Gilbert started a mortgage business that he turned into Quicken Loans, amassing a fortune of $4 billion. He owns about 100 companies, multiple casinos and hotels, and much of downtown Detroit. Yet here's what comes up first about him on Google: the 434 splenetic words he wrote four years ago in "The Letter." [which conviced LeBron to come back]

Conclusion

The mainstream view of the Midwest crisis, as reflected in Sugrue's book, is myopic. It looks at Detroit and its problems solely through the prism of race and housing issues. But these issues are symptoms, not causes, of Detroit's problems. This difference in point of view about what is important makes a lot of difference. Many Detroiters think like Sugrue, and as a result, the people of Detroit can't fix their problems even in the 2010s. Not recognizing that race and housing are just symptoms, that the root problem is too much grief in conducting business in Detroit, is what has kept Detroit constantly declining for the last sixty years.

40

The North American Colonial Experience

In the 1600s, many people in western Europe were doing something crazy—pulling up stakes, leaving their villages, towns, and farms, and spending a lot to immigrate to the unknown—North and South America. The Spanish and Portuguese headed to South America, and the northern Europeans headed to North America. The iconic first voyages to North America were the 1607 settling of Jamestown in what would become Virginia and the *Mayflower* going in 1620 from England and Holland to Plymouth Bay in what would become Massachusetts.

It was crazy, but one curious part of this craziness is that the urge to pull up stakes is still very much alive and well today. Consider that about two thousand people signed up in 2013 to be considered for a one-way trip to Mars as part of a reality TV project (Mars One). It's an instinct only a few people in any community feel strongly, but those few feel it quite strongly.

A November 16, 2013 article in the *Economist* discussed colonial museums in the United States. A different story dealt with how ethnically mixed the early colonial experience was and how different it was from the European experience of its day.

The first efforts to exploit the Americas, an unknown wilderness, were near disasters if not complete disasters. But in the end, thanks to the persistent pioneering spirit, constant learning from mistakes, and technological advances, these adventurers transformed the Americas to what they are today.

This transformation took time; the nature of the colonizing experience changed greatly between 1600 and 1800, and it led to the immigrant experience, which has also been changing dramatically over the last two centuries.

Christopher Columbus was far from the first European to discover America. What made his discovery different was what people around him did when they heard the news; tens of thousands listened, invested millions, and migrated.

Consider what has happened since Neil Armstrong and Buzz Aldrin landed on the moon in 1969: very little. If this continues, it will be some later Columbus who will wake up the exploiting wave that washes over the moon and the rest of the solar system and becomes the remembered person.

The Crazy Man from Italy

During the 1400s, sailing technology in Europe had been steadily improving; people could sail the Atlantic as well as the Mediterranean. Merchants traveled south down the coast of Africa and north into the North Sea. Marco Polo types were traveling the Silk Road through Asia and returning with stories and riches from China. At the center of this activity were the Renaissance Italians such as Polo and Columbus.

Christopher Columbus was a crazy Italian explorer. The scientists of the Spanish court knew he was crazy. He was saying the world was half the size they knew it was. (The flat-earth theory was comfortable legend, not real.)

But if he were right, if he could sail west and reach Japan, wow! The riches! The Spanish wouldn't have to deal with Indian, Arab, and Italian middlemen to get Chinese silks and Indonesian spices. Instead, *they* would become the middlemen.

In 1492, the Christian Spanish had just fought the final of several successful wars to unify Spain and subdue the Moors there. This was a civil war in nature, which meant there were still many restive people in Spain, and the court needed big, unifying projects to keep the unrest from growing and rekindling the conflicts. Columbus might be crazy, but if he were right, developing prosperous trade was just the kind of project

189

that would grow peace. The king and queen sidestepped their court and gambled on him, and three ships headed west.

Well, Columbus was wrong, but he was very lucky. He ran into the Caribbean islands just before he ran so low on food that the crew would have mutinied and turned back. So in the early 1500s, it was learned that there was some land, big and mostly unknown, five weeks west of Spain and Portugal and six weeks coming back by sailing far to the north or south before heading east due to the trade winds and the westerlies.

"What to do about this ... this ... new world?" became the question for the wildly ambitious explorers and exploiters of Europe of the early 1500s.

Adding Information

Other explorers headed west and returned with reports to western European nations. In 1497, John Cabot, another Italian, brought a sketchy report to the king of England of a landmass well north of where Columbus was exploring. His son, Sebastian Cabot, continued the family tradition and added much more information about our East Coast.

Making Money

The Cabots were not particularly interested in North America; they were looking for a way around it to get to China. In 1520, Magellan made a tough journey around the tip of South America and circumnavigated the world for the first time.

Other adventurers were looking for different ways to make money. Gold, silver, and civilized Native Americans were discovered in Central and South America. Interesting plants such as tomatoes, potatoes, and tobacco were found there too. All these the Spanish and Portuguese exploited; they brought European cultures to South America and took back riches. Central America and the Caribbean islands turned into the hemisphere's free-for-all zone for many European nations.

The situation wasn't as dramatic in North America. The Native Americans there didn't have as much agriculture, infrastructure, or population as did their southern cousins. The eastern side of North America was mostly primordial—heavily forested wilderness. The first attractions there were certain kinds of wood for shipbuilding, certain kinds of fish that could be cured, and some specialty plants such as tobacco. These were what brought the first commercial adventurers to the Virginia and Massachusetts areas.

Spreading the Word and Practicing the Word

Potential riches were one compelling reason to come; religion and lifestyle were others. Puritans and Quakers traveled to North America, and Spanish and Portuguese priests and conquistadors went to South America. The same instinct that today prompts people to help the poor empowered religious people to "help" the natives learn about the Christian God.

Protestants traveled to North America because they felt the Catholics and some other Protestants were doing things wrong; their feeling was related to the counterculture feelings of the 1960s such as the hippies in northern California.

Skinning Cats in Different Ways

Each of the thirteen colonies here was set up for a different reason by different people.

- Massachusetts was established by Puritans of eastern England who were disgusted with how religion and politics were mixing in England and Holland.
- Virginia was established by southern English gentlemen who were adventurous and unhappy with the religion/political mix in England but in ways different from the Puritans.
- Another unhappy group was the Society of Friends, the Quakers, who established themselves in the Philadelphia region.
- Maryland was set up to be a home for unhappy English Catholics.

And so on. And adding even more flavors to this mix were the French, German, and Scandinavian malcontents in the 1700s who came to North America.

What these settlers had in common was that they wanted to prosper, and they did compared to their European counterparts. This transformation from a collection of strange places inhabited by weirdoes in the 1600s to prosperous folk in the late 1700s attracted the attention of the English Parliament. "It's taxing time, baby!" they announced, "time to pull your weight in keeping this British Empire going."

"Taxation without representation is tyranny," the colonists responded.

These conflicting viewpoints led to the Revolutionary War and the formation of the United States of America.

The Transformation Didn't Stop

Transforming the colonies into a united nation didn't stop the transforming that was going on; it made the experimentation become even more exciting. Immigrants were entering the Industrial Revolution. An iconic figure for this was Ben Franklin. A Wikipedia article reads, "A noted polymath, Franklin was a leading author, printer, political theorist, politician, postmaster, scientist, musician, inventor, satirist, civic activist, statesman, and diplomat." He also had time and attention available to be a Founding Father.

Technologies spread as fast and furiously as did new settlers. Steamboats and canals opened up the Mississippi River basin to amazing exploitation. The canal and factory combination fueled upstate New York's transformation into a prosperous area that became the center of the religious Second Great Awakening. And the cotton gin transformed slavery in the South into a social system that had never before been experienced—something I call Industrial Age slavery (though chattel slavery is a more common term). But these changes had social consequences—"This is letting *what* happen?"

Working the Kinks Out

These huge changes were not all for the better; they caused arguments and raised fears. The most famous argument in history books of the 2010s was the slavery issue, but in those times, it had competition. How to run factories, how to handle immigration, how to manage settling the West, and how to run importing and exporting were all equally hot national topics, and there were plenty of local hot topics as well. These issues had special interest groups vigorously fighting for and against them. <u>Tammany Hall</u> was famous as a powerful special interest group in New York City politics.

What Made the Colonial Experience Different?

What made the North American colonial experience different from the western European experience of the same era? Everyone's experience of that era was different. Each region of a European nation had a different experience as did each North American colony, so what comes next is generalizations.

In the 1600s and 1700s, western and central Europe were undergoing big social changes. In the 1600s, merchants were prospering due to expanded trading opportunities, and in the 1700s, the Industrial Revolution was shaking everyone in England, France, and the German lands as vigorously as it was everyone in the North American colonies.

What was different between the European and American experiences was the mix of resources available and the social environment. North America had many untapped resources but little infrastructure to conduct the tapping; in Europe, the situation was reversed.

The Europeans had existing social structures that had to be accommodated in many ways by those bringing disruptive technologies to the various communities—the new merchants and industrialists had to keep the peace with the landed nobility, clerics, artisans, and farmers. In the colonies, the existing social structures were as new as were the disruptive technologies; this made it a lot easier to make changes, recover from mistakes, and try again.

Conclusion

The North American colonial experience was a fascinating series of social experiments. The primordial wilderness of the eastern coast of North America proved to be a wonderful place to mix social experimenting and try out Industrial Revolution technologies. It was exciting. And scary. But it was an environment that easily said okay to new and different ways of doing things.

Is the North American experience likely to be a repeating pattern? Not likely on earth. There are no unexplored areas with bountiful, untapped resources left here. It could happen in other parts of the solar system if resources are out there. And plentiful resources are a necessary ingredient. Lots of commerce is a key element in making any kind of colonization worthwhile.

41

Slavery and the Reconstruction Era

The <u>Reconstruction Era</u> (1865–77) in the United States has a lot in common with the post–World War I, <u>Treaty of Versailles</u> era (1918–1939) in western Europe. In both cases, the conduct of the preceding war was much longer and more emotional than anyone had expected. The conduct of the war was also a surprise, and as a result, figuring out how to conduct the postwar peacemaking was also very difficult. In both cases, leaders took their people into unknown social territories, and not surprisingly, there were many disappointments.

One big difference between these two eras was slavery. How to deal with the end slavery was a high priority during Reconstruction. Simply saying it was over wasn't enough. Dealing with the fallout was a challenge.

Industrial Age Slavery

Slavery, which has been around since prehistory, has been conducted in different ways at different times. Slavery in the antebellum South stands out for being the newest twist in its day. Southerners then called slavery "our peculiar institution," and it was, in spite of the euphemism. This was Industrial Age slavery, quite different from Stone or Agricultural Age slavery; it's often called chattel slavery.

Because Industrial Age slavery was different, how to end it was difficult. <u>Barbados,</u> <u>Haiti,</u> and The South engaged in large-scale slavery to operate plantations in the seventeenth and early eighteenth centuries, and all had a difficult time migrating from their slave-based plantation societies to prosperous, modern economies and societies that used modern agricultural and industrial technologies and techniques. The South didn't really "get over" slavery until the 1960s and '70s. Barbados took off on sugar and slaves starting in the 1640s but freed the slaves in the 1830s; however, the economy didn't fully modernize and become prosperous until the 1970s.

Haiti's experience illustrates this issue the most. It was thickly settled by the French in the 1700s, and like Barbados, it developed a sugar-is-king social system. In Haiti's case, we have a historic accident mixing in: while the French were engaged in revolution in the 1790s, Haiti had a spectacular slave revolt that led to its independence in 1804, and the first with black leadership. The French *liberté, égalité, fraternité* types were shouting, "Three cheers for that!" But sadly, even to this day, modernization hasn't followed. Haiti has been the poorest part of the western hemisphere for most of the twentieth century and all the twenty-first. Why has it been so hard to follow Industrial Age slavery with modernization? Here are my speculations.

A big obstacle is the change in attention-focus.

Slaveholders want to profit from their slaves and avoid revolts and runaways. Curiosity and diverse thinking are two big casualties of the latter goal. And it's not just the slaves who suffer; those who guard the slaves do so as well. The slave society is an intensely focused one on all levels.

Ignorance becomes a virtue.

Slaves who don't know where to flee are less likely to run. Why run away if you have no information about where you are going to run to? Keeping them ignorant is important for their masters, but if the masters don't know any more than their slaves do, they can't let slip hopeful information to the slaves and don't have to feel uncomfortable with the cognitive dissonance of knowing there are more-varied ways of doing things.

The result of these peculiarities is that when the system ends, getting the community transitioned into non-slave, Industrial Age thinking is tough for everyone involved because no one in the community knows how to do it. In the Barbados and the South, this transition took generations, and in Haiti, it's still a work in progress.

The Bitterness Doesn't End

The acrimony between North and South didn't end when the Civil War did. Southerners still felt Northerners were taking cheap shots at them and weren't minding their own business. The Northerners wanted to make sure the South gave up slavery and moved on to newer and better ways of doing things.

The Lincoln assassination took a lot of wind out of moderate sails on both sides; "Live and let live" became a small voice crying in the wilderness. Starting with the election of 1866 and lasting ten years, Congress was in the hands of radical Republicans, and the rest of federal government followed their lead. The radicals were interventionist; they supported actively showing Southerners how to do things right.

Northern Idealism vs. Southern Pragmatism

After the war, Northerners were definitely in a mood to fix the South by replacing slavery with modern techniques that would bless all Southerners. The problems were that this was expensive and there was little agreement on what modern techniques would work well throughout the South. That didn't stop many enthusiastic Northerners from going to the South and helping out; terms from this era include carpetbaggers, scalawags, and freedmen.

The South changed, but the result was not harmony or prosperity. The Ku Klux Klan was spawned in this era. With the Compromise of 1877, the North and the federal government moved on, to focus attention on other pressing problems. The Redeemers took over in the South, and what followed was called the Jim Crow era (1876–1965) by those unhappy with the result. In that era, separate but equal became the slogan for race relations in the South.

Other Disruptive Issues

Technology remained an exciting and disruptive element North and South. Rising prosperity caused much of the disruption. During the war, Northern exports increased, and in 1867, the United States bought Alaska from the Russians for $7.2 million. Postwar building of the transcontinental railroads was an optimistic symbol of this disruptive change—financial booms and busts and violent labor disputes not so much so.

Other prewar disputes continued as well. Immigration, money, and tax issues continued to generate heat. This was the era when the potato blight and British farming policies brought on famine in Ireland, and the Irish replaced the Germans as the iconic undesirable immigrants east of the Mississippi. In the West, the Chinese were flooding in due to the Taiping Rebellion, China's massive civil war that was part of its coping with the invasion of Western ideas that left hundreds of thousands of Chinese unhappy with their situation. Many came to work on railroads in the western United States and became the iconic undesirable immigrants.

This was when homesteading became a large-scale way of settling the Great Plains. This was also the era of Thomas Edison, inventor of hundreds of interesting devices that changed how Americans lived.

Moving West: The Great Social Safety Valve

"You won, right? Why the long face?" One social phenomenon rarely commented on is that in a case like the Civil War, there are many unhappy people on the winning side too. These wars are surprising, and the victors are just as surprised at the outcome as the vanquished. The unhappy winners are looking for relief just as vigorously as are the unhappy losers.

This produces unrest. In the case of the United States, much unrest could be worked off by moving West and settling untamed wilderness,

as many Northerners and Southerners did. It was sometimes called the
safety-valve theory.

This social valve theory also got some play after World War I ended
and Europe was enduring the Treaty of Versailles era. One of the programs
Hitler and the Nazis talked about implementing for the Germans was
moving east into sparsely settled areas of southern Russia. In fact, there was
considerable but quiet migration of this nature happening even without a
formal program.

Hard-fought civil wars are hard on winners as well as losers, and people
on both sides pick up, move, and start over.

Conclusion

The Reconstruction Era was not a happy one for the North or South.
Though the war was over, there were still plenty of unanswered questions
and many unhappy people. The radical Republicans tried to supply
answers, and how people lived in the North and the South changed. Many
idealistic Northerners went south to help fix things there.

The era ended when other pressing issues pushed ahead of fixing the
South in the national attention. Federal troops were withdrawn, and the
South went back to being in charge of itself.

But Industrial Age slavery is a surprisingly hard lifestyle to transition
from, and the transition didn't finish for many generations. Reconstruction
was replaced with Jim Crow, and that era didn't end until in the civil rights
movement of the 1960s.

42

Korea: How Did It Get Where It Is Today?

Korea is in a fascinating state, a divided nation whose halves are pursuing radically different ways of developing. The interesting part, the mystery, is that both ways are quite different but stable.

Teaser

Imagine you're in a college classroom.

Suddenly the ground shakes and rumbles and a huge whoosh sound comes from outside the building. You run outside and see a giant flying saucer—a city block wide—hovering over campus. A voice comes over a speaker on the flying saucer: "We mean no harm to your planet." Aliens from outer space!

What do *you* do when you first see the saucer? A week later? A year later?

This relates to Korea's situation today, but let's consider the time line.

- 1839–42: the First Opium War sets the stage. British high tech trashes the Chinese military response. (Opportunity knocking?)
- 1854: Commodore Perry visits Tokyo with a high-tech fleet of warships and opens Japan.
- 1864: China's response: panic. Taiping Rebellion.
- 1868–1912: Japan's response: "We can adapt." Meiji Restoration ends Tokugawa shogunate.

- 1866: Korea's response: "Strong national will will protect us." General Sherman incident.
- 1899: Open-Door policy opens China to all comers. This is different from India, Korea, Indonesia, and other places that get just one colonial master.
- 1894–95: First Sino-Japanese War. More humiliation for China; Japan colonizes Korea; China's 1911 revolution occurs (Sun Yat-sen).
- 1910–1945: Japan annexes Korea; "We're all Japanese now."
- 1937–1945: Second Sino-Japanese War; the big one; becomes part of World War II.
- 1945: Japan surrenders and Korea is divided.
- 1950–1953: The Korean War makes the accident permanent; "The wrong war, at the wrong place, at the wrong time, and with the wrong enemy"—Gen. Omar Bradley.
- 1953– 2010s: Life evolves in the two Koreas—the experiment continues.
  - Southern evolution: accommodate the world—military dictatorship evolves into democracy and a globalized economy.
  - Northern evolution: isolate from the world—military dictatorship, juche, and Korean values preserved.

- 1994: Enter Roger's unsolved mystery: Kim Il-sung dies, Kim Jong-il simply takes over.
- 2011: Kim Jong-un succeeds Kim Jong-il in a smooth succession.

Setting the Stage

Starting in the mid-1850s, the nations and cultures of East Asia faced a huge challenge. The Europeans who had previously come to trade in sailing ships started showing up in steamships armed with big guns. That was just the beginning of the new strangeness. They were also bringing new, marvelous products and talking about the new ways products were being made in Europe.

The question of the century for China, Korea, and Japan was how to deal with the Europeans, whom they considered as strange as we would consider aliens from outer space. There were basically three choices.

- Plan A: Pay attention to the change and respect it. Assume it was worth learning about and work hard at integrating the new products and new ideas into the existing culture.
- Plan B: Strongly regulate the change to keep it from endangering the culture.
- Plan C: Do nothing meaningful about it; focus on more-important issues.

All three choices had proponents in the three cultures; each chose differently. The Japanese picked plan A. They paid attention, adopted, and adapted. This formally started with the Meiji Restoration in 1868, which ended the shogunate government that had chosen plan B.

The Koreans picked plan B. The Chosun (Joseun) dynasty has been ruling Korea stably since the 1400s and had implemented silhak—a policy of strict control starting in the 1600s. But this high-tech alien invasion of Europeans was something new, and it wasn't clear the old ways would keep working. At one point as the crisis built, the plan A folk staged a coup but stayed in power for only two days before the plan B folk staged a countercoup. Heungseon Daewongun, the regent during the 1860s, led the plan B'ers back to power.

The Chinese picked plan C. The government, the Manchu Dynasty (also called the Qing Dynasty) was in the process of losing the Mandate of Heaven and dissolving. The Manchu government was corrupt and ineffectual. But after its first big challenge in this era of crisis, the Taiping rebellion of the 1860s, was even more so.

The rebellion started strong in the south and gained enough support to capture Nanking, the southern capital. But after this success, it lost focus and didn't move on Beijing, the northern capital. The rebellion sputtered, and the Manchus survived for another five decades … sort of. What resulted was chaos similar to Somalia's in the 2000s, with local warlords picking up a lot of power.

Various European nations carved trade zones out of the chaos; this carving up was called the <u>Open Door Policy</u> and made China's fate different from that of India, Indonesia, and French Indochina.

Korea suffered a different fate as well. It became the first colony of a Far East nation following in these European footsteps. In the Sino-Japanese War of 1895, Japan took on Korea as a protectorate, and in 1910, it annexed Korea. "We're all Japanese now" became the formal policy, and Japan started pushing Korea hard down the plan A road.

Ah, well … so much for plan B it seems.

But plan A wasn't inevitable or smooth sailing. After 1905, the Japanese were on something of a sugar high: they had defeated the Chinese and the Russians. But there was still much uncertainty and controversy in Japan and its newly acquired colonies—Korea, Manchuria (northeast China), and Formosa (Taiwan). Not everybody in these areas was winning; there was much arguing and terrorist violence.

This controversy and uncertainty led to a militarist-style government in Japan that was as ruthless and full of propaganda as were its European counterparts. But like them, there was optimism supporting this revolutionary government. Part of this optimism came across as trying to assimilate Korea and make it fully Japanese. This bright-eyed enthusiasm brought just as much controversy to the Koreans—some loved it, some hated it.

All this starry-eyed enthusiasm led the Japanese government a step too far: it renewed war with China with the intent of making all China as enthusiastic about these new ways as the Japanese were. This started the 1937 Second Sino-Japanese War, which merged into World War II.

It was a big undertaking … too big … and the Japanese surrendered in August 1945.

The Beginning of Two Koreas

The question in late August 1945 for the Japanese armed forces was, "Who do we surrender to?" This became an issue when the Russians had declared war and conducted a blitzkrieg through most of northeast China, which, along with the northern half of Korea, surrendered to the Russians. Taiwan and the other Chinese areas surrendered to the

Nationalist Chinese. Japan and the south half of Korea surrendered to the US Pacific fleet with the formal ceremony taking place aboard the USS *Enterprise*.

This should have been mostly an administrative matter, but the Cold War was getting ready to launch. Korea split in two—the north under Kim Il-sung and the south under Syngman Rhee. That wasn't according to anyone's plan.

After five years of trying to deal with this deep confusion, Kim Il-sung, with Stalin's blessing, training, and tanks, took the bull by the horns and invaded South Korea to unify the country.

Surprise! Instead of rolling over and accepting this, as it had in East Europe and China, the United States convinced the UN to condemn this and sent troops to vigorously defend the south. But the North Koreans were well prepared for this campaign, and they kept advancing. The UN forces were repeatedly defeated until they were hanging on by their fingernails in a small area around Busan (Pusan) at the south end of the peninsula.

More surprise. General MacArthur, commanding UN troops, and with a bunch more available, invaded Inchon harbor and captured Seoul, cutting the North Koreans' supply and retreat line. MacArthur headed north, way north, to the Korean border with Manchuria. Game over for the North Koreans? No. Instead another surprise.

The Chinese Communists did what the Soviets weren't willing to do—send in ground troops, lots of them. They began with a big win; the UN forces "bugged out" and hastily retreated to south of Seoul.

More surprise. MacArthur was relieved of command by President Truman. General Ridgeway, MacArthur's replacement, advanced UN forces to roughly the north-south border before the war started, the 38th parallel, then stopped. (Seoul changed hands four times in this war.)

The war then became a Chinese vs. UN slugfest, a proxy war, and it stalemated. It became much like World War I: trenches, tunnels, lots of shooting but no moving. (My theory on why the Chinese were willing to do this stalemate part was that Mao and the Chinese Communists needed a final bloodletting to consolidate their win in mainland China of the year before. Big social revolutions need one.)

A year later, the fighting wound down. In 1953, an armistice was signed, but no peace treaty followed. Instead, the demilitarized zone (DMZ) remained the most heavily fortified and militarized border in the world for more than sixty years. All through the 1950s and into the 1960s, much small-scale violence occurred back and forth across it.

Two Cultures Evolve: Plan A and Plan B Are Back

Over the six decades since the Korean War wound down, the DMZ has remained an icon of the Cold War. Panmunjom, the negotiating point, is a popular tourist destination, and pictures of the DMZ being fenced and patrolled by vigilant South Korean soldiers were a cultural icon in South Korea into the 2010s. Both Koreas have maintained strong militaries. The Chinese went home, just north of the border, but the United States has maintained roughly 30,000 troops in Korea over these many decades. And away from the DMZ, the two Koreas have been developing their cultures in dramatically different ways.

The history twisting continues: Plans A and B are revived, and the experiment as to which is better has been running for six decades now.

In this version of the experiment, South Korea has been pursuing Plan A. It embraces the rest of the world and has looked to Japan's success as an exporting nation as a model. The results have been impressive. South Korea is now considered a developed nation and can produce smartphones and Gangnam Style K-Pop videos. Its government has moved from military dictatorship to democracy. And its economy from a chaebol-based handful of companies to being broad based with many small- and medium-sized enterprises as well.

North Korea has been pursuing Plan B. They embraced growing a strong national will (my term) as the heart of its development and vigorously control contact with the outside world. Kim Il-sung developed a philosophy of self-reliance, juche, which has been the philosophic center of the North's development. The culture depends on a lot of self-delusion in the form of teaching the people that the rest of the world envies North Korea's prowess and progress.

For three and a half decades, the Soviet Union subsidized Kim and the North Koreans. They paid for Kim to have a strong military and engage in periodic saber-rattling to keep America and Western Europe on edge. (They also paid Cuba and various Eastern European states.) During that time, Kim developed a leadership style that was a mix of Soviet communism and the Japanese militarism that Korea had been subjected to during the colony years.

Then in 1989, crisis! The Soviet Union went bankrupt and dissolved. The Russian nation that took its place said, "Sorry, folks, we're no longer going to be your sugar daddy. You're on your own."

Cuba and North Korea adapted to this harsh new reality, but it wasn't easy. North Korea adapted by transforming its saber-rattling into extortion. It got the United States and China in the habit of paying it off to end its temper tantrums. This is why nuke developing has been so important to the government.

Kim Il-sung Dies: Enter the Roger Mystery

Kim Il-sung died in July 1994. I remember the day well. I was midway through my first year of teaching English in Korea. I was on a weekend trip to visit caves in the center of South Korea, and I had been befriended by a Korean family. We were taking a taxi from one cave to another when the father of the family announced, "The news on the radio just said Kim Il-sung has died."

My first thought was, *Whoa! Here I am in Korea and the dictator just two hundred miles north has croaked! Where's my plane ticket?*

What gave this thought even more importance was that Marcos of the Philippines, Papa Doc of Haiti, Ceausescu of Romania, and the whole Soviet Union had all been replaced by new styles of government in the decade before this. Was this about to happen in North Korea? Would this newbie Kim Jong-il last a year or so before being ousted?

I decided to risk staying. But I held my breath and watched the news. I predicted regime change.

Nothing happened. Kim Jong-il came in smoothly and stayed smoothly. Whoa! How could nothing have happened? I had a mystery on my hands. This was way off pattern. Usually, when strongmen died, they were succeeded by short-lived tyrant wannabees followed by blander leaders. Stalin, Mao, Ho Chi Minh, Churchill—all followed this pattern.

Churchill was voted out right after World War II. Roosevelt died, but his successor, Truman, proved himself such an able, conventional leader that he survived.

The answer to this mystery of why tyrant successfully followed tyrant in North Korea came in time. Clues popped up in surprising places: I read a North Korea travel guide that boasted of the pride the North Koreans in their "genuine Korean culture," and I learned more about Korean history as I taught English to my students and traveled the country. The result was an insight.

Insight

One of the distinctive facets of Korean culture is its location, right between China and Japan. When either China or Japan was feeling its oats, it looked at the other as a fertile field to conquer, with Korea being in the path. The result was that Korea was invaded twice as often as its neighbors, and resisting invasion has always been high on its list of priorities.

The consistent way to fend off invasion is to appear unified and strong; for this reason, Koreans do their political arguing behind closed doors. If they appealed to China or Japan for help in solving internal issues, they'd be inviting long-term intervention. This keeping the dirty laundry covered is why North Korean successions go so smoothly. They keep up the appearance of strength and unity. They are taught that they are surrounded by aggressive foreign powers that could easily bring on Colonization 2 if the Koreans showed weakness. In the eyes of the North, the South sold out and was already in Colonization 2; the South had become the running-dog lackeys of American imperialism.

These days, the North survives on self-sufficiency and what it can extort by rattling sabers.

When Will It Change?

Company presidents rule with the consent of their boards of directors, and elected politicians rule with the consent of the voters. Tyrants lead with the consent of the opinion-controlling elements of their communities;

North Korea is no exception. It will change its governing style when the influential people of North Korea decide that this militarist, self-deluding style is no longer serving them and their children well. Predicting when this will happen is difficult, but when they decide that keeping a "pure" culture is not working, that saber rattling has become too risky and is not producing enough income, that they aren't going to be colonized if they start arguing in public, and that they aren't doing the best they can for their children, they will change.

And the world will then be in for more surprises from Korea.

Potemkin Village

One of the likely surprises is that the North Korean army is a <u>Potemkin village</u>. While North Korea is savvy in its public relations visible military, the low-profile parts are likely to be underfinanced and dysfunctional. North Korean PR routinely extols the virtue of the military in ways that make external watchers sit up, listen, and report breathlessly. But this is a country that has been impoverished for decades, at peace for decades, and quite willing to lie to itself and its neighbors for decades. This could mean that current North Korean military prowess consists of conducting massive parades through the main square in Pyongyang, harassing fishing boats off the coast, and showing off along the DMZ at the South Korean border. Much of the rest is a sham.

Conclusion

Korea has a remarkable recent history. The stable split into two parts that evolved into very different but stable cultures, an uncommon occurrence. Likewise, the orderly succession of the Kims and their maintaining ruthless leader–style governments is very uncommon. But their geography—being a small culture nestled between two much larger cultures—explains a lot of the mystery.

43

Why the Middle East and Africa Are Having Such a Hard Time with Nationhood

One of the foundational assumptions of people living now in developed nations is that nationhood is the most desirable form of government for people all over the world. But as good as it has been for the Americas and Western Europe for the last couple of centuries, some parts of the world have had a hard time making nationhood work in modern times—violence-torn regions in the Middle East and Africa come to mind. Why is this?

A Key Ingredient of Betrayal vs. Cooperation

Based on the patterns of where nationhood seems to work and where it doesn't, I think one key ingredient to making it work seems to be a culture that supports widespread cooperation among diverse groups. The converse is supporting widespread betrayal between groups—Us vs. Them thinking. The more it's okay to betray strangers, the harder it is for many modern institutions to thrive, and one of these is nationhood.

Many Possible Solutions vs. Many Possible Betrayals

Betrayal of strangers worked in the Neolithic Age environments and became instinctual behavior. It still worked well in and Agricultural Age environments so it hasn't been suppressed. But it doesn't work well today, when we rely heavily on cooperation on many levels for society to function.

When betrayal occurs in modern organizations, it's considered corruption and organized crime. Conversely, dissent can be a virtue today; we need loyal opposition to shake things up at times and devise solutions to new problems or figure out ways of doing things better. This, however, is a skill that has to be learned and then taught.

If a community hasn't learned how to cooperate in Industrial Age ways, is nationhood the best governing choice? Probably not. And so for a few generations in certain places in the Middle East and Africa other governing forms may work better. There is so much betrayal going on in these regions that building diverse and thriving Industrial Age communities is not happening. Instead, violence and chaos are thriving.

Those who want to help these regions evolve into supporters of nationhood should focus on teaching the virtues of tolerance and cooperation and recognize that these are social skills that won't come about instinctively—betrayal is what instinct teaches.

44

The Roaring Twenties and the Great Depression

The post–World War I era—the 1920s and '30s—was as surprising as World War I was but in a very different way. The United States experienced a series of booms and busts in the Roaring Twenties until the big one, the Great Depression. Americans underwent many changes in how they lived, what they worked for, and what they thought about the world.

Western Europe grappled with economic cycles similar to those of the United States and felt the shock of the huge casualty count and destruction World War I caused. The French and British faced the problem of managing their empires after they had called upon so much help from them to fight the war. There was lots of thinking changing going on there, but it was different from what was happening in the United States. They were more Socialist oriented in its many flavors.

In Central and Eastern Europe, the war didn't end with the German surrender in 1918. It continued for a few years in the form of chaotic revolutionary fighting and the social and economic turmoil caused by the social revolutions that were carving up the empires. These were more earthshaking than those the United States was going through caused by the Great Depression.

Dealing with Another Industrial Revolution

The Industrial Revolution in the 1800s was initiated by the invention and use of the steam engine. In the 1920s, cars and trucks and the adoption of household appliances were even more life changing than the steam engine had been.

These innovations meant that jobs were changing—being created and disappearing—as well, and the relations people had with their communities were changing. *The Great Gatsby* (1925) talked about the social changes happening in these times—how they amazed the people living through them. (The book, not the movies—the movies are about how to party hearty.)

Tractors produced big gains in agricultural productivity but also displaced many farm workers and lowered the prices farmers received. Food exports became vital in maintaining whatever prosperity could be found in the industry. Steinbeck's *Grapes of Wrath* (1939) described the farmers' plight of the 1920s and '30s.

But even with all this turmoil, things kept getting better. The key to all this improvement was widening cooperation.

The Lesson of World War I: Cooperation

World War I was surprising in many ways. One of those was using the war threat to promote Big Cooperation (my term). Thanks to the new communications techniques of the era (propaganda), Americans and Western Europeans learned how to cooperate in many new ways. Because of the war threat, they put aside their prewar differences, and everyone came together to do what it took to win the Great War (as it was called then).

The lesson learned continued through the 1920s and became the foundation for much prosperity—the booms were spectacular, the busts were small, the recoveries from them were fast, and the overall optimism remained high. This is why the 1920s were roaring.

Slipping from Prosperity into Acrimony

The Great Depression was something different, the Big Cooperation ended. The bust didn't disappear quickly as previous busts had. It lingered and lingered on. Hoover tried to fix it and failed. Roosevelt was elected in the 1932 election because Americans were scared at what was happening economically. Conventional solutions hadn't worked; Hoover solutions hadn't worked; Americans were ready to try something different, including Roosevelt.

What was different was people were arguing and defecting—in the prisoners' dilemma meaning of that word—they weren't working together to solve problems; they were pursuing and defending their own interests and letting others fend for themselves.

One example of this "defecting" was nations enacting high protective tariffs, for instance, the Smoot-Hawley Tariff Act of 1930. The thinking behind this was, "If we don't import stuff, we'll make it at home and protect and create jobs." There was good logic in that in the scary context of the day, but in practice, this thinking led to a deep cut in total jobs worldwide as international trade dropped to near zero. This thinking had the opposite effect of what it was supposed to have, but the people of the day didn't see it that way. It was an example of an acrimonious solution. In the same way, farm policies and labor relations were becoming more acrimonious and not solving the problem of how to recover, grow the economy, and create more jobs.

What Roosevelt offered in place of a business recovery was a government recovery—the government would create jobs and hire many people to do them to stimulate the economy. He also invited business and labor groups to set up business-controlling boards that would enact regulations to restrict business and labor practices so more people would have to be employed to accomplish specific tasks. If workers could work for only eight hours on ten-hour tasks, other workers would have to be hired to finish them.

In 1936, he received academic justification for this instinctive solution when John Maynard Keynes published his theories on how the economy was affected by government stimulation, but still the results were poor. Jobs were created, and Roosevelt became a hero for that, but the economy didn't prosper—business wasn't growing, so it wasn't creating many jobs. In 1937, what little growth that had occurred since 1933 was lost again in another recession. The times were acrimonious indeed.

Europe Slipped from Socialism into Acrimony

The western Europeans, much more than the Americans, were enamored with the ideals of socialism; they were much more concerned about social safety nets to protect workers from the dislocating traumas this new industrial revolution was creating.

When the depression spread to western Europe, the solutions were just as acrimonious as those enacted in America. Europeans, for instance, invented the <u>sit-down strike</u>. In spite of the acrimony, Britain and France hung on to democracy as the governing form. Italians and Germans took a different road.

Fascism

Fascism these days is looked upon as a spooky way of governing people that created terrible wars and even more terrible concentration camps. It did, but those were late developments in the concept's short history. In its early days, fascism was just another form of socialism and the product of the early 1930s Time of Nutcases in Italy, then Germany. (Another name for fascism is National Socialism)

What it had going for it in the early days was a way of providing a big vision that people could get behind. This was a revolution. The goal was for government to tell big business what to do, help that happen, provide some spectacular bread and circuses programs directly to the people, and grow national pride by growing the military; the thought was that this combination would grow the economy better than conventional Liberal-oriented solutions would.

It worked for a while, but it turned out to be a slippery slope. The leaders couldn't keep delivering on their promises, so they reverted to blaming others. This led to starting wars aimed at those others and basking in the nationalist glow of winning them. Producing warm, fuzzy feelings at home was the goal of Germany's blitzkrieg style of war making.

The Russian Solution to Acrimony

The Russians started down the road of a Communist solution even before World War I ended—which sure added a lot of confusion to what was happening on the Eastern Front in the last months of the war. The road to a supposed workers' paradise in Russia was rocky and violent from the beginning. At first, competing warlords and political groups fought over their competing views as to what communism demanded of businesses, farmers, and government.

As the outright fighting wound down, the solution to these differences of opinion took the form of violent purges aimed at those labeled counterrevolutionaries. The result was a violence-filled transition from a monarchical and mostly agricultural Russia to a Russia that was a mix of communism with heavy industry. The change happened, but these were dramatic days in what was then called the USSR.

As did the governments that chose fascism, the Soviets found themselves on a slippery slope but not quite as steep as were the Fascist forms. This allowed Stalin to follow Hitler's lead when he got adventurous and reap similar advantages without looking quite as scary internationally. In the end, his adventurism led to the Soviets fighting Hitler. Thanks to Blame Them thinking, both sides looked upon this as a contest quite worth fighting.

The End to Acrimony

World War II was surprising in many ways, but one big way was how it ended the acrimonious era in Western Europe and America. As Hitler's adventurism was dramatically succeeding around the German borders starting in the mid-1930s, Germans were as surprised as Brits and Americans were. But in time, all these people started thinking about cooperating to solve their domestic disputes so they could unify to deal with this surprisingly successful international threat.

The cooperation became pervasive under various forms of "Win the War" slogans as had happened in World War I. But this time, people had practiced this, so the results were even more spectacular. This cooperation continued after the war was won because the Cold War kicked in so quickly after World War II ended, and based on what had been learned in the lead-up to World War II, it also provided powerful incentive to cooperate.

The Cold War years were economically boom times for most of the world because the feeling of needing to continue to cooperate remained strong.

Conclusion

During the 1920s, people were healing from World War I and continued to cooperate. A decade later, thoughts of cooperation were replaced by thoughts of "I got my rights" and the resultant acrimony that made it tough to recover from the stock market crash of 1929 and the following Great Depression. This became a Time of the Nutcases and their strange ideas about how to solve problems—fascism, communism, and the New Deal. All the solutions turned downright scary by the late 1930s, and Fascist and Communist solutions turned to military adventurism and caused World War II.

World War II solved the Great Depression by changing people's thinking. People got scared in a different way and started cooperating again. This led to increased productivity and economic growth that continued through the Cold War years because the United States and USSR threatened each other in ways that were similar to the prewar threats of the 1930s.

And then came the 1960s and the Generation Gap, time for yet more new thinking to take center stage.

45

The Next NBTs Will Be Tough

In these post-2007 crash years, we're still searching for the next generation of NBTs, the next big things. Economic growth has been anemic throughout the developed world since the 2007 bust. Antiterrorism, housing, and "green" are not positive-feedback industries, so what we invest in these is not firing the economy. This means that the last boom ended in the 1990s. The boom of the 2000s was a war- and mortgage-powered bubble, not an NBT-powered, positive-feedback boom.

What comes next in positive feedback hasn't been easy to find; it will most likely be on the heavy side and quite disruptive. We got off easy in the last part of the twentieth century with the medium electronics and software boom. It's not likely to be so easy the next time, but here are some possibilities.

Another round of intense industrialization that adds even more automation to manufacturing and service processes

This will let us make more things and services faster, better, and cheaper—very positive feedback. The gotcha is that it does so without increasing human employment, so the world gets more to consume, but people work less and have less to pay for this bounty. This sure qualifies as disruptive, and it's not clear who the new winners will be. One loser will be the social thinking linkage between self-worth and a good-paying job in service or manufacturing. Shouting "Get a job!" at someone is going to change its meaning a lot.

Another transportation revolution built around driverless cars and other vehicles

This will involve not just redesigning cars, buses, and trucks but also roads, road networks, and parking. The current light rail and bicycle schemes popular in gentrifying urban cores are resource saving but not positive feedback. These won't sustain a boom, but driverless vehicles will when they transform the car culture into something much more transparent and effortless. Welcome to a world of 90 percent robot-driven taxis, buses, and trucks traveling new and much more efficient road networks. Boston, San Francisco, and Los Angeles will be dream places to drive.

The losers in this transformation will be those who take pride in owning a car and their driving skills. The new road networks will change to suit driverless cars—very different.

Air travel and air traffic revolution

Getting to airports and getting on and off planes will become much simpler and quicker, and getting planes from A to B will also become much simpler and quicker. Drones are part of this revolution. The losers here will be those involved in the airport security rituals put in place to calm the fear-of-flying emotion many passengers have.[3]

A health care revolution

Health care is positive feedback in that it helps people work more consistently and for more years. We're rapidly learning so much more about how life works, but we're slow at transforming this knowledge into tangible products that help humans stay healthier, which hinders positive feedback.

---

[3] This is covered in my *Evolution and Thought* book.

The revolution here will be in delivering health care without the encumbrance of existing professional guilds, regulations, and the insurance-centric procedural framework. The losers will be the existing health care infrastructure and the current rituals for getting health care—the health insurance industry as we know it today.[4] The winners will be the more-numerous health care employees. This will continue to be a growth industry for people as well as machines. Health care has much emotion involved with it, so it will remain a place where people can still be valuable workers.

Energy revolutions that spread fracking and nuclear technologies

Cheap energy lets us get things done faster, better, and cheaper; we're aware of this due to media chatter. But because the oil industry is so emotional, myth wraps itself around the topic. The old "I'm selling my breakthrough carburetor to the oil companies because they want to keep it off the market" story and current fracking controversies are examples of the potency of this mythology around oil. And the stark terror of nuclear has stopped us from exploiting the nuclear NBT opportunity for more than half a century. I don't include wind or solar because they aren't cheap enough yet to produce positive feedback. Until their pricing comes down dramatically, they are feel-good rather than positive-feedback technologies.

Employment revolution made possible by dramatically simplifying employment regulations

Employment suffers deeply from The Curse of Being Important (my term), and the suffering seems to increase with each decade. Too many people have a say in how a job is conducted. Simplifying employer-employee relations will be a huge step in allowing new NBTs to be discovered and exploited. The sharing economy is an example of a step in this direction.

---

[4] I've written more about this as the concept "Patient Pays," an article on the White World website.

Obstacles to Implementing NBT

The next boom hasn't happened yet because barriers must be overcome. Here's what needs to be done.

Recognize and remove The Curse of Being Important.

One of the big barriers is the complex employer-employee relation that every business has to deal with in the 2010s. Getting a job should be more like getting groceries and less like getting married. This complexity is another manifestation of Us thinking. "We want team players" is a way of expressing the Us instinct.

Recognize that growth is important.

Another Roger truism: fairness is nice; growth is necessary. Communities get distracted, and their leaders tend to confuse spectacle with growth, so they promote spectacles rather than the next big thing. Community leaders should not pick winners; the market should do that. The leaders should promote laissez-faire simplicity and a transparent, level, legal playing field to attract the NBT.

Recognize that NBT growth is a messy process.

Finding and exploiting NBTs involve experimenting and learning from the failures. That's disruptive, scary, messy, and disorderly, but if the community can train itself to work though that period, the roller-coaster ride will have an excitingly good ending.

Figure out what to do with people.

We need to make sure people feel enfranchised so they'll stay committed to the NBT. If not, we'll create a spectacular bread-and-circus lifestyle that would make even Nero blush. This is distraction, not positive feedback.

Further Reading

"Technology and our standard of living: Are we really better off than the numbers show?" (*Economist*, August 8, 2013) made the point that this last boom has been different from previous ones and less disruptive.

"Net Gains and Losses" (*Economist*, August 17, 2013) talked about how "The internet has not yet produced the hoped-for productivity miracle."

"America Faces the Shock of the Old: Future Economic Growth May Depend on Innovation" (*Wall Street Journal*, September 8, 2013) by Justin Lahart was a fret about the decline in productivity growth over the last couple of decades.

> [Robert Gordon] argues that even with the boost provided by personal computers and the Web in the late 1990s through the early part of the last decade, innovation since the 1970s hasn't been as strong as in earlier decades when products like the internal combustion engine filtered through the economy.

"The Politics of Distrust: What explains the weird unpredictability of the 2016 presidential race? An anemic economy that has Americans questioning incumbents, doubting experts and worrying about their own prospects" (*Wall Street Journal*, October 16, 2015) by Jay Cost was about the frustration being felt in the search for an NBT in 2015 and how it was being expressed as a Time of Nutcases politics.

> Until quite recently, our politics seemed to function much more smoothly. Most adults can remember a time when government actually seemed to work. Now we all struggle to explain what has gone wrong.

Conclusion

Our economic growth will fire up again when we discover and develop our next NBTs. These new NBTs are very likely to be heavy industries, which means disruption will accompany their implementation. We should once again expect a boom that leads us down a rough but exciting and surprising road. But the other end will be just as dazzling as our twentieth-century progress has been.

Part 3b

Case Studies—Wars

46

Proxy Wars

A proxy war is one in which those in conflict are helped by outsiders' money, equipment, and manpower. If only one side is getting help, the conflict usually ends more quickly and the result is not a proxy war. An example of this happening is Russia supporting rebels in Georgia in 2008. The war lasted five days.

Proxy wars are some of the bloodiest and most damaging kinds of wars. If they're better understood, they may be prevented or be mitigated in their conduct.

I will discuss three examples: the Spanish Civil War of 1936, the Korean War of 1950, and the Syrian Civil War of 2011.

The Spanish Civil War

The Spanish Civil War started in July 1936 and lasted until April 1939, nearly to the beginning of World War II, which started in September that year. At the start of the war there were many well-established political and regional factions in Spain, but when the fighting became serious, these narrowed down to the Republicans, who represented the recently elected government, and the Nationalists, who felt the new government was deeply flawed and should be replaced by something more conservative. The war started as a half-bungled coup attempt by the proto-Nationalists.

The conflict gained international attention; both sides had enthusiastic supporters outside Spain from which they picked up tangible support. The Republicans picked up support from Europe's intelligentsia as well as the USSR and Mexico. Many of the intelligentsia came to fight in person; they formed what were called International Brigades, which became a famous part of this war. The Nationalists picked up support from the Nazis and Fascists of Germany and Italy, who donated military hardware and technical people. The Nationalists won, and General Francisco Franco became head of state, a title he kept until his death in 1975.

The external help made the war much longer and bloodier than it would have otherwise been. Another surprising result of all the intelligentsia getting directly involved was much being written about the war. Ernest Hemingway ended up being the most famous writer of this group.

The Korean War

Between 1945 and 1953, East Asia was full of history-making surprises; the Korean War (1950–53) was the capper. At the end of World War II, Korea was split in half. In the north, the Japanese surrendered to the Russians, while in the south, the Japanese surrendered to the United States. Much to the surprise of all involved, that split turned into two countries.

The Chinese Civil War wound up in 1948 with the Chinese Communists winning a series of big victories that gave them control of the mainland and left the Chinese Nationalists holding out only on the island of Taiwan. This Nationalist/Communist conflict had been going on and off since 1924, so this series of successes and the decisive victory came out of the blue. This surprise of losing China to the Communists and the surprise of the Iron Curtain coming down in Europe to turn half of it Communist scared Americans; the fear of communism ushered in the McCarthy era.

North Korea's leader, Kim Il-sung, launched a blitzkrieg against South Korea in the summer of 1950 that took his forces to the outskirts of the southern port of Pusan (now called Busan) in just two months. His plan almost worked; he almost won a quick war, but it turned into a proxy war. US and UN forces backed the South Koreans and were led by General Douglas MacArthur, who drove the North Koreans all the way back to their border on the north with China, which alarmed China. They worried that MacArthur would invade it. They in turn launched a counterattack that drove these potential invaders back. That was the end of the flashy maneuvering; the front stabilized; the border was once again in the center of Korea, but the fighting continued for two years.

The proxy part of this conflict was that tens of thousands of UN and Chinese soldiers were fighting and dying on Korean soil, and the Korean soldiers and civilians had to live with wartime conditions for three years. By the time the armistice was signed in 1953, Korea was a very poor nation.

The Syrian War

The Syrian Civil War started as part of the Arab Spring of 2011, a time of popular protests that spread through Arab countries from Morocco to Syria. The protests toppled many governments in the area starting with Tunisia's. Syria's leader, Bashar al-Assad, was expected to be one of those toppled, but he called upon and received military aid, mostly from Russia. He stayed in power and conducted a shooting war. Bashar's many enemies inside Syria found outside supporters, and the fighting continued and was much more damaging.

By 2015, this conflict resembled the Spanish Civil War. It had been going on a long time and had been supported by outsiders. The many factions involved attracted allies from outside the country who became personally involved. As in all proxy wars, the civilians suffered the worst; over 100,000 people were killed and millions became refugees out of the total population of about 17 million.

One difference between the Syrian and Spanish civil wars is that there remained many sides in the Syrian version; they didn't become just two. Another difference was how many Syrian refugees decided to emigrate, many to Europe, because the war wouldn't end.

What Can We Learn?

Here are the common patterns I see in these three conflicts.

Proxy wars start as social revolutions.

These wars are the children of chaos. The communities vulnerable to proxy wars are those that undergo a time of uncertainty greater than usual. This uncertainty becomes violence, and the government is threatened. There's much outside interest in what is happening.

Outside interests send support.

This is why many police officials dealing with protesting fear "outside agitators" exacerbating the conflict. Thailand weathered a coup in 2014 due to unrest, but no outsiders were involved.

More than one side gets support.

Of these three, the Syrian conflict involved many factions; the chaos was so high that it was hard to count how many sides there were and how many got outside support.

The more outside enthusiasm, the more damage the locals suffer.

Sad but true. "I'm an outside supporter and I'm here to help you" sounds great until you watch the damage done by such escalations.

The war ends when the outsiders' interests move on.

When the outsiders tire of contributing money, troops, and equipment, the war will wind down, but this is usually a frustratingly slow process. The Korean War armistice took months of negotiating and one-upmanship delaying tactics. This silliness happened because when the negotiations started, neither side was ready to end the bloodletting.

Conclusion

The most distinctive feature of proxy wars is that they turn very ugly for the locals and can be lengthy. For this reason, it's good to avoid getting involved in one if possible.

47

Characteristics of Bloodletting Wars That Follow Social Revolution Wins

When difficult social challenges face a community, it might choose revolution as a way to solve them. Whether the revolution is short or long, the victors enforce their will. But the fighting doesn't stop with the victory; it's usually followed by another war, a bloodletting war. Its purpose seems to be to let those discontented with the win of the revolution have an opportunity to fight and even die for this new social order, even if they don't like it.

These bloodletting wars are most often long and indecisive; a good example is the Iran-Iraq War (1980–88) that followed the Iranian Revolution of 1979. They can occasionally be spectacularly successful—the best example of this being the Napoleonic Wars (1803–1815) following the French Revolution (1789).

The three examples I will discuss are the <u>Iran-Iraq War</u>, <u>World War II</u>, and the <u>Korean War</u>.

Iran-Iraq War

Prior to the Iran-Iraq War, the bloodletting war after the <u>Iranian Revolution</u> of 1979, Iran's shah was guiding his country through an industrializing phase that was transforming its social fabric; amid the growing prosperity were many discontented people, one of whom was

Ayatollah Khomeini. When the shah lost control in 1979, moderates replaced him, but they also lost control. This was the time of the <u>Iran Hostage Crisis</u>; the US embassy was taken over by Iranian radicals. Ultimately, it was Khomeini and a mix of theocrats and republicans who took control.

But that didn't end the discontentment or the uncertainty in the country; many factions demonstrated and engaged in some violence. Next-door strongman Saddam Hussein decided the time was ripe to reap some benefit from all this chaos; his army occupied some of Iran's oil fields on the Persian Gulf next to Iraq. In addition to being an opportunist, he was dealing with the challenges of his own social revolution too. Winning a quick war against a traditional enemy would help his prestige.

This invasion didn't go well for Saddam. The Iranian army, still in good shape, drove him back. A panic on the Iraqi side ensued, and Hussein hollered for help. And he got it from his Sunni neighbors, the Saudi Arabians, who very much didn't want the Shiite religious theocracy in Iran to gain any ground in the Middle East. Later, other Sunni groups also contributed, and during this time, Hussein was considered a hero in the United States for his role in containing those nasty Iranians.

Geography in this case was squarely on the side of stalemate; the river delta between Iran and Iraq was a swampy, miserable place to fight. But for eight years, the Iranians kept trying to defeat the Iraqis and advance into their homeland, and for eight years, the Iraqis found people who would finance their defense line and held fast.

The Iranians found a place for bloodletting where Iranians who were proud to be Iranian but frustrated with the choice of Khomeini and the mullahs could demonstrate their dedication to the motherland. The Iraqis were also gaining this same kind of benefit, but not as obviously.

When the war ended, the Iranians finally found peace but the Iraqis didn't. Saddam was too adventurist at heart to let things lie, and he felt the world owed him a lot for holding off the Iranians as he had. He invaded Kuwait and started the <u>First Gulf War</u>.

World War II

World War II was the bloodletting war for the social revolutions of Central and Eastern Europe that followed World War I—Germany, Italy, and Russia in particular—and for Japan. The long, mostly stalemated World War I unleashed social revolutions all through Central and Eastern Europe and in the Ottoman Empire in the Middle East, where the fighting continued for up to four more years and resulted in new governments with many variations on Socialist ideas.

But these new ideas and governments upset many people. These winners of the mid-twenties violence had won the right to choose new governments, but they hadn't won the respect or peacefulness of the peoples they governed. Then came the worldwide Great Depression, and the unhappiness kept growing.

The solution to all this unhappiness was a series of bloodletting wars that are now lumped together and called World War II. In these wars, the unhappy people of Germany, Italy, Japan, and Russia got a chance to show their patriotism by fighting vigorously for their country against neighboring enemies—first small ones, then huge ones.

In the end, Germany, Italy, and Japan lost and had to start their social revolutions all over again from different foundations dictated by the Allies. This second time, these revolutions evolved much more peacefully. Russia won and kept its revolution going for another forty years.

Korean War

The Korean War (1950–53) was the bloodletting war for the Chinese Communist victory in China in 1948.

The First Opium War (1839–42) was in response to Western traders (primarily the British) showing the Chinese Manchu/Qing dynasty rulers how potent Western military technology had become. Coping with these virulent Western ideas and techniques started a crisis in China that lasted a hundred years.

In 1927, another civil war pitted Nationalist Chiang Kai-shek against Communist Mao Tse-tung. The fight continued off and on, interrupted by the Japanese invasion of 1936, until 1948, when the Communists won a series of decisive victories and occupied the Chinese mainland. The Nationalists withdrew to Taiwan and hoped for a triumphant return to the mainland, but that was just wishing and dreaming; the Communists had won.

But many Chinese who were unhappy about the choices the Chinese Communists were making protested and had to face bloody crackdowns by the Communists.

Then came an opportunity for a distraction. Neighboring North Korea's leader, Kim Il-sung, started a war to take over South Korea. He nearly succeeded, but he was pushed back by UN forces, who seemed on the verge of defeating the North. As the battle moved north, the Chinese Communists got nervous; would the UN stop at the border or keep moving north to help the Nationalists back onto the mainland?

The Chinese responded by jumping into the Korean War wholeheartedly but sneakily. They called their soldiers "volunteers" and never officially admitted to helping out. After they got involved, the war went on another two years, and about 300,000 Chinese lost their lives. This was a bloodletting war that followed the winning of the Chinese Revolution.

Note that this function of the war in Chinese social fabric explains the difference in how the Chinese reacted to the Vietnam War. They no longer needed a bloodletting, so they offered lots of moral support and some materiel to North Vietnam but no soldiers.

The Safety-Valve Alternative

The American Civil War was not followed by a bloodletting war; I think this was because everyone, particularly those who were discontent with the outcome—had a safety valve—migration westward. This kept them busy and gave them something to think about other than their outrage. This safety valve helped America recover more peacefully from the trauma of the Civil War. More peacefully but not completely peacefully. The Reconstruction Era still produced lots of arguing and disputing.

Extending the Concept: The Syrian War

The Arab Spring (2010–12) was a series of decentralized protests and revolts throughout North Africa and the Middle East. Each country experienced it differently; Tunisia changed government style while Libya slipped into tribal chaos.

The Syrian War could be the bloodletting war for all this Arab Spring frustration. It has many of the earmarks: lots of fighting, lots of causes, and no progress to speak of. If it's a bloodletting war, as it winds down, it should bring relative peace to North Africa and the Middle East for at least a decade.

Further Reading

"The rule of the gunman: Why post-colonial Arab states are breaking down" (*Economist*, October 11, 2014) indirectly supported my contention that Syria was a bloodletting war. It basically said that much of the North Africa and Middle East region hit by the Arab Spring movement was suffering from dissolving governments.

Conclusion

Bloodletting wars often follow social revolutions. Their purpose is to allow still-discontented members of the community to find a patriotic outlet for their discontent. When these wars work well, they're followed by a relative peace, and people get on with the challenges of adapting to a new regime.

But they are expensive. I call them bloodletting for good reason.

48

Long Wars—Surprise Enemies and Protected Resources

The United States has been involved in many conflicts, from small actions such as the Indian Wars of the American West to huge actions such as the two world wars.

In many cases, Americans have been aware of the magnitude of the wars they were getting involved in. Americans knew the world wars would be long and hard-fought months before the United States became involved. Sometimes, there have been pleasant surprises—the First Gulf War, fought by Bush Sr.'s administration, was surprisingly short and sweet.

But three of America's wars—the Korean War, the Vietnam War, and the Iraq War—have been surprising the other direction: they were all supposed to be short and relatively low cost, but they turned into long, high-cost, and difficult entanglements.

What do surprisingly long wars have in common? What makes them different from "average" wars?

The Average War

Wars start when two communities led by their politicians think it's time to fight. When one refuses to fight, a border conflict—a local conflict—ensues. These are common but not memorable. One example is the fighting between the Soviet Union and Japan prior to World War II.

Currently, the most famous is the <u>Kashmir conflict</u>, which has been an off-and-on, often bloody, dispute between India and Pakistan that started in 1947. If only one side agrees to fight, the other side loses bloodlessly. Examples of times when only one side chose to fight are Germany's taking over the <u>Rhineland</u>, <u>Austria</u>, and <u>Czechoslovakia</u> before World War II.

No politician in his right mind invites his community to start a long war. One way of telling who really started a war (something often disputed after the fact) is to compare the prewar statements of the leading politicians on both sides. Whoever was promising a short war ("I'll have the troops home by Christmas" is an infamous war-starting pledge) is the one who started it. If politicians on both sides were promising a short war, both sides started it.

The German Experience after World War I and Leading to the Russian Invasion of World War II

The conflicts Hitler started are examples of <u>splendid little wars</u>. All the battles from militarizing the Rhineland up to and including invading Russia were planned as short wars, and all except invading Russia were executed as short wars as well. The Germans developed the term <u>blitzkrieg</u>—lightning war—for internal consumption. The Nazis were explaining to the German people that they had figured a way to make wars short and relatively painless, and this is why it was okay to go to war.

After World War I and before Hitler, the average German was just as war-shy as any other European because all Europeans had experienced the long World War I. But seeing blitzkrieg in action in Poland, Norway, France, Yugoslavia, and Greece allowed the average German to become more war-tolerant.

Following the Vietnam War, America was also war-shy. Consider Carter's feeble response to the Iranian radicals taking the <u>US embassy hostage</u> in 1978 in the middle of the Iranian Revolution. But then came a change. Just as Hitler reversed Germany's war-shyness with a series of short, contained, and very successful military engagements leading to the fall of France, so Reagan reversed America's war-shyness with a series of short, contained, and very successful military engagements starting with <u>Grenada</u> and leading to the First Gulf War. In both cases, following this build-up of confidence, the leaders then led their nations into long, difficult, quagmires with surprise enemies and protected resources.

The average war lasts from days to a month or two. In those days or months, one side takes enough of a hit that it sues for peace, and the other side looks at the cost of continuing the fight, sees peace as the more profitable alternative, and takes the peace offer.

The Long War—An Average War Plus a Surprise Enemy

A long war happens because one or both sides get a surprise enemy that upsets the plans for the short war. The Korean War was supposed to be short and sweet for the North Koreans because the Americans had indicated Korea was not part of their vital defense line (Japan and the Philippines were) and the Americans had not equipped the South Koreans to take on a surprisingly well-equipped and well-trained North Korean army.

Then surprise! The United States got involved under the auspices of the UN. That war was supposed to be short and sweet because either the North Koreans would drive the UN forces into the sea before they could get organized or the US and UN forces would stop that from happening and launch a massive counterstroke.

MacArthur's landing at Incheon in September cut off the North Korean army from the north, and in the following month, it dissolved. The UN forces marched north, and MacArthur made the famous pledge all soldiers and their families love to hear: "We'll have the boys home by Christmas."

Then surprise! The Red Chinese Army came to rescue the North Koreans in November with two full armies with the aspiration of driving the US and UN forces into the sea. That didn't happen because the United States sent more troops in; the Chinese advance was stopped south of Seoul in December.

After the Chinese intervention was halted, the war devolved into a bloody stalemate because both sides had large protected resources (discussed in the next chapter). In the end, both sides claimed victory. The Americans said, "We stopped North Korean–Chinese aggression and saved South Korea." The Chinese said, "We stopped US/UN aggression and saved China." The South Koreans said, "Thank you," and the North Koreans said, "The revolution lives on!"

The Vietnam War was to be short and sweet because the US forces would quickly chase out the local guerrillas, the Viet Cong. That war turned long and ugly when the North Vietnamese Army (NVA), supported by lots of war materiel from China and Russia, came south to rescue the Viet Cong. Like Korea, the war evolved into a long, bloody stalemate. Unlike Korea, the stalemate ended with astonishing speed in 1975 when Congress voted to pull the plug on the billions of dollars a year the United States was sending to South Vietnam to support its army. Just weeks after that was announced, the South Vietnamese Army became the incredible vanishing army and disappeared in a couple of months. It was one of the largest and fastest routs in history.

The Iraq War—the Bush Jr. version of the First Gulf War—was going to be short and sweet as well because the United States planned on facing only Saddam's field army, which collapsed on schedule as US forces rolled north from Kuwait. Then surprise! The war turned long and ugly when the Iraq internal security structure (various police forces) vaporized along with the field army and various insurgent groups sprang up to fill the security vacuum.

The surprise got worse when a year or so later, these local insurgents started getting serious aid from everyone in the Middle East with an ax to grind with the United States (or some other Iraqi faction). Iraq turned into the perfect place to tweak the United States' nose.

The Biggest Losers: The Countries Themselves

In the Korean War, China hurt some, America hurt some, but Korea was devastated. Under Japanese rulership (1900–1945), Korea had transformed from almost completely agrarian to modestly industrial and moderately prosperous, benefits the Korean War took away. It's miraculous that in the fifty years following, South Korea has become a world-class manufacturing powerhouse surpassing Italy in GNP and per-capita income.

In Vietnam, America's blood and pride were injured, North Vietnam's blood was spilled, but South Vietnam was ripped apart. North Vietnam won, but it had no resources comparable to America's to rebuild South

Vietnam after the victory. Thirty years later, the unified Vietnam was still a poor nation, but it has been slowly and steadily prospering.

The Korean and Vietnam experiences suggested Iraq was going to take this one on the chin. No matter who won, the Iraqis would suffer the most, and it would take them decades to recover. On the negative side, Iraq, like Vietnam but unlike Korea, had no industrial tradition to aspire to or to remember and rebuild. On the positive side, it had oil, but it was surrounded by dozens of interest groups that would support more fighting in the region. Iraq was flattened, and its cultural and geographical neighbor Syria joined the mess. The regional chaos became spectacularly long running and widespread.

A Surprise Enemy and a Protected Resource

A surprise enemy is not enough to make a war long; there must also be protected military resources that neither side can effectively turn off. America is the world's largest protected resource. Historically, if you fight America, expect to fight a long war against a well-financed enemy.

In Korea and Vietnam, America's enemies were fighting with a large part of their military resources protected from American firepower. In Korea, the Chinese could stage their military resources in northeast China (former Manchuria) and then sneak those resources across the border when American air power and firepower were nullified by darkness or bad weather. In Vietnam, the NVA could stage in North Vietnam and sneak men and materiel into South Vietnam by sea or by the Ho Chi Minh trail. These protected resources on both sides of the conflict were the major reason the war was conducted in a bloody and intense fashion for a long time.

The Iraq War went on and on because various insurgent groups were assisted by protected resources—nearby active suppliers. The media was diligent in reporting deaths, suicide bombings, and occasional military operations but said little about where the outside supplies were coming from. This was a serious shortcoming in reporting. It may also reflect poor understanding on the part of top Bush officials. If Secretary of Defense Rumsfeld and Vice President Cheney were routinely reporting, "The insurgency is on its last legs" (which they did through most of 2005) and yet it kept fighting strongly, they didn't understand where the insurgency's protected resources were either. This was probably because the answer was an unpleasant one for the media and the Bush administration.

Americans count on firepower to win the day, but its successful enemies have found ways around that advantage. The Chinese and North Vietnamese used weather, darkness, and shovels to counter the American firepower advantage. The Iraqis used the cover of civilians, hopelessly weak police forces, and ignorance as to whom the true enemy was to do the same.

Even Long Wars Are Fought as Short Wars

No politician makes points by saying, "This war I'm about to get you involved in will be a long one." George W. Bush constantly said in the post-9/11 days, "This war will be a long one," but he was very careful never to define "long" or "war," so most people thought the fighting would last a matter of months and that the war he mentioned was the war on terrorism, a chronic state like that of the war on drugs.

Every war is fought with a plan to make the enemy sue for peace in a matter of months. This was true of both world wars, but they went on much longer because the plans didn't work; the enemy was always more resilient than had been expected.

Hitler's Russian campaign is a good example. The first move into Russia was supposed to have Stalin (or his replacement because of his disgrace at the huge defeat they would suffer) suing for peace by Christmas. And the Russian counteroffensive was supposed to break the overly proud German army that was shivering through a Russian winter. The Russians thought the Germans would retreat as had Napoleon and sue for peace before the cherry blossoms bloomed. Hitler's summer offensive the next year was supposed to gore Russia economically and force it to sue for peace by Christmas. And so on. Long wars tend to be a series of short wars none of which go as planned.

The Middle East: A Record-Breaking Mess

The Iraq War became messy, went on and on, and spread to Syria, where conflict as well became long and messy. The Second Gulf War was the biggest blunder caused by the panic that followed 9/11; it was hastily planned from the beginning, and sadly, the planning never got better.

For centuries, this part of the Middle East has been home for many cultures happy to compete with and betray each other. When Saddam was scraped off the top and not replaced with any kind of imperialist structure (such as the Ottomans had been before World War I), the competition kicked in full force. Many nearby outsiders were happy to add their resources to the competition and violence, a perfect storm of protected resources and surprise enemies.

When the Arab Spring of 2012 brought unrest to Syria, it added to the Iraqi chaos. When Syria swirled into this mess, another previous pattern was added—that of the Spanish Civil War.

The Spanish Civil War Pattern

The Spanish Civil War of 1936 provides a pattern for the rise of ISIS in Syria and Iraq. This war is like the Syrian part of the war because of the role of the International Brigades, those the European intelligentsia formed because they felt so strongly about this conflict.

The Iraqi/Syrian War is attracting the same kind of interest among Islamic intellectuals. The Middle East's growing prosperity is creating a fresh, new, expanding middle class that is experiencing the growing pains Europe's middle class went through at the beginning of the Industrial Revolution (roughly the 1800s through the 1840s—the era of supporting the Greek revolt from the Ottoman Empire and the beginnings of the anarchist and socialist movements).

The Iraqi/Syrian War will become a pivotal part of the Islamic experience and Middle East Islamic culture for decades no matter who wins or loses. Given that this is a new middle class, what will come from this new cultural force will be something never seen before. This war is shaping up to be something as influential in the Islamic world thinking as was the American Civil War in American thinking.

This Syrian-Iraq war is overloaded with surprise enemies and protected resources and is becoming a defining cultural world event. What a situation!

49

The American Revolution

The Americans' victory in the <u>Revolutionary War</u> (1775–1783) was a big surprise for the people on the American continents and the governments of western Europe then.

Prior to this surprise and for many decades following, western European kingdoms such as England, France, Spain, and Portugal had been on a roll; they had extended their power and influence south and west and had established colonies—the Spanish in the Philippines, the Portuguese in India, and the Dutch in the Indonesian archipelago.

The American Revolution was a bump in this colonizing and imperializing path, not a turning point. European domination became more intense for another century and a half, up until World War I. As an example, the First Opium War didn't happen until 1839–41; the British defeated the Chinese Empire for the first time.

But the American Revolution was quite a bump, and the British learned important lessons about handling their empire.

Background

Agricultural Age cultures had been improving in prosperity and technological diversity around the world for centuries. There was overall progress, but it was uneven. The rise and breakup of the Roman Empire was an example of the unevenness.

The key technology that allowed western Europe's colonial expansion efforts to grow mightily starting in the 1500s was improved sailing technology that allowed for travel on the stormy Atlantic as well as the relatively calm Mediterranean and increased commercial opportunities.

The "commercial" part is important. When exploration opens up new markets, commerce beckons, and ships will be built to take advantage of this. If you don't have commerce following an exploring effort, you get one-shot deals such as a single brave explorer or scientist backed by an eccentric, rich person making discoveries that are ultimately forgotten. The astronauts made it to the moon and back in 1969; that was exciting, but people later asked, "Great! But what's it doing for me today?"

What made Columbus different from Eric the Red (both discoverers of North America) was the millions of people and dollars that followed Columbus's discovery. And the key technology that made that Columbus follow-up possible was better sailing technology.

For these trading opportunities to be exploited, the rank-and-file of European kingdoms needed to learn how to cooperate more widely. Long-distance trading ships would be gone for a year or more, and the people back at their home ports needed to deal with these long departures in ways that didn't discourage young folk from becoming sailors. One famous example of that learning happening was creating Lloyd's of London in 1688—the invention of insuring the ships and cargos.

Thanks to this combination of improving technology and improving social skills, colonizing North America after 1500 proved steadily more profitable and attractive to many different people in western Europe. By 1770, there were about twenty colonies on the eastern coasts and islands of North America because many people were going over for different reasons and were prospering in different ways. The people on Barbados were prospering by growing sugar cane and making rum from it, and those in Virginia were growing tobacco and making cigars.

By the 1770s, North America was a prosperous and innovative place, but the people living there had several bones to pick with the British, who claimed ownership.

The Root Problems

The root problems that caused the American Revolution were differences in thinking about what a colonial empire and its subjects should do for each other. The root cause for this difference in thinking was the difference in environment between western Europe (England in particular) and the areas being colonized.

The British Point of View

The western European governments became colonizers because it was profitable for not only the sailors and merchants behind them but also for their ports and the governments controlling them. As technology allowed for better and more ships, profits increased and colonizing became even more attractive for western European powers.

People were learning how to cooperate more, but betrayal still had its attractions. Merchants, ports, and governments engaged in cheap shots to restrict competition in the expanding marketplaces. In the 1600s, the Spanish were notorious for their <u>mercantilist</u> policies concerning trading around the Caribbean. They weren't alone; other countries came up with similar restrictions, but the Spanish had the highest profile in this matter. One result of these policies was a lot of hypocrisy and corruption among those in charge of colonies. And this was a time (1650s–1720s) when pirating flourished whenever the Spanish went to war with the other western European powers.

While overseas trading was profitable, it was a lot of work, and it was causing big social changes at home. Those who accumulated wealth were different from the warriors, priests, and landed nobility, the powerful classes in the Agricultural Age. These newly wealthy people thought quite differently about how their societies should work. The <u>nouveau riche,</u> as they came to be called in France, became more numerous and important as the boom continued.

In Britain, these social changes mixed with religion, which caused much unrest. The highest-profile unrest went on between Catholics and Church of England/Anglican Protestants. This split, which started in the 1530s, was still generating heat in the 1700s. Mary Queen of Scots and Queen Elizabeth I contested who should rule England and Scotland in the late 1500s. In the 1640s, religion, politics, and money mixed vigorously again to cause the <u>English Civil War</u>, which deposed Charles I. England tried parliamentary rule for a couple of years and then brought Oliver Cromwell to power as Lord Protector, not king. After he died, the monarchy was restored—the people of England were not ready to give up on kings yet. Contemporary with the unrest leading to the American Revolution was the arguing between Parliament and King George III (1760–1820) over how the United Kingdom should be ruled.

Just prior to the American Revolutionary War, the western European kingdoms had fought the <u>Seven Years' War</u>, a bloody affair in which England and Prussia fought Austria, France, and Russia and later several other European countries. The British and Prussians won; the latter consolidated their claims to Silesia and managed to avoid losing, which was a big surprise at the time. The British won colonial regions from the various losing kingdoms in North America, Africa, and the Far East. This was when England pushed the French out of North America and India.

The British were happy with the result, but the war had been very expensive, and there was still much to argue about domestically. It was paying for the war and these domestic arguments spilling over into the North American colonies that brought this "How should we be ruled?" crisis to a boiling point.

The Other Regions' Point of View

Other regions, India being the most important to the British, were experiencing different relations with Britain. The British were importing to these other regions mountains of high-tech merchandise such as textiles in exchange for silks and spices.

These regions had strong cultures based on Agricultural Age technologies, and the locals didn't mind mixing competition and scheming in their governing styles. When the western Europeans showed up with trade goods and high-tech military equipment, the locals readily invited them to join in on their disputes with neighbors.

At first, the traders held off—they were there to trade, and fighting made enemies as well as friends. But as the substantial fruits for participating became clear and the logic of "If we don't, some other western Europeans will" became stronger, western Europeans became more active in the imperialist game. They found that bringing order to other regions widened markets.

Later in the evolution came the desire of some of the locals to imitate the industrial success of the western Europeans. "Why buy their goods? Why not make them here?" In general, western Europeans didn't mind; they were happy to educate the brightest and best in their colonial lands so they could go home and transplant the success. But in practice, the results of the transplanting were widely mixed. There were a handful of successes such as Japan but many failures such as in the various Ottoman Empire regions.

Success or failure, the efforts to industrialize caused social discontent that went on for decades. The Chinese effort to industrialize was an example; it continued for over a hundred years and supported at least three civil wars—in the chaos, it was hard to tell when one ended and another began.

The American Point of View

Thinking in the American environment was dominated by the wilderness: it was close, it was big, and it offered many opportunities for exploitation assisted by a spirit of cooperation and European technology. The colonists wanted safe trade routes to markets, and as long as the empire was doing this, everything was just fine.

The two biggest sore points were when the empire closed markets and when it asked the Americans to participate in wars it was fighting with enemies such as the French and Spanish. That spread the wars to North America, including the French and Indian Wars (1689–1763) that became locally nicknamed King William's War and the War of Jenkins's Ear. The Americans weren't happy to be spilling blood, money, time, and attention over what they saw as European arguments such as the Seven Years' War (1754–1763).

The British action that started serious protesting was its levying taxes on the colonies. The Boston Tea Party was a partly theatrical protest against a tax on tea purchases that came at the end of the Seven Years'

War. The British had won, but it had been expensive, and they wanted the colonies to help pay for it.

The War

The protesting transformed into armed insurrection in 1775. Boston became the early hotbed. In July 1776, the American colonies declared what they were fighting for: the Continental Congress voted for the Declaration of Independence. Prior to that declaration, the colonials were fighting for better treatment while still remaining part of the empire—"Taxation without representation is tyranny" was the thinking.

The battles fought on the coast from Boston to Savannah involved much maneuvering and marching. As the conflict progressed, Britain picked up more enemies; the French entered the war in 1778 and the Spanish in 1779, and the fighting spread around the world to places such as India. Ironically, this was a conflict that had begun in North America and then spread to Europe and beyond. As this happened, the importance of the outcome in North America diminished for the British; winning in Europe and India became higher priority.

After the colonials' victory at the siege of Yorktown in 1781, the fighting in North America wound down. It took a while for tempers to cool, but in 1783, a treaty was signed; Britain recognized the thirteen colonies as the United States of America.

The Aftermath

This conflict is called a revolution for good reason. Much thinking around the world was changed by its outcome. The colonials had cast out the imperialists, a first in the previous two hundred years. The Americans chose to experiment with becoming a republic and a democracy rather than installing a king. This wasn't the first democracy—the Swiss had one—but it was a first for a former colony that became a large country.

This outcome was a surprise, and the rest of the world took notice—especially those people who were industrializing such as those nouveau-riche

French. This outcome was a big inspiration for these other people to think about doing things differently.

Changes in British Thinking

The British did some soul-searching too and realized that the imperialism and colonialism adventure they were on—white-hot as it was at the time—wouldn't last forever and that they had to prepare for the aftermath. Their colonial policy shifted to preparing the colonies for independence, and the result was a good one: the post–World War II British Commonwealth. British post-imperial governing structures worked out much better than had those set up by the French, Spanish, or Dutch in terms of fostering smooth transitions to independence for their colonies and retaining their goodwill.

Conclusion

The American victory in the Revolutionary War was the big, worldwide surprise of its day. It inspired people all over the world to change their thinking about their relation with their empires. The "shot heard round the world" is an apt description of it.

50

The Civil War

In the 2010s, the American Civil War is often taught as being fought over whether to continue or end slavery—end of story. Hardly! Slavery became the hottest issue as the war dragged on, but it was not at the top of the list when the line was drawn on the Potomac River in 1860 and both sides decided fighting was better than talking.

This war was about many issues; it was about all Americans getting scared; they panicked and blundered into a long war. In the end, as is almost always the case in drawn-out wars, neither side got what it expected; they had to deal with big changes in how they lived and conducted their politics.

The Lead-Up to the War

North America is a big and diverse place. The United States had been formed by thirteen colonies because that size and diversity made these smaller units the most workable arrangement. Each colony ruled itself because that worked better in an era before telegraphs, railroads, and fast clipper ships.

That diversity didn't go away just because those colonies united under the Constitution; they still had much to learn about nation making, which was a moving target. Much of the political experimenting going on in the

United States from the 1770s to the 1850s was dealing with the effects of a triple whammy.

The growing size of the United States in land area, number of states, and population

The United States started out as just the <u>strip of land</u> on the east coast of North America between the Atlantic and the Appalachians. It grew across the mountains into places such as Ohio, Kentucky, and Alabama. The <u>Louisiana Purchase</u> (1803) doubled the land area, and the <u>Mexican-American War</u> in 1846 doubled it again. The states grew from thirteen to thirty; the population grew from 4 million to 31 million. Huge changes. <u>Rip Van Winkle</u> was a contemporary story about all that change.

The changing nature of the technology being used in day-to-day living

This was an age of industrial and agricultural revolutions. Canals, railroads, steamboats, telegraphs, steel mills, and <u>cotton gins</u> all grew from essentially zero to widespread use in this era. This made huge changes in what people could do. Profitable cotton and tobacco flourished in the South, and steamboats could transport them to markets up or down rivers.

The changing nature of the social structures in all the states

The combination of new technologies and constantly growing immigrant populations meant that the states were never your old grandpa's state anywhere in the United States. Dramatic change was the constant; the Washington-Jefferson-Adams style of governing changed dramatically as Andrew Jackson and his Democrats were voted in in 1829.

What the colonies/states/territories had in common over this entire era was a lot of prosperity. Gone were the days of the 1600s when people were coming mostly for religious freedom (<u>Puritans</u>) or to try new styles of living in an untamed wilderness (<u>Quakers</u>). People were coming because first the British Empire colonists and then the citizens of this newly created country were prospering. This is why the United States could afford $15 million for the Louisiana Purchase from the French in 1803 and pay the Mexican government $18 million for California, Texas, and the Mountain West in 1848. (They paid this even after they had already occupied Mexico City and had won the war! Yet another example of how strange this American way was.)

From diversity to acrimony

When it took two weeks to travel from Boston to Washington, it was hard to meddle meaningfully in the affairs of people in other states. This was even more so when the business in Boston didn't depend much on what was happening in Washington. And that was the easy trip! Getting from Boston to Cleveland (Ohio was the West in those days) was a harrowing journey through wilderness and mountains that resembled crossing the Misty Mountains in *The Hobbit* and the *Lord of the Rings* and took a month.

But this was a time of change. Canals, railroads, and steamboats made traveling faster, cheaper, and easier in the early 1800s. And later, telegraphs allowed for the quick exchange of information over vast distances, another first for the world.

All these developments meant that business relations and meddling in the neighbor's business became easier and more important. This turned the live-and-let-live attitude of the 1780s into the serious meddling and acrimony of the 1850s.

This unsettling was enhanced by all the other emerging technologies. "How should we farm the rivers and build the towns of the Mississippi watershed now that we have steam-powered riverboats available?" And because there was so much new happening, cheap shots became endemic.

One of the sources of acrimony was how to handle slavery. This is considered today as the highest-profile issue of back then, but it wasn't. In those times, many other equally or more-important issues were raging. Here are some examples.

How to handle factory working conditions in the North

The conditions were new and unregulated. Child and women labor conditions were as controversial in the North as slavery was in the South.

How to handle customs duties

The North wanted duty structures that would favor building factories, particularly textile factories. The factory builders came up with the bright idea of putting a tax on exporting cotton. The South thought this was a terrible idea, a Yankee cheap shot. They wanted to sell to all comers, including the equally new and booming English and French textile factories. This category of difference in opinions came to be called states' rights issues.

How to handle money

Industrialists and traders in the northeast wanted a strong dollar to promote profitable trading. The farmers and settlers wanted the dollars widely spread so they could better develop their farms, which meant a weaker dollar. This issue pitted the South and the West against the Northeast. The new railroads, canals, and mines gobbled up money as fast as they created vivid dreams of wealth and prosperity. But the various booms all cycled with busts, and the bust that started just before the fighting was a doozy.

As mentioned in the April 2014 *Economist* article "The Slumps that Shaped Modern Finance," 1857 was the start of a severe slump in America—the boom dreams turned into bust nightmares. The one in 1857 changed finance and enflamed separatist passions as Americans and the world tried to figure out how to deal with the broken dreams and emptied purses.

> But this time things were different. A shock in America's
> Midwest tore across the country and jumped from New York to
> Liverpool and Glasgow, and then London. From there it led to

crashes in Paris, Hamburg, Copenhagen and Vienna. Financial collapses were not merely regular—now they were global, too.

Imagine how twitchy you would be if a big chunk of your life savings was wiped out by a string of bank failures. In the following couple of years, politicians were campaigning by pointing fingers and shouting about who should keep paying out "to save the rest of us."

How to handle immigration

Many of those in the United States got huffy about newcomers. The issues brought up at the time were eerily similar to the immigration issues brought up in the 2010s. The term "Dutch treat" comes out of this time; it was one of a series of jokes about how newcomers would say one thing and do another. Dutch in this usage was a mispronunciation of Deutsche—they were mocking German immigrants. The icon for these immigration issues was the <u>Know Nothing movement</u> of this era.

Religion

This was the time of the <u>Second Great Awakening</u>. New religious ideas were spouting like toadstools after rain. The Southern Baptists formed in this era. The Upstate New York region along the newly built <u>Erie Canal</u> became a hotbed of new religions, including Mormonism, Christian Science, and Seventh Day Adventism.

Money rights, land rights, human rights—ouch! These were deeply emotional things to be arguing over. And by the 1850s, there were many heated emotions on many sides of many issues, but the North-South issues took the limelight.

Enter Panic and Blunder

The political parties were having a hard time as this acrimony grew. The Whig party had such a hard time that it dissolved in the early 1850s. The Democrats gloated for only a short time because the Whigs were replaced in 1854 by the new, virulent Republican Party, a mix of former Whigs, ex-Free Soilers, ex-Know Nothings, and Abolitionists. It spread like wildfire through the North, and the mix of policies it was advocating terrified the South. The crash of 1857 made matters worse.

The South panicked. Before the election in 1860, many Southern leaders declared that if a Republican were elected president, they would secede. The Republican candidate was Abraham Lincoln; he won, and the Southern leaders made good on their promise.

A Different War

This was a war of many firsts. It was the first time railroads and riverboats played a big role. Their effect was to make the battles much bigger than they would have been otherwise. They made it possible to even consider conquering a quarter of a continent—The South was that big.

It had the first battles utilizing steam-powered ironclads that in the next fifty years evolved into the battleships of World War I navies.

This was the first time so many people on both sides participated so enthusiastically in conducting a war; it's sometimes cited as the first example of modern total war.

Late in the war, static trench warfare was first conducted.

The Conduct of the War

As does every long, drawn-out war, this one changed its nature as it progressed. At first, no one was sure what was going to happen or what had to be done. One example of this was the reaction to General Winfield Scott's plan. Scott, a hero of the Indian Wars and the Mexican-American war, was well respected, but he was old. He came up with a plan but did not implement it. He outlined a massive plan that called for huge expense, time, and effort. Scott's Anaconda, as his plan was called, was mocked. Everyone wanted a lightning-fast, highly decisive strike on a much smaller scale. But the winning Northern strategy ended up being much like what Scott had forecast.

The big issue for the Lincoln administration was keeping the North enthusiastic about conducting the war. A related issue in the first year of the war was keeping more states from seceding. Because so many issues were simmering, if Lincoln and his freshmen Republican party got too zealous, too arrogant, and stumbled too badly, other states could easily join the protest.

On the Southern side, the big issue was keeping the Confederacy running smoothly while the war was in progress. The Southerners were doing the seceding because they felt the Northerners were seriously crimping their style and taking cheap shots. If Jefferson Davis and his administration bumbled running the Confederacy too badly, this secession would be of no benefit to the Southerners, and they might as well stay in a union.

One historic accident that dramatically shaped the war's destiny was the purely political choice to move the Confederacy's capital from Jackson, Mississippi, to Richmond, Virginia. Virginia was an important state, but that move put the North and South capitals only a day's ride apart. This provided the opportunity for the lightning strike everyone in the North was looking for. Fighting to take Richmond competed with the Anaconda scheme for attention and resources—it seemed like something that would be faster to accomplish than subduing a quarter of a continent.

The first year of the war looked like sparring—the battles were small and the casualties light because both sides were still gearing up physically and emotionally.

The battle that made everyone realize this was going to be serious was fought at Shiloh, Tennessee, in April 1862—23,000 casualties over the two-day fight. Neither side was outraged enough at this casualty count to call for peace. This one was going to be long and hard fought.

The next major change in thinking came at the Battle of Antietam, Maryland, four months after Shiloh. This was another shockingly bloody battle with casualties a bit higher than Shiloh's. But this one was very close to Washington, not in some midcontinent backwater. It got even more attention, and this was when Lincoln pushed slavery up the priority list with the Emancipation Proclamation. He was still being discreet and political. This proclamation freed slaves only in the Confederacy, not in the Union.

In July 1863, the South suffered two harsh blows: Vicksburg, on the Mississippi, was lost, and the battle of Gettysburg was lost. The former was the last Confederate stronghold on the Mississippi, and afterward, the Union controlled the river; the latter was another big bloodfest. The Anaconda was squeezing hard. Lee at Gettysburg had tried to force a spectacular showdown that would seriously discourage the North; it didn't work. The question was, would the North have the dedication to finish this?

Adding to the South's problems was that the Davis administration wasn't successful at keeping business as usual going in the South. The Northern blockades of Southern ports were crimping commerce, and the Davis administration was financing the war by printing money, not floating war bonds—the South was suffering from hyperinflation. The South's armies were shrinking while the North's kept growing.

In 1864, the nature of the war changed again; it became deeply frustrating. "The South isn't going to win. Why doesn't it give up or negotiate?" was the feeling of cooler heads in the North, South, and those watching in Europe. But it became a grudge match; the people of the North and the South backed their governments' conduct of the war. Lincoln was reelected over former General McClellan, who ran as a peace party candidate.

As a result, the conduct of the war became more hotheaded. The icon for this was <u>Sherman's march to the sea</u> in December 1864 after he took Atlanta. It was a bold and audacious military choice designed to make civilians suffer as much as the military had.

In April 1865, harsh reality finally caught up and dashed cold water over all this emotional heat. Richmond was lost, and Lee couldn't evade the pursuing Union forces to fight another day though he tried. He surrendered at Appomattox Courthouse in western Virginia.

The Aftermath

The war was over, but the hard feelings were not by any means. Lincoln was trying to pursue a moderate postwar policy when the hotheaded postwar feelings swept him away: he was assassinated by John Wilkes

Booth a week after Lee's surrender—Booth was one of many who couldn't accept that the South had lost fair and square.

The assassination of a beloved wartime leader at such a celebratory moment fired even more emotion and the post–Civil War time, <u>the Reconstruction Era</u>, became famous for how badly it worked out.

51

The War of 1870

Germany and France fought this war, the crowning achievement of <u>Otto Von Bismarck</u>, chancellor of Prussia and the newly created North German Confederation led by Prussia. It was a splendid, short war that resulted in a surprise, <u>the Paris Commune</u>. This commune experience was unexpected at the time but inspired the socialist and communist revolutionaries in the first half of the twentieth century.

Background

Germany and Italy of the 1650s through the 1850s were the playgrounds for the sport of kings: war. As France and England evolved from collections of feudal domains into nation states, the areas that are now Italy and Germany stayed politically fragmented and stayed the places where wars were fought. Aspiring kingdoms on all sides took their turns marching armies across these lands—French, Austrians, Prussians, Swedes, Poles, and Russians.

In the 1750s and '60s, the <u>Seven Years' War</u> rocked the region harder than usual. In addition to being an exciting war in German lands, this was in fact a world war. Western European colonies such as those of the Spanish, French, and English in North America partook in the fighting as well, as part of the <u>French and Indian Wars</u>. The British were on the winning side in this one, but it nearly bankrupted them. In part because of the austerity forced upon the British Empire, this war was followed quickly by the <u>Revolutionary War</u>. This one also spread worldwide and ended in 1783. This one France and allies won. But unlike Britain in the Seven Years' War, the French government was fully bankrupted by this effort, and in 1789, the <u>French Revolution</u> began as French citizens vented their outrage.

In the 1800s, the first stage of the Industrial Revolution was sweeping through France, England, and the German lands and was a game changer. The first example of how much this would change the game was the dramatic sweep of French Revolution armies across Europe right to the edge of Russia. France had industrial muscle, revolutionary zeal, and <u>Napoleon's military brilliance</u>, an unbeatable and legendary combination until the combined Russian and Spanish campaigns of 1812 showed that Napoleon could overreach himself.

The end of this era was the famous <u>Battle of Waterloo</u>, a historical curiosity. The era actually ended in 1813, when Napoleon recognized he was beaten and abdicated. But that ending was so smooth and painless that it couldn't make a good story end. Two years later, Napoleon returned to rule France and fought a desperate battle at Waterloo. He was tangibly defeated there, and that is the ending event history remembers.

Napoleon's brief rule of the German area rekindled hope for a unified German state. In 1848, another big surprise rocked the world. <u>Popular unrest</u> swept across Europe from France to the Russian borders. It also spread in China and Latin America. But the zeal did not transform into concrete changes—the zealots of the time couldn't agree on what to turn this zeal into, so instead, they squabbled. Over the following couple of years, reactionary forces regained control and clamped down. For the conservatives, the monarchists in particular, this was a deeply scary time.

The reactionaries were back in control, but the causes for the unrest were still there, and better solutions were needed in the face of the industrialization that was changing the way things were done.

In the German area, two men rose to the occasion and took full advantage of the circumstances: the Prussian Otto Von Bismarck became chancellor, and <u>William I</u> was king. They worked hard and ingeniously to work out effective, government-run social programs for the Prussians to settle the unrest in their homeland, and they tried to unify the lands between Prussia and the Rhine into what would become the German Empire.

These tasks took a heady mix of diplomacy, social understanding, and military prowess, but this pair plus the Prussian military had the talent to accomplish them. History gives Bismarck most of the credit, but all were necessary.

The Lead-Up to 1870

The Germans wanted unification; the big question was who would do it. The two major contenders were Austria under the Hapsburgs and Prussia. Other contenders, and in this era of uncertainty they could not be counted out, were the other midsize states of Germany such as Bavaria and a pan-German movement that wasn't connected with any state. This was what the unrest of 1848 had almost brought about.

The Hapsburgs had been dominant in the German lands for a long time; they had contested with the French, Russians, and Prussians for over a century. Getting them out of the running was the first success of the Bismarck/William team. In some fancy diplomatic footwork in 1865–66 concerning the succession of Schleswig and Holstein, lands between Denmark and Germany, Prussia first allied with then turned on Austria and won the Austro-Prussian War. This splendid little war put Austria out of the running and let Prussia dominate what was then called the North German Confederation.

Bismarck and team were careful all through this period to cultivate good relations with the Russians, but the French were another matter. Trying to maintain good relations with France was like trying to maintain good relations with a schizophrenic neighbor. Ever since the French Revolution began in 1789, the government of France had flip-flopped between republic, monarchy, and a few other styles of governance roughly every decade. In 1870, it was a monarchy again under Emperor Napoleon III, nephew of Napoleon I. As the Austro-Prussian war ended, Napoleon III was not happy about this sudden resurgence of Prussia and this new confederation.

Napoleon III had started his rulership with a lot of respect, but in these crucial years of the late 1860s, Bismarck played him like a fiddle. Through various maneuvers and deceits, he isolated Napoleon and the French from potential European allies and even got the French to declare the war.

The War and the Surprise

The fighting part of this was another splendid little war for the Prussians and their enthusiastic German allies. The French armies were defeated and surrounded, and they surrendered in two months. Neat stuff!

Then came the surprises. Rather than surrendering along with the armies, the French people decided to keep fighting. They formed yet another French republic, the fourth. The Prussians responded by surrounding Paris and besieging it. At first they didn't even bombard the city. They waited for the French to come to their senses and sign a peace treaty. That sort of happened in January 1871, and the Prussians left. But the French kept arguing among themselves.

In Paris, the Paris Commune started. In the countryside south of Paris, the citizens argued over whether this Fourth Republic/Commune was a good idea, and many didn't think so.

Times got strange even for those strange times. Bismarck and team got the Germans to agree to a German Empire. While that was happening, the Parisians were doing more experimenting with radical governing styles. The commune itself lasted for only two months—March through May 1871, but it became legendary as the first attempt at a socialist government with some anarchy and internationalism mixed in as well. People such as Karl Marx followed its progress closely. At the end of those two months, the conservatives of France became well-enough organized to attack Paris. In May, the fighting got very nasty and became known as *La Semaine Sanglante*, and the conservatives ousted the communes.

But the commune legend lived on vividly and inspired many socialists and communists of the early twentieth century. The War of 1870 was another small war with big surprises.

52

World War I: The Most Surprising War of the Twentieth Century

World War I was the most surprising war of the twentieth century. It wasn't surprising that the war was fought; Europeans were all expecting one. But the way it and its aftermath played out were not in anyone's turn-of-the-century playbook.

The Rise of Italy and Germany before the War

The French Revolution a hundred years earlier had shown Europe that industrialization meant big social change and disruption was on its way. The surprising string of French victories of the Napoleonic Wars spread that awareness all the way to Moscow.

Industrializing meant millions of Europeans would be transformed from farmers and farmers' wives into factory workers and factory workers' wives. It meant a new and influential social class would come into the various communities—industrialists. It also meant the landscape would be transformed by railroads, improved roads, factories, sanitation systems, new mines, and bicycles. This wasn't going to be your grandpa's Europe anymore.

The change started in England and France and moved east. One surprise fallout of this wave of change was Italy's and Germany's unifying into nation-states. Since the decline of the Holy Roman Empire 400 years earlier, these areas had been a patchwork of city-states and small kingdoms and the sporting grounds for whomever in the surrounding areas decided it was time for a war.

The social ground shook in the Revolutions of 1848, but the status quo was maintained. Then in 1866, Italy unified under the leadership of Garibaldi, Cavour, Victor Emmanuel II, and Mazzini. The next year, Germany unified. But here, a historical accident came to the fore. Germany unified under Prussian rule, not Austrian or Bavarian, because of the brilliance of Bismarck as a diplomat as well as a warrior—he was a rock star of diplomacy up against an ADHD-style Napoleon III in France. He outmaneuvered Napoleon III and the Austrian Hapsburgs during the 1850s and '60s. The coup de grâce was the War of 1870, covered in previous chapter.

Multicultural Monarchies under Siege

The Paris Commune, which followed the War of 1870, was a vision of things to come. And the people most scared of that vision where the rulers of the empires that spanned many agrarian cultures in eastern Europe: Austrians, Russians, and Turks. Even before World War I, these governing systems were having a hard time coping with the disruptions of industrializing. Austria transformed into Austria-Hungary in 1867. Russia had serious unrest in 1905. And the area where interests of all three converged, the Balkans, was suffering much conflict in the 1910s.

The Balkans had been dominated by the Ottoman Turkish Empire during the 1700s. All through the 1800s, it was losing its grip, and by 1900, Russia and Austria were looking to replace it as regional hegemon. But as of 1910, there was a power vacuum, not a hegemony, and much violence. Small wars had been fought there in 1912 and 1913. What would have been the third Balkan war of this time became World War I when it spread to the rest of Europe.

A New Style of Militarizing

Industrialization allowed for quicker mobilizations of armies. The German army started mobilizing on July 30, 1914, and was fighting the Battle of the Frontiers with France just two weeks later. In contrast, the first big battle of the Civil War took place six months after war was declared, and people were criticizing Lincoln's government for being hasty. Declarations of war spread swiftly once Russia declared war on Austria-Hungary in support of Serbia—if a government was slow to decide, it lost advantage on the battlefield.

A second big change was that weaponry had become much faster at firing and more accurate. Bullets, as we know them today, became commonplace in the 1900s for rifles and artillery, and machine guns became commonplace. Marching in mass formations over open fields became an invitation to get soldiers killed in huge numbers, but no better tactic for attacking had yet been developed, that happened late in the war. The result was a casualty count ten times higher than anyone had been expecting. And when the war became static trench warfare, the casualty problem multiplied every month—not the kind of war anyone was expecting in 1910.

New Styles of Socializing

Monarchies set atop a mesh of landed nobility work well for governing preindustrial, agrarian societies, but the disruptive changes of industrializing don't mesh well with the timeless rituals at the heart of that ruling system. But what should replace it? This was subject to a lot of experimenting all through the 1800s and 1900s. America was trying the republican democratic system and found it was stable for its circumstance of being a growing nation next to a giant wilderness it could settle—except for the vicious Civil War, that is. That was one pole. On the other was France. After the French Revolution, the French government oscillated between monarchy and republic about four times, and as written about above, had tried the Paris Commune in 1870.

France was far from alone in this chaos and confusion. This was the era when <u>Marx</u> and Engels wrote about communism as an alternative to monarchy, and the British were trying a constitutional monarchy with an active Parliament based on liberal ideals. There were dozens and dozens of other ideas being advocated and tried on smaller scales.

New and Old Bad Blood

The rise of Germany and Italy changed the bad-blood relations in Europe. England and France had had bad blood between them since William the Conqueror invaded England from France in 1066. It was ferociously bad during the 1700s and 1800s when they were competing as world colonizers. But the unification of Germany and its rise to being a first-rate industrial and military power pushed the British and French to become strange bedfellows.

Likewise, there had been long-standing bad blood between the Austrians and the Italians. The Italians considered the Austrians chronic meddlers in their affairs and as bad as the French. But when Germany went shopping for allies in Europe after it unified, Austria and Italy signed up—the trio became the Central Powers, the Triple Alliance. This was another collection of strange bedfellows.

The Turks had been having governing problems for a hundred years. They went from an unstoppable Islamic wave, besieging Vienna in 1529, their high point, to losing Greece in 1832. It was being called the sick man of Europe starting in the 1850s. There was long-standing bad blood between them and the Russians and Austrians—they all contested for influence in the chronically chaotic Balkans.

This newly unified Germany was sandwiched between Russia and France. It feared and planned for a two-front war. In self-fulfilling prophecy, those plans made the French and Russians pay much more attention to each other as potential allies.

The Alliances' Shakeout

Of the many alliances in 1910, no one knew for sure which ones counted. There were overt as well as secret alliances. All these great powers were wheeling and dealing with several different agendas in mind, so it wasn't clear who would back up whom when push came to shove.

Italy was allied with Austria and Germany as a Central Power, but it stayed neutral in the first round of war-declaring and fighting and turned on Austria and Germany a year after the war had started. Conversely, Britain had much influence at the Ottoman court, which was expected to stay neutral or join the allies. Surprise! They decided it was a great time to take a swing at Russia, so it joined Germany.

During the War

During the fighting in 1914, no nation's plan went as expected; no one won a splendid little war. Nor did anyone win in 1915, or 1916, or 1917. It wasn't until November 1918 that the Allies brought Germany to unconditional surrender.

This ended war on the Western Front and started the negotiations that produced the Treaty of Versailles. But the fighting that continued in eastern Europe lasted into the 1920s as the Russians, Poles, Finns, and others decided boundaries and social systems. This continuing unrest completely disintegrated the Austrian and Ottoman Turkish Empires. The Russian Empire disintegrated too, but much of it was subsequently unified under the Union of Soviet Socialist Republics (USSR). The Germans also had a deep social revolution and ended up trying multiparty democracy during the Weimar Republic era.

The United States, France, and England were all too busy recovering from the war and the damage it had caused to worry about events in eastern Europe. As I wrote earlier, this war was seen as having had an off-the-charts bad result.

After the War

World War I was so surprising that when it finally ended in western Europe, no one was sure what to do next amid the hugely damaging outcome. This meant the negotiators came to the Versailles table with lots of emotion and idealism in mind but little analysis or pragmatism.

The Ottoman Empire shattered as Russia and Austria had, but the rebuilding was shaped by more British and French colonial influence than was true in eastern Europe. The British and French drew the lines on the map. Sometimes, the lines reflected the culture of the area, but often, they didn't because the cultures in the Middle East were thoroughly mixed.

But technological change went on and resulted in the Roaring Twenties and then the Great Depression, and it paved the way for World War II—a completely different style of war.

In the West: Too Scared to Figure Out a Good Peace

In the west, the victors assembled in Paris in 1919 to figure out what to do next. They didn't handle this process well; the <u>Treaty of Versailles</u> has been condemned as a masterwork of bad choices. One good element of the treaty was trying to set up an organization to prevent future worldwide conflicts; <u>the League of Nations</u> was modeled after the <u>Congress of Vienna</u> that followed the Napoleonic Wars, but it didn't work out.

Everyone played the blame game. Germany was to pay reparations to France, which made sense to the French. But it laid the foundation for a financial crisis for Germany that ultimately brought the Nazis to power in the 1930s. Germany didn't strongly object to the treaty because it hadn't been invited to it and it was in the throes of building up a post-Kaiser, democratic government; all the leaders were busy, and it wasn't clear who should be its voice.

The League of Nations turned out to be controversial and ineffectual. The US Senate wouldn't let the United States join it, and it wasn't good at resolving the international disputes that came on hot and heavy in the 1930s as all nations tried to figure ways out of the Great Depression.

In the East: Empires Disintegrating

In eastern Europe, the fighting continued. In Russia, civil wars were raging in the cultural regions of the old empire. Russians fought among themselves, and the Poles, Finns, Ukrainians, and many others.

The Austrian Empire pieces didn't fight as much. The empire quickly transformed into smaller nation-states, and the Treaty of Versailles/League of Nations did good work in this area to make this transition fairly smooth.

The Ottoman Empire violently disintegrated, and the national boundaries of the Middle East as we know them today were laid out in this era except for Israel, which was created after World War II.

New Social Orders

The most exciting new experiment that started after World War I was the communist experiment in Russia, which changed its name to the USSR. The <u>Bolsheviks</u> were just one of a dozen or so factions that had ideas about how to replace the Romanovs. By historical accident, they ended up on top, and communism burst on to the world scene. For some people, it was as new and scary as World War I had been, and America experienced its first <u>Red Scare</u>.

But the Bolsheviks were just the most spectacular. Following the war, new governing systems were tried all over Europe.

New Technologies, New Prosperities

There was lots of experimenting going on with new technologies as well. Oil was replacing coal as the best way to power engines. (The *Titanic*, an icon of modern technology in 1912, had been powered by coal.) Electricity and electric motors were replacing steam engines and belts and pulleys as the way to power industrial machines. Henry Ford started automobile mass production. Disease was becoming better understood; medical treatments such as diphtheria vaccinations and better sanitation systems such as flush toilets made changes in how people lived.

New Disruption, New Paranoia

This change was good but unsettling. People could make money in more ways, and government was called upon to regulate what was happening. This was an era that vigorously supported class warfare—fat-cat capitalists vs. workers joining in solidarity. Political parties and the governments they supported vigorously chose sides in this class warfare.

But after the crash of '29, during the Great Depression, no one could figure out how to get the boom back. People in America, Europe, and Japan became frustrated and scared and turned to radical, unconventional solutions—the New Deal, Fascism, Nazism, Communism, and others that were less successful and famous.

These new movements brought famous strong men to power—Roosevelt, Mussolini, Hitler, Stalin, and others—and some of these proved "adventurous" to understate the matter. World War II was the result.

Conclusion

The 1910s brought the world to a place it had never been before. Sadly, one part of that place was a style of war-making that shocked the world with its ability to kill and damage. Again, the big surprise of World War I was how long it lasted, not that it started in the first place. That surprise lead to a Blunder Chain, next step of which was the Treaty of Versailles. After the war the world stayed shocked with all sorts of new ideas, technologies, and social movements that led up to World War II.

53

World War II

<u>World War II</u> was completely different from World War I. Britain, France, Russia, and the United States again lined up against Germany, but the unfolding and aftermath were completely different.

One of the big differences is that World War II was no surprise. People had experienced World War I, and as Hitler, Mussolini, and Stalin became more bellicose and as many other world hot spots festered and flared, a big war was expected years before it started. One of the important goals of the players was to avoid World War I–style trench warfare and slaughter. There were indeed fewer trenches, but new technologies brought new ways to slaughter.

The internal combustion engine went into the vehicles of war—trucks, tanks, and planes. Oil displaced coal as the energy resource and turned the Middle East into a strategic area rather than a backwater. And the world witnessed nuclear power in a most scary way.

Between the wars, social orders standardized as choices were made. The Italians and Spanish chose fascism; Germany chose Nazism; Japan chose militarism, and Russia chose the Stalinist form of communism. Two standards emerged as the postwar developed into the Cold War: capitalism and communism. Experimenting was underway in these two frameworks.

Now let's look at the details.

Before the War

Though people were in chaos and confusion after World War I, they benefitted from the spread of new technologies but wondered how the benefits and wealth should be spread. Who should get better sanitation? Who should get decent-paying jobs? Who should decide the work rules for a job?

This led to strange new ways of spreading wealth, the most famous of which were fascism in Italy, Nazism in Germany, and communism in Russia. The heady mix of fear and optimism in the people led their rulers to be adventurous, and that's what started the war.

Wild Booms and Busts

When the boys came home from the Great War, the economy transitioned from making military stuff to making civilian stuff—labor-saving home appliances such as washing machines. This successful transition fired a boom in prosperity in the developed nations that lasted throughout the Roaring Twenties.

But the boom had weaknesses, notably in the agriculture arena, and when the bust came in '29, no one knew how to resuscitate the stock market and banks. During the Great Depression, the average people of the world were unemployed, frightened, and frustrated.

Conventional and unconventional solutions didn't work. Hoover failed in this regard, but Hitler, Mussolini, Stalin, and Roosevelt rose to power on their promises to fix everything. Some of the ideas bandied about during this Time of Nutcases were visionary, but most were crazy. Which were which was determined through experimentation.

New Style of Militarizing

Industrial advancements led from planes during World War I that could carry one or two people with some armament to planes that could carry large crews better armed and able to drop enough bombs to destroy cities. Ultimately, it led to single bombs that could each destroy a city.

Exciting but not necessarily cost effective. "<u>A costly, brutal failure</u>" (*Economist*, September 21, 2013) reviewed the book *The Bombing War: Europe 1939–1945* by Richard Overy that considered how exciting strategic bombing was while the fighting was going on but concluded it accomplished little for either side.

New Styles of Socializing

Movies and radio were the mass-communication media of the day. People would listen to radios and watch "News of the Week" before feature films at theaters. Both of these forms were vivid compared to reading newspapers, but they were expensive. This made them easy for governments to manipulate, and they did. Hitler's speeches and Nazi newsreels are still memorable to this day as mass-communication icons of the time.

This was a time when many people were moving into cities for industrial jobs, a dramatic change in lifestyle for the average European and American. (Two movies of this era that dramatized these new lifestyles were Fritz Lang's dark sci-fi <u>Metropolis</u> and Charlie Chaplin's comedy sci-fi <u>Modern Times</u>.)

But particularly in the '30s, there was great frustration in the air with such newfangled ways. There was talk of the <u>Forgotten Man</u> who was not getting his fair share, and this supported populist politicians and movements. The huge mass rallies put on by political parties were ways of building support and enfranchisement.

Blitzkrieg

One of the tricks Hitler was masterful at was conducting splendid little wars. The Germans called it <u>blitzkrieg</u>—lightning war. This was an important skill. After World War I, the Germans were as war-shy as the rest of Western Europe was. Hitler started his series of wars in 1936 with the bloodless reoccupation of the Rhineland, which had been demilitarized by the Treaty of Versailles. His series of splendid little wars started in peacetime and continued into what became World War II. Each success allowed Germans to gain confidence in the viability of military solutions to its national problems.

The chain of success was broken in two ways. The first, a small one at the time, was when the British refused to sue for peace after Germany blitzed France in the summer of 1940. The British army was as thoroughly defeated as the French army had been and had been forced at Dunkirk to evacuate to England without its equipment. Instead of suing for peace, the British elected Churchill as prime minister and chose to keep fighting.

The much bigger chain break was in late summer 1941, when Germany invaded Russia and that war didn't end in six months with Russia suing for peace. Woops! Both Britain and Russia were in it for the long haul. War-making was going to get seriously hard on Germany.

The Germans stayed game, and their attacks remained potent and scary for another two years. But the combined forces of Britain, Russia, and then the United States were too much.

Japan likewise was an early master of blitzkrieg. Its opening campaigns after Pearl Harbor captured the Philippines, Singapore, Indonesia, and those coastal cities of China they didn't already control. But historic accident cost them their hammer fleet (my term) at the Battle of Midway in 1942, and it was steadily downhill from there—the United States was just too big an industrial power for them to battle with long term. They surrendered three months after the Germans did.

After the War

This war was not the surprise World War I was; this meant the aftermath was much better planned. There were still many scared people, but clearly, the blame game hadn't worked as a peace plan after World War I, so different solutions were tried. These solutions paid a lot more attention to nation building and devoted many more resources to it.

Sorting through the Ruins

All the European countries involved in the war suffered from heavy bombing, but America didn't. This is partly why America became the biggest industrial power right after the war. It was followed in size by Russia.

New Social Orders

Another way the world wars differed was that few new social orders emerged. Instead, the Cold War started, and that was a contest between just two flavors of social order: communism and capitalism. There were many variations within those two flavors, but much of the world chose between them. India was vigorous about not taking a side, and that is why India of this era was called a Third World nation or a nonaligned nation.

The Soviets and the Western powers were much better about organizing the societies of the postwar world. America and the Western powers did a good job of setting up Japan and West Germany to recover from the war as capitalist-oriented democracies. Russia did a good job of setting up central Europe and China as Communist workers' paradises. Both sides pointed fingers at the other and shouted, "You're doing a terrible job! Look at the abuse! Look at the injustice!" but both organized societies that were stable for the next fifty years.

New Technologies, New Prosperities

As was the case after World War I, the post–World Wars II era fostered prosperity, and people benefitted from new technologies. Cars became faster, cheaper, and better. TV displaced radio and newsreels at movies as the hot, new broadcast communication technology. Telephones got cheaper and easier to use and could call worldwide; direct dial started replacing operators and switchboards.

In the Communist countries, the emphasis was on building heavy industries such as steel making. In the Western world, the emphasis was on making consumer goods such as TVs. Both spent heavily on military, each fearing the other. This spending was feeding back on itself. In 1961, departing President Eisenhower warned about the dangers of the military-industrial complex overreaching itself. This was a warning the West took to heart but the Communist states ignored, and the Communists continued to outspend the West as a percentage of their economy.

New Disruption, New Paranoia

The worrying of the postwar era in the United States centered on sneaky Communists. The United States and the Russians were allies in fighting Hitler, but after the war, the Russians under Stalin installed Communist governments throughout central Europe. This surprised many people in the United States, and Churchill came up with the phrase Iron Curtain to describe those nations that had been converted. And in 1949, the Chinese Communists drove the Chinese Nationalists from the mainland and left them controlling only the island of Formosa/Taiwan. Double extra scary! When would this spread of communism stop?

In 1950, the North Koreans started rolling troops and tanks through South Korea until the United States and the UN drew the line; the Korean War ensued and went on until 1953.

Meanwhile, in the United States, many people started seriously worrying about who was a Red in US government and businesses. If you were, that was a big problem. It would likely cost you your job; you'd be blacklisted. The second Red Scare came to America. This worry was called McCarthyism, named after Senator Joe McCarthy of Wisconsin, who became the icon of worrying about Communist plotters.

And as in previous times of stress in the twentieth century, many words were coined to cope with these new situations. In this era, if you weren't a full-fledged Red but sympathized with the cause, you were a Pinko.

Conclusion

World War II had the same major fighters—France, Britain, Russia, and the United States vs. Germany—but it was otherwise completely different from World War I. The civilian and military technologies were different, how the war and peace were conducted was different, and how the postwar era turned out was different.

World War I turned into a time of social chaos and experimenting that continued for twenty years after the war and ultimately created the conditions that led to World War II. World War II ended with just three sides emerging—the Capitalist side, the Communist side, and the Third World side—those who didn't want to be either Capitalist or Communist.

Technology changed dramatically during and after both wars, and after both wars, there were still many questions about how people should live. But the peacemaking after World War II proved more durable, and by the 2010s, we had been living with sixty-plus years without World War III.

54

Comparing the Two Gulf Wars

Some wars go well, and some go poorly, but all wars are surprising in how they turn out.

In the case of the two Gulf Wars America participated in during the 1990s and 2000s, we have examples of wars being conducted and ending in dramatically different fashions. From the American point of view, the First Gulf War conducted by George H. W. Bush was a well-conducted war. From that same American point of view, the Second Gulf War conducted by George W. Bush came out miserably.

The lessons provided by comparing these two apply to many other wars that have been fought and will be fought.

First War Background

The First Gulf War occurred just after the eight-year-long Iran-Iraq war had wound down. That had been a bloodletting war (my term) after the Iranian Revolution. The Iraqis got to play the part of the bloodletters and were supported in this effort by the Sunni Arabs of the region and the United States.

Note that this should have been a bloodletter for the Iraqis as well, and produced a lasting peace. But one of those surprise twists in history happened. Saddam chose to continue being an adventurist at this point rather than becoming a conciliator. He was an adventurist eight years earlier when he started the Iran-Iraq War by invading Iran's oil provinces when the Iranians looked to be so deep in their revolution chaos that they could not respond well. And he did his adventuring again when he invaded Kuwait after the war ended.

Another big change in the world situation just before this war started was the dissolution of the USSR in 1989–91; the former Soviet Union states were concentrating on internal issues and not willing to devote much time, effort, or attention to Middle East issues.

Yet another change was that Bush's predecessor, Ronald Reagan, had been doing much to get American thinking moving beyond the post-Vietnam war shyness that was a Nixon/Carter legacy. Specifically, he had conducted a series of quick-win military engagements to restore American's confidence in the ability of the American military to win wars quickly and well. The first in this series was on <u>Grenada</u> in 1983.

Reagan and Bush had been doing things right; Saddam had been doing them wrong. Saddam started this war by invading and occupying Kuwait in the summer of 1990 and declaring it was part of Iraq. He felt the world owed him even more than it had already paid him for holding off the Iranians for eight long years, and giving him Kuwait was suitable payment.

The invasion was a surprise, but the Bush administration responded very well to it.

The Virtues of the First Gulf War

Here are the commendable elements of what Bush Sr. put together.

- He mustered sufficient (overwhelming) force to make it a short and decisive war.
- He was masterful at gaining allies for the cause; this list included the UN. Hussein was delusional in starting the war in the first place, but Bush Sr. showed wonderful skill at taking advantage of his diplomatic blundering.
- He let the generals conduct the war; he didn't micromanage it.
- He and the generals set specific and reachable goals for the war that didn't drift.

Compared to Bush Sr., Saddam Hussein came across looking like Bozo the Clown. In the eyes of the US media, he transformed from controversial hero into full-fledged arch-villain. Still, in spite of that transition and the deep embarrassment of losing so quickly, he survived as ruler of Iraq. At the time, that was a surprise to the Bush administration. This turned out to be a waving yellow flag (my term).

Watch for Yellow Flags

Saddam's survival was a mystery at the time. One of the interesting lessons from this element of the war is that mysteries of this nature need to be examined carefully. The mystery is that though there is a good reason for it, that reason isn't clear to the people being surprised—in this case, the Bush administration. They had expected the embarrassment of the defeat to cost him his job. It should have, but it didn't. Why became an unsolved mystery, until the aftermath of the Second Gulf War explained it.

Quickly forgetting a war

Quickly forgetting a war.

This trend isn't often talked about in history books, but when this evolution of thinking about a war happens, it's a hallmark of a well-fought war, and this phenomenon has important consequences: it was this quick forgetting about his spectacular victory that cost Bush Sr. his reelection. In the United States, it's usually a given that winning a war will give you the presidency, but Bush Sr. managed to break that rule.

Second War Background

It's ten years later. The post-USSR states and Iran have had ten years of recovering from their weakened and distracted conditions at the start of the First Gulf War. Russia and Iran are ready to do some meddling in the Middle East again.

But the big change is in America. America has been deeply and scarily surprised by the 9/11 disaster. This has caused the American people, the media, and the Bush Jr. administration to panic and commit blunders. Starting the Second Gulf War was just one of many blunders, another was the Patriot Act, but the war has become the most memorable.

The Vices of the Second Gulf War

Bush Jr. did so much wrong compared to his father that it was almost as if he had wished to make a "do's and don'ts" statement that could be passed down. Here is a quick list.

- The war was stared in response to the 9/11 panic. Unlike Saddam invading Kuwait, 9/11 surprised and scared Americans; as a result, the war was hastily planned by people who were deeply scared. The war ended up as much a blunder as Saddam's starting the First Gulf War had been.
- Bush Jr. didn't spend much time or effort lining up allies. He didn't have the excuse of Saddam's blundering to get him started on this, and he spent very little time on crafting or spreading some alternative message that other leaders could get behind and support. The result was the WMD fiasco that the war is now famous for.
- Bush Jr.'s goals were grandiose and changed with time. As a result, there was no way to fight for a short time, declare, "We won," and bring the troops home.
- He didn't start the war with overwhelming force, and the military stayed on a tight budget for years thereafter.
- When the Iraqi governing structure vanished as US troops moved across the land, it surprised him; this made post-fighting recovery even more expensive and more chaotic.

This is a great list of ways not to conduct a war. But again, this is not purely and simply a matter of blaming Bush. A forgotten element in the story of the Second Gulf War is that the sloppy planning was enthusiastically supported by a deeply scared nation that demanded revenge for 9/11 and government actions that would ensure it never happened again. Blaming Bush for this sloppily conducted war is convenient but a mistake. He had the will of the American people firmly behind him when he started this affair, and he had record-high approval ratings when he made his <u>Mission Accomplished</u> speech.

Mystery solved

As noted above, the mystery of Saddam not falling from power after the First Gulf War was a yellow flag waving concerning conditions in Iraq. The solution to the mystery was that there was no one to replace him among the behind-the-scenes Iraqi leaders who supported him. They knew even in 1991 that it was either Saddam, someone even crazier than he was, or complete warlord chaos, so they continued to back him. But given the deep panic caused by 9/11, it's not too surprising the Bush Jr. administration chose to ignore this waving yellow flag.

Conclusion

These two wars were fought over the same ground between the same contenders only a decade apart. But the conduct of the wars was night-and-day different. In those differences are some great lessons about how wars should and shouldn't be conducted and when to be really careful before starting a war.

Part 3c

Case Studies—Other Memorable Times

55

Mania and Markets explaining
the 2008 Crash

This is an example of some predicting I did using the mania and markets model I wrote as the Iraq War and the 2000s bubble evolved. This is a real-world example using the patterns to predict.

2003: Major Crisis

The number-one crisis of 2003 is the Iraq War crisis. There is every sign that this crisis will reach some kind of resolution during 2003. So it is not only a crisis, it's a mania marker as well. In my thinking, the Iraq War will represent "closure" on the mania that the 9/11 disaster brought into being and thus end that mania. (Note: I later had to change my mind on this presumption. These days I see 2008 as ending the 9/11 Mania.)

Are We in a Mania?

Is there a big mania building in 2003? I think so! It's being built around the Iraq War scare. Unlike the Hong Kong and Y2K examples, this mania has had a short gestation. Bush's saber rattling started in September 2001, so the event has been running only eighteen months, not thirty years. But it makes up for its short duration and unknown ending date by being a very exciting event.

So lesson one is in place: we have a mania situation. What about lesson two: what investment trend has the mania latched onto?

As I look at the news, I see one industry that is clearly in an unnaturally prosperous condition: real estate, in particular the new housing market.

My experience over the last forty years is that a recession trashes the new housing market. But this trashing hasn't happened in 2001 or 2002. What's holding this market up? Conventional wisdom is that low interest rates are, but my vote is mania. (Note again that this is an example of quiet investing running contrary to public doom and gloom.)

My prediction based on the mania model is as follows. We're in a mania period that started with the shock of 9/11 and with the expectation that something would happen as a consequence. With time, the mania has become focused on G. W. Bush's saber rattling (War on Terrorism) and on the Iraq crisis in particular. This is the doom-and-gloom element.

Now that the mania is focused, the mania will end when the Iraq crisis is solved in some fashion—war is fought, Saddam leaves, or some new crisis takes its place. If the crisis winds down, that means some other crisis has taken its place as a headline maker and the Iraq crisis will no longer support mania. That counts as ending the crisis and will mark the end of the mania.

When the Iraq crisis resolves, the mania will end. The mania could end earlier than solving the Iraq crisis if a credit crunch starts for some other reason, such as a Greenspan announcement that fighting inflation is now a Fed policy, and interest rates will go up.

When the mania ends, the new housing market will tank because easy money will dry up. Coincident with this drying up will be a serious readjustment of credit in the United States, which will first cause great pain in the construction and finance industries, and then the pain will spread. Scandals comparable to Arthur Anderson and Enron will likely be uncovered.

This readjustment will go on for years and will be characterized by the housing market being soft and slow compared to the markets of 2001 and 2002. There is no upside to jumping at real estate bargains. Wait at least a year, and more likely two or more, to see a bottom.

The contagion will likely spread to the large-appliance and auto industries since these are also based on easy credit and consumer confidence; the end of the mania will be marked by a collapse in consumer confidence and general economic malaise.

In other words, just as it seemed to be safe to get back into the investing waters. (Cue theme song from *Jaws*.)

June 2003 Update

The Iraq War has and come and gone. The big surprises of the war were its speedy and cheap conclusion and that the main justification for going to war seems to have been bogus: Iraq didn't have huge stockpiles of weapons of mass destruction or any at all.

Viewed from the mania model

The mania should be ending. There is a good chance it is, but if Bush is ruthless and adroit, he may succeed in keeping the mania burning on for years longer as the war on terrorism. With the mania ending, consumer enthusiasm (confidence) should wane—it's recovery time.

The housing bubble hasn't burst yet, but that's because it's being deliberately sustained by Greenspan and the Fed's actions. Greenspan wants to see housing remain the engine for an economic recovery, and he's more worried about deflation than inflation, so he's lowering the prime rate again, which is encouraging another round of mortgage activity and pumping more paper wealth into the system. This is delaying the burst of the housing bubble, and it's going to make it worse.

Other news: due to severe earnings drops in 2002, the S&P P/E ratio is still well over twenty, which means the stock market is still behaving as if we're in a boom.

Other significant news: the Freddie Mac scandal. Freddie Mac is a key component in the mortgage industry. As of this date, the three top people at Freddie Mac have been summarily dismissed. That's a huge amount of smoke in a critical place at a critical time. I predict this news is the fluttering of the butterfly wings that will evolve into a housing hurricane.

Remember lesson three: when the housing market tanks, the effect will be long lasting, and it will mark a major change in how the housing industry does business. I don't know the housing industry well enough to predict what kinds of changes are likely, but if it fits post-bubble patterns, there will be many consolidations and it's likely Freddie Mac and Fannie Mae will be restructured to change their privileged charter positions.

December 2011 update

My goodness! That crystal ball was crystal clear! It's spooky in retrospect. One thing I didn't catch in June 2003 was that Iraq would turn into a long and deep quagmire. That extended the mania. The hangover didn't begin until 2007, and then, whew! I've been surprised at the depth of the bust. Another interesting element is what I called a housing boom transformed into a mortgage boom as the CDO (collateralized debt obligation), a new financial invention, became popular.

And finally, the hangover is transforming into our new worry of the decade. We're moving from worrying about terrorism to worrying about debt and income distribution. This is an example of not going back.

Conclusion

This is a real-world example of doing some predicting based on the mania and markets model. The predicting is not perfect in terms of timing, and there were surprises. But the pattern was fulfilled. This is a good example of how history can help in predicting the near future.

56

Enfranchisement and gangs

Introduction

Why do some communities become infested with corruption, gangs and organized crime, and others do not?

In this section I will propose that the key to the crime rate is community enfranchisement. When enfranchisement is strong, crime is low, when enfranchisement is weak, crime is high.

I will further propose that organized crime is a symptom that the conventional community government is dysfunctional in the areas where organized crime has taken over. Organized crime thrives when it is acting as a shadow government and filling in where conventional government has dropped the ball because the conventional government's rules are so disenfranchising that it can no longer govern a popular community activity.

Why Crime?

Why do we have crime? In particular, why do we have crimes against property? Crimes such as stealing, burglary, pick pocketing do huge damage to the victim and gain the perpetrator comparatively little. My guess is that, on the average, the damage done to the victim is roughly a hundred times the value gained by the perpetrator. It is this huge disparity between damage and reward that makes property crime so senseless and emotionally threatening. The community would be hurt a whole lot less if a burglar knocked on the door and politely said to the resident, "Excuse me, I will be burgling your place later tonight, why don't you give me a hundred dollars instead, and I'll be on my way."

So... why as a community don't we accept this knock-on-the-door solution? It would be a whole lot cheaper.

Yeah, I know, we don't accept it because it wouldn't work.... But why not?

Part of the answer comes from asking why the criminal commits the crime in the first place. The criminal steals from a person he or she doesn't respect. For pickpockets and fare-jacking taxi drivers, the victim is a face in the crowd who will never be seen again. The best victim is an obvious out-of-towner, and one that can be laughed at later for his or her gullibility.

For a home burglar it's either a stranger's home or the home of a person they have some kind of grudge against. Even then, it's common for a home burglar to "trade" something for what they steal, something such as a piece of shit they leave behind.

The point being that these crimes are not without attached emotion.

So, what is the emotion? The emotion is disenfranchisement. It springs from Us versus Them thinking, "I'm stealing from someone who is not Us and so it's OK."

This Us versus Them emotion goes one step further: It is also acceptable thinking to the community around the thieves -- when the thieves finish a day's adventure and have a drink with their pals, the pals' reaction is acceptance, not horror. Likewise, the family of the thieves do not feel great discomfort at their activity. They may fret a little, but they don't do anything drastic enough to convince the thief that his activities are not profitable by his personal measure.

This revelation came to me after I was pick pocketed while visiting Istanbul. I saw who did it, I chased them, (but not well, old age had finished off my knees by then) and got pictures of them! And, amazingly there was a cop there when I needed him! Two of them, in fact. What was a jaw-dropper for me was that the cops would not chase the pickpockets across the street and into the next neighborhood. As one of them put it, "They may have friends over there."

As I thought about this incident, I realized that those cops did not feel enfranchised once they crossed that street. Enfranchisement... it's so important when dealing with crime. Likewise, those pick pockets did feel enfranchised when they got across the street -- their neighbors and family would stand by them.

Here is the difference enfranchisement makes:

- o   If a typical citizen who feels enfranchised sees a crime in progress, they report it to the police, or they gather neighbors and try to prevent it.
- o   If that typical citizen does not feel enfranchised then their reaction is, "Meh... so what? It's not my concern." and they do nothing to try and prevent it.

========
Pop Quiz
========

Question:

Given this definition of crime and enfranchisement, what newsworthy community of the 2007-2009 timeframe is famously disenfranchised?

Answer:

The Gaza Strip. There is a community that has been without an enfranchised government since 1948. So, if an average citizen there sees a neighbor building a car bomb or setting up a mortar, what is their reaction?

"... Meh..."

And this is why the violence there is endemic.

Organized Crime, Corruption and Enfranchisement

One of the functions of organized crime in a community is to function as a shadow government which handles disputes and activities that the formal community government has disenfranchised, and thus no longer handles well.

The formal community disenfranchises an activity when it refuses to deal with it in a way that almost all of the community thinks is working well. To put this another way, if there is a substantial minority of a community that thinks a law is total bullshit, then there is room for criminal activity in meeting demand to circumvent that law.

If the activity is large, complex and profitable, then the criminals will organize to manage it better, and organized crime emerges.

Vice crimes -- drugs, prostitution, loan-sharking -- are areas of human activity about which there is sharp disagreement in most communities. Some members say let's get rid of these activities entirely by banning them, others say, "That's fine! That's right! For sure!... Except I want to do them once in a while....Well, maybe more often than just once in while." So there is a constant demand for these activities. (The loan sharking demand comes about because community-approved money lenders can't service the kind of demand that many loan-seeking customers are asking for.)

If the community forces the powers-that-be to ignore these demands and the people that service them, then we are looking at a gaping disenfranchisement situation, and an organized crime shadow government will spring up to service the demand for some kind of government to do things such as organize distribution, enforce acceptable rules, and handle dispute resolution.

The moral of this is that it is disenfranchisement that is empowering organized crime. A community can reduce organized crime by extending community enfranchisement so that it includes more community members and more activities. To many this will sound like having the government make a deal with the devil, and it is. But that devil doesn't go away if you don't deal with him -- if you don't deal with him, he makes crime grow.

Closely related to this is the issue of government officials getting corrupted. If a government official is charged with enforcing a law that a substantial minority of community thinks is bullshit, he or she will feel the temptation to agree and get discouraged about enforcing the law. If that happens, then the temptation to get paid to support the shadow government—organized crime—becomes pretty strong.

Here are a couple of examples of places where I wonder if a careful reexamination of the enfranchisement issue might produce dramatic changes in the crime rate:

○ The construction industry in East Coast US and other places is notorious for being linked to organized crime. If that is true, it suggests that the laws/codes the government inspectors are trying to enforce are ill-suited to current conditions, and so those laws are disenfranchising the people they effect. But enfranchised or not, completing a building still takes a lot of coordination and dispute resolution. So a shadow government—organized crime—springs up to fill the enfranchisement gap.

○ The Red and The Black, an article in the October 4-9th, 2009 issue of The Economist talks about the problem China is having with "Black and Red" issues—gangs (Black) and government corruption (Red). This suggests that China's local governments are not doing a good job of enfranchising their residents. Their actions, organization and regulations have created an enfranchisement gap and gangs are springing up to fill it. It suggests that Beijing needs to look hard at reforming local government structure so that it better represents and enfranchises the people it is governing. When they do that, the Black and Red problem will diminish on its own because the shadow government is no longer needed.

○ Here is an article about the enfranchisement issue here in the US, the city of Salinas, CA. Iraq's Lessons on the Home Front The Washington Post Nov 15, 2009

○ Here is another Wall Street Journal article The End of Bolivian Democracy (Nov 22, 2009) explaining how President Evo Morales of Bolivia is leading Bolivia into a populist dictatorship. His power base for this power grab? Coca growers, who have been disenfranchised by previous governments. Article writer Ms. O'Grady states at the end, *"Mr. Morales is South America's latest dictator, but he is not the ideological communist that many fear. He's more akin to a mob boss, having risen to power by promising to protect the coca business. Now he has the capacity to do it.*

Under his rule, coca cultivation is legal and he collects a licensing fee from all farmers, whose harvests are sold through a centralized market. MAS officials [Morales' political party] also regulate cocaine production and trafficking which now reaches down to the household level."

Whatever else he's doing, he's bringing more enfranchisement to the coca growing industry in Bolivia, and this has made him and his party popular.

- o And here is an article about a step backwards. In northern Mexico the disenfranchisement surrounding the War on Drugs has gotten so bad that drug lords are attacking military bases! <u>Mexico drug gangs turn weapons on army</u> by Tracy Wilkinson, 2 Apr 10, LA Times.

- o And a 27 Jun 11 WSJ article, <u>City's Ban on Smoking Called 'an Absolute Joke'</u> by Michael Howard Saul and Richard Autry, about a busybodyish good-intentioned step towards disenfranchisement—banning smoking in outdoor public places. The good news is that thus far the enforcement people have chosen not to take even the first step down this particular slippery slope. They are keeping enfranchisement high for now.

- o Update: A 19 Jul 13 WSJ article, <u>The Rise of the Warrior Cop</u> by Radly Balko, which describes the militarization of US polices forces over the decades since the 1960's. No knock assaults on homes and other civil-rights-trampling SWAT team tactics are highly disenfranchising. They aren't worth it! They do much more damage to enfranchisement with their frightening tactics than they do benefit in capturing criminals. Rather than forming more SWAT teams, we need to be building live and let live tolerance in our communities, with police that support that tolerance and thus become part of the community fabric.

Summary

Enfranchisement and crime are tightly related. If crime is booming it's because enfranchisement is declining, and Us versus Them thinking is becoming appropriate for the circumstance.

One of the common ways to start disenfranchising is by enacting bullshit laws that ignore the fact that part of the community thinks what is being banned is an acceptable activity. If there is demand for an activity, but the powers-that-be refuse to enfranchise activities centering around that demand, then a shadow government will spring up to do the regulating, and that shadow government will be called organized crime.

If government officials become discouraged as they try to enforce disenfranchising laws, they will be strongly tempted to become corrupt.

As citizens become discouraged they will stop caring of crime is being committed around them, and they will not discourage their family or neighbors from becoming criminals.

57

Roger's Answer to Fermi's Question – Thoughts on the Fermi Paradox

Introduction

"Where is everybody?"

-- Enrico Fermi, 1950

The "everybody" in this quote is intelligent aliens who are engaged in interstellar space travel, and should have been discovered in some fashion by people on earth by now. This is the <u>Fermi Paradox</u>: the galaxy is a big place, filled with many stars which have many planets. Why haven't many of those planets developed civilized life, then interstellar space travel, and at least one of them made contact with people here on earth?

Here is how patterns of history can explain this paradox.

Where is everybody?

As astronomy improved during the 20th century, it became clearer and clearer that the Earth was orbiting a star, The Sun, and that The Sun was just one of billions in the Milky Way galaxy.

If The Sun was nothing special in the way of being a star, then there should be billions of planets orbiting those other stars, and if even one in a million was capable of creating civilized life—the sort we have here on Earth—then the Milky Way should be crowded with civilized life.

By 1950 it was clear that space travel was likely to come soon to humanity, and if humans could space travel, shouldn't many of those other beings also be capable of space travel?

This question is the root of the Fermi Paradox: If there are many interstellar space-traveling civilizations in the Milky Way galaxy, how come we Earthlings have not detected any?

The role of commerce

The answer I have to the Fermi Question is: "We haven't seen any others because no civilization has discovered space commerce, as in, discovered a way to move "things" (of some nature, any nature) from star system to star system for a handsome profit."

To see why space commerce is so important, look at the history of exploring Earth. Prior to the development of sturdy ocean-crossing merchant ships, the peoples of all continents were experiencing an earthly form of the Fermi Paradox. There were people on all the continents (except Antarctica), but the interchange between them happened rarely. If the peoples were separated by an ocean it happened once or twice a millennia, so infrequently that contact was routinely forgotten.

Then came the sturdy sailing ships, and commerce. Hundreds of sailing ships got built because there was huge profit in doing so. These sailed, and the cultures all over the earth were changed by lots and lots of contact with each other. They became much more aware of each other and much more interconnected. Today we call this globalization.

The important point here is: *Commerce changed these cultures. Commerce made this contact happen on a large scale.*

We are at a similar point in interstellar exploration. Without commerce, only a handful of ships will get built by any planetary civilization, and only a handful of star systems will get explored. (We are also at a similar point in interplanetary exploration. If we don't discover more ways of doing commerce between our sun's planets, moons, comets and asteroids, our interplanetary space traveling fleet will also remain small.)

The galaxy is a big place. If we are talking just handfuls of explorers and stars explored, it is not surprising we haven't been visited. The further implication of our not being visited yet is that both of these skills -- the traveling and the commerce -- are difficult to master, so few, if any, current civilizations in our galaxy have succeeded in doing so. This is a sad implication for a science fiction buff such as myself who loves the idea of the wonder of traveling to distant worlds.

Conclusion

The moral of this tale is that just developing ways of flying between stars is not enough for civilizations to spread across the galaxy. In addition to interstellar traveling technology, good reasons to engage in trade are also needed.

When reasons to trade between the stars are found, then we will get a positive answer to Fermi's Question.

Conclusion

58

Conclusion

And there you have it—history told as a series of patterns. Along with those patterns, we see the fabric the patterns are composed of—human thinking, technologies, circumstances, and surprises.

With these historical patterns in mind, the patterns that dominate current events become clearer and so does the future; we'll have a much better chance of getting on the right side of any fences we find ourselves sitting on.

Helping you become more a master of your current events is the goal of this book. If you know the patterns of history, you can pick which ones you'd like to become part of and make your own history come true.

I hope you have a fun, exciting time making the good patterns of history come true for you.

Printed in the United States
By Bookmasters